Stress in Social Work

of related interest

Negotiation for Health and Social Service Professionals
Keith Fletcher
1 85302 549 6

Good Practice in Risk Assessment and Risk Management 1
Edited by Hazel Kemshall and Jacki Pritchard
1 85302 338 8

Good Practice in Risk Assessment and Risk Management 2
Edited by Hazel Kemshall and Jacki Pritchard
1 85302 441 4

Competence in Social Work Practice
Edited by Kieran O' Hagan
1 85302 332 9

Handbook of Theory for Practice Teachers in Social Work
Edited by Joyce Lishman
1 85302 098 2

Stress in Social Work

Edited by Richard Davies

Foreword by Isabel Menzies Lyth

Jessica Kingsley Publishers
London and Philadelphia

First published in the United Kingdom in 1998 by
Jessica Kingsley Publishers Ltd
116 Pentonville Road
London N1 9JB, England
and
1900 Frost Road, Suite 101
Bristol, PA 19007, USA

Copyright © 1998 Jessica Kingsley Publishers

Library of Congress Cataloguing in Publication Data
A CIP catalogue record for this book is available from the Library of Congress

British Library Cataloguing in Publication Data
Davies, Richard L.
Stress in Social Work
1. Social Workers – Mental Health.
2. Social workers – Job stress. I. Title.
ISBN 1 85302 390 6

Printed and Bound in Great Britain by
Athenaeum Press, Gateshead, Tyne and Wear

Contents

Acknowledgements

First, I particularly wish to acknowledge Ved Varma who approached me with the idea for this book. His prolific and important contributions as editor of many books relevant to social work and allied professions has given him much experience and expertise which he generously made available to me in producing this book. I thank him for his support and encouragement.

I would like to acknowledge the help of a number of colleagues who helped me in my task by adding perspectives to my editing either through discussion or reading of chapters. In particular I am grateful to Robert Fleming and Dorothy Lloyd-Owen.

Finally I wish to thank all the authors for their hard work and in some cases, endurance, and for their unique contributions to the subject of stress based in all cases on a background of experience in social work at one level or another. I particularly want to acknowledge the contributions of Sonia Appleby and David Townsend who each produced chapters in a matter of weeks after other contributors had unfortunately to withdraw.

Foreword

There appears to have been a subtle change in the meaning of the word 'stress' as it is applied to the social and other public services. Its original meaning, the application of force or pressure to an object to impel or constrain it, carries no implication about the effect of the stress on the object: it is neutral. However, stress, as now frequently used, has subtly acquired the implication that stress is, by its nature, harmful. Stress has also been subtly extended to cover the effects of (harmful) stress. It is now understood as an undesirable or even pathological state that arises in the object of stress as in 'Stress in Social Work'.

These may well be significant changes in that they may tend to confuse thinking about the problem and lead to inappropriate measures towards its solution. It confuses the effects with the cause of which it is not the inevitable effect. Thus, to reduce stress, the effect, one should reduce stress, the cause. This is muddled thinking. Indeed, one can quote examples that disprove that connection. In the Royal National Orthopaedic Hospital, changes in the nursing care of patients and their families, such as the introduction of case-assignment, considerably increased the stress on the nursery nurses. They came into much more intimate and continuous contact with the distress of patients and families. The result was not greater stress in the nurses. Instead, they blossomed. They enjoyed the new challenge, valued their new skills and grew more confident. They felt rewarded by the affection and respect of patients, families and colleagues. There was little absence and no labour turnover. This was achieved by the careful management of the circumstances in which the role-change took place; clear definition of the roles of all concerned and of the nature of delegation, support and training where necessary, the development of a culture where people talked.

Using 'stress' as the effect confuses the issue about the effect of stress. It is a portmanteau word that covers a wide variety of symptoms, psychological, physical and behavioural. It is, in effect, an 'illness' though it would not be judicious to use that word in public. The illness may be temporary, episodic or chronic and of all degrees of severity. It has much in common with other 'illnesses' not usually described as such. Mourning or maternal preoccupation, it is said, would be described as an illness if one did not know the circumstances. This brings us back to the circumstances under which stress may bring about harmful effects on the individual in an organisation. Bion made a similar point when he held that whether or not troops in battle developed panic depended on circumstances, whether the battle was properly managed.

I doubt whether the level of stress inherent in social work is any greater than in some other professions; if this is so, then one is forced to seek an explanation for the high level of stress in individuals in the circumstances. Our society is characterised by a high degree of dependency: pressure on Government to provide excessively is linked to a scarcity of resources to do so. Both of these features are passed down to the Social Services. Be that as it may, the responsibility to manage the conflict still falls on the Social Services. It is clear that they are not generally succeeding in managing the conflict without undue stress to social workers. The stress is in the circumstances. It is not easy to see from the outside how these might be changed. There is no lack of suggestions and prescriptions. Many have already been tried and seem to have made little improvement. These are too often in the nature of placebos, 'which humour rather than cure', the patient. They help people to feel they are doing something.

Among the placebos is the increasingly common practice of providing counselling or psychotherapy and very generous sick leave for those who have succumbed to the inadequately managed stress, the symptoms of the organisation's disease. This approach may be a sign that the Social Services are themselves caught up in the overriding dependency culture. They give *care* which may be inappropriate. In the Walker case, the local authority was blamed for not providing care when it seemed to me it was rather that they had failed to provide proper professional circumstances for good professional work to be done without excessive cost to workers. Care seems to me to disrespect and diminish those who without proper professional support cannot carry the burden. The casualties are exported from the system which thus tries to absolve itself from further responsibility and, perhaps more importantly, from its responsibility for preventing future casualties.

The basic disease is harder to cure. It needs more drastic remedies. It may be of little benefit to sit and think what could be done. One may need to get in there and see what needs to be done and to stay there and help it to be done. This was what happened in a small way in the Royal National Orthopaedic Hospital – 'An Experience in the Art·of the Possible' – a long, slow and often painful process.

Reading this book has immensely evoked my sympathy for social workers in their present plight. I wish I could do more to help.

Isabel Menzies Lyth

Introduction: Stress in Social Work

Richard Davies

Modern social work is in a state of crisis. It has always been a profession towards which society has displayed ambivalence and it is now grossly underfunded and understaffed. Tragedies and subsequent vilification of social workers and their managers are reported with increasing frequency. The profession attempts to function in an environment of obstructive administrative 'systems', the anachronistic 'community care' philosophy, severe financial restrictions and conflicting demands emanating from confused legislation and a concomitant plethora of guidelines, 'standards' and procedures.

Against this background it seems hardly surprising that 'stress in social work' appears in the press, regularly among the top three in the stress 'charts'. Even in 1987 the problem had been considered 'widespread' (Baker 1987). But what is 'stress'? Most people seem to know and many think 'it' is getting worse but there seems to be no consensus about what 'it' is. A general practitioner or psychiatrist may describe it as a condition with various symptoms, such as lethargy, inability to function, loss of appetite, loss of weight or hair, high blood pressure, high anxiety, depression and so on. A social work manager may describe it as a state of being caught in the 'middle', unable to satisfy anybody and being unable to sleep at night. A social worker may describe it in terms of some entity that has its origins in managers or clients and, somehow passed on to them, makes it practically impossible to do their job.

Many valuable thoughts and ideas on the subject of stress are offered by the authors from their unique professional experiences. In particular, some authors have addressed the functioning of organisations and their structural context while others have focused either on the role of social work or on the interactions at the various interfaces of client, practitioner, manager, director or chief, political overseers and, finally, the 'public' – who are also the 'users', the clients, of social service. I should be clear at this point that my use of the terms 'social work' and 'social service' in this chapter is generic.

This book is an attempt to address what I believe to be a complex subject that is often treated as if a simple matter. It does not pretend to be comprehensive or to offer simple explanations or remedies. It is my hope that, taken as a whole, it will offer a framework for serious discussion towards understanding the nature of stress in social work. The aim is that it might facilitate a thoughtful and constructive attitude to the problem rather than the customary and dismissive approach of 'treatment without diagnosis'. A typical example of this kind of simplistic approach is the lists of tips on 'how to tackle stress' which have frequently appeared in the press and, I understand, are also issued by some authorities to their employees. An equally dismissive approach is the assumed diagnosis of 'overwork' that does not consider the nature of the work or how the 'overworking' arises and for which the 'cure' is 'less work'.

From my understanding of the various contributions by the authors, and also from my own experience, I am led to think that a 'solution' for stress cannot simply be prescribed by one party for another for the reason that it seems common for the 'prescriber' to be held accountable for the stress by the sufferer. While in the wider context there are many versions of what 'stress' means to people, it seems to acquire a certain meaning when discussed in relation to social work. Its identification as an experience, a 'state of suffering from stress', whatever that may be to an individual, seems to occur simultaneously with an identification of 'somebody', an individual or an organisation, that can be held responsible. The suggestion is that there has been an experience of something harmful having been done to somebody either through action or, possibly, lack of action.

Stress, when thought of in terms of 'a state of suffering', can exist anywhere on the continuum from 'stressed out, taking a day off' to 'burnout, incapable of functioning'. It is, perhaps, used as a shortened form of (di)stress in this usage. The 'cause' is frequently seen either in terms of 'too much work' or an ill-defined 'the work itself', hence the ubiquitous 'work-related stress'. Here the term 'stress' has acquired a quality independent of people – the cause, the 'stressor', is invested with a life of its own. We might have the situation between employee and employer:

> I am working too much and feel stressed and tired and need a few weeks off.

> I agree that you need a break as you have had a lot to contend with lately.

Here both 'sides' agree implicitly that 'work' is the aggressor, that the employee is the victim of work and that the employer is likely to suffer also in the longer term if he risks having an under-functioning employee. In this scenario neither holds the other responsible; excessive work, perhaps due to external demands of the 'market-place', is to blame. An agreement of this nature may briefly be tolerated in a social work environment but it is likely to break down quickly for reasons that I believe pertain specifically to the nature of social work.

In relation to the workplace, there would at first glance seem to be a basis for some common ground between all concerned about the 'state of being stressed'. It may sometimes be thought of as a sort of illness, that when people 'phone in sick' has euphemisms such as 'flu', 'domestic crisis' and 'bad back'. There is also likely to be some agreement in principle about undesirable stressors, such as a level of work beyond the capacity of a 'human being', dangerous working environment or lack of tools and resources. One might suppose, therefore, that it would be possible to hammer out some basis for reducing stress since employers and employees would have a mutual investment in such a pursuit. The evidence seems to be to the contrary.

Through my teaching, supervision and consultancy work I am told of the increasing frequency of sick leave or of those who persist at work while chronically under-functioning. I am also told about 'good departments' and 'bad departments'. I am then told about 'bad' managers who, 'unable to do their job', pass their stress down to social workers and of 'bad' social workers who, through constant complaint about lack of resources or failure to follow procedures, 'pass' their stress up to managers. The less critical talk of different perceptions of task between management and practitioners, resulting in such complaints by practitioners of 'inappropriate or absent supervision' or, from managers, 'too demanding of supervision and resistant to what is offered' or 'failure to understand the task'.

The complaint of 'something having been done to somebody', whether implicit or explicit, seems to be central to the subject of stress in social work. I will go on to explore the nature of the 'complaint' and of the polarity that, as a consequence, emerges between individuals and groups within organisations.

Several authors in this volume refer to the well-known case of Walker, a Northumberland social worker who sued his authority for the stress that he suffered. In this case there was, presumably, sufficient agreement, initially, about overwork being the source of stress, such that some extra support was arranged on his return from sick leave. When Walker became ill again he was dismissed on grounds of permanent ill-health. Walker sued his authority and won. It was judged that the cause of his stress was an authority who had overworked him. In defending their dismissal of Walker on grounds of permanent ill-health, the council, who no longer agreed with the earlier notion of 'overwork', would have presumably located the cause elsewhere, possibly, for example, in an inherent weakness in an employee.

In this case the agreement of 'overwork' had broken down as it was no longer mutually satisfactory to both parties to retain an externally identified 'aggressor'. The relationship between employer and employee had become polarised, each denied responsibility for the state of affairs and in some way held the other responsible. The necessity for the matter to go to a court, an adversarial arena, only served to reinforce the polarisation and achieved nothing towards understanding stress.

An organisation may sometimes seem united against the 'common foe'. They may hold central and local government responsible for under-functioning departments, high staff turnover, high rate of sickness absence and complaints from users. Unworkable policies as well as reduction in staff and resources may be blamed. On the other 'side', politicians and the press criticise the profession for not providing what they and the public demand. This conflict, that many may feel resigned to as being institutional, is, nevertheless, in my view, another manifestation of what I have referred to as the 'polarised relationship'.

In the attempt to identify the basis for the polarised relationship it may be useful to begin with 'the public'.

The public, by definition, demands everything and hence presents conflictual demands. For example, affecting the social worker's task there exist such demands as: child protection vs. parents 'rights' protection; child protection vs. adoption made easier for all those who wish to adopt; mental health community day centres vs. more asylums (miles from habitation); greater care for children the elderly and disabled vs. tax cuts; civil liberties vs. the dangers of 'high risk' offenders in the community. Such impossible demands might be thought of in terms of a child caught between two parents in violent opposition – a polarised relationship. To please one parent is to displease the other and so, with no possibility of resolution, a sado-masochistic process ensues where the child effectively becomes a victim of psychic torture. I think social workers and their managers frequently experience themselves in a position tantamount to that of a victim torn between two aggressors with no presence of a sane and caring authority.

One example of the above may be a social worker who having listened to the disclosure of a child's horrendous abuse by a parent has to 'allow' the abuse to continue while he or she contends with the Children Act 1989 (which leans towards the rights of parents), attempts to gather watertight evidence for a court and experience the frustration of the child who withdraws the 'disclosure' because, left in the same abusive environment, it seems safer to do so. Eventually, if 'lucky', the social worker then has to negotiate with his or her own manager for a proper placement to be funded from a pitifully inadequate budget and has the continued anxiety about a child placed in a possibly unsuitable foster home and prays that the abuse is not repeated.

One such case is, arguably, too much for another human being to bear knowing about, let alone to find a way to act 'professionally', even if the 'system' could be made to be less obstructive. With multiples of such cases and with ever decreasing available support from his or her own organisation or those who fund it, it seems an entirely sane act for a professional to wish to 'cut off' from the experience. The anxiety that is intolerable to the conscious mind, in becoming unconscious, takes with it the capacity to think properly, the capacity to 'remember' what once might have felt engraved on the mind. 'Mistakes' may be made, a tragedy may occur, enquiries and press coverage enhance an already paranoid situation. Weighed down with corporate guilt, and even more anxious than before, the social worker may attempt to avoid being exposed to such feelings and experiences again and may welcome the warm illusory safety of 'wooden' guidelines and procedures that can be applied unthinkingly. Supervision that is becoming more concerned with 'case management', throughput outcomes and finances reinforces the temptation for the social worker to behave in this mechanistic way.

Managers too may have to defend themselves from 'knowing' too much, while also knowing, as in the case above, the inevitability of a crisis around the corner which may signal the end of their career. They are in an invidious position in relation to their staff in that they may effectively have to ignore the intrinsically risky way staff are forced to try and cope with their work, feeling in a similar situation themselves of trying to cope with unrealistic and conflicting demands. The internal pressures that arise from this, as well as the more tangible pressures on them from councils and government, may be resolved through a mechanical style of management more easily concerned with budgets than people and preoccupied with procedures rather than their purpose.

Politicians and executives responsible for social work organisations are not immune. In what I would see as the attempt to manage their own anxiety about a high volume of cases of sexual abuse, one London council, while ignoring the effect of stringent cuts on 'service delivery' concomitant with poor morale and high staff turnover, produced countless memos issuing trivial dictats, including one concerning 'dress codes in summer'.

In the context of the 'polarised relationship', a number of 'complaints' emerge from the above relating to the quality of 'care' – including unfairness, neglect, chaos, abandonment, impossible demands, cruelty and contempt.

Of particular interest in the Walker case was that the County Council was judged to be in 'breach of its duty of care for an employee'. In search of more graphic prose to describe what kind of relationship this implies, there seems to be a central complaint of 'You don't care about me' with a counter along the lines of 'You need to be looked after but not by me'. It suggests a neglectful or disowning parent with a dependent child. While this analogy may be obvious in terms of parent-manager and child-employee, it also holds true for the employer who may feel at risk from, and neglected by, the employee on whose actions the employer, and thus the organisation, is dependent. An example of this might be the impact of Leeson's actions upon Barings Bank.

It is unsurprising to note that managers, some of whom have contributed here, similarly describe how they may feel disregarded by those to whom they are accountable and who could also be considered in breach of duty of care.

The statement 'duty of care' is important to this discussion, not so much in terms of Health and Safety at work legislation but because the term is applicable to the central task of Social Work. 'Users' demand and require 'care', either actually, in the case of an abandoned child, or, less literally, through some form of assistance to make their lives more manageable. The polarisation between Walker and his employers might be understood as having arisen when the 'demand for care' became too overwhelming, both for Walker in relation to his staff and clients and for his employers in relation to him. Each of the parties might argue differently about responsibilities for 'care' and where it should 'begin'. However, I simply wish to make, perhaps, the obvious point that many 'users' of services feel overwhelmed with their own difficulties and thus carry the potential to overwhelm others, particularly through their unmet emotional needs. When this 'impact' is not fully taken into account, the effect on both the individual worker and the organisation is likely to be deleterious.

Many people within the profession might disagree with any idea that they are not aware of the needs of their clientele and would say they make every attempt to fulfil their obligations. While I am sure the latter in one sense is true, I also think that the profession, within an organisational context, and perhaps more so, in the statutory sector, has felt it necessary to create defensive structures in proportion to increasing demands for 'care' in an increasingly 'unsympathetic' environment. In the way that I have described how individuals have had to distance themselves from the 'threat' of being overwhelmed, so too have organisations erected structures to avoid being overwhelmed. I am also suggesting that the individual and organisational defences reinforce each other and, in doing so, provide an environment that engenders stress. If this is true then there is a concomitant defence against properly recognising the potential for stress.

In relation to the above it may be useful to explore two suppositions:

1. Yes, there is stress in social work. The potential for stress is inherent to the job. 'Somewhere' in the work is stress. It is something that is accepted along with the contract, salary and the car loan. It has certainty as an occupational hazard – as much an expected part of the deal as, say, 'oily hands to the car mechanic'. One would therefore expect something analogous to hand-cleanser to be available somehow to wash away the grime at the end of the day. If the 'somewhere(s)' could be located, and if this view was shared by all, then, as with 'ordinary' Health and Safety schemes, there could be a similar shared agreement to establish integrated 'psychic' welfare schemes to 'wash away' the stress. Such 'schemes' might include the availability of regular casework-centred supervision, counselling, psychotherapy, regular supervision for all levels of management,

regular consultancy for staff and managers and the means to share acknowledgement of impact of work and how it can lead to polarisation. The lack of such schemes suggests that this interpretation is not shared by 'all'.

2. The second supposition is more of a question: 'Stress in Social Work?' One would not, or should not, normally expect to find stress in this work. It was not part of the contract. When it is experienced it may thus be denied by the 'victim' and by his/her colleagues, hence superficial statements such as 'frequently off sick' or 'under-functioning in the team'.

I think a 'state of mind' exists in individuals and organisations that incorporates both the above suppositions. The first, that potential for stress is inherent to the work, is not fully recognised but is, nevertheless, (unconsciously) 'known'. The second supposition, then, represents the defence against 'knowing' the first to be true. There may be many reasons, some that I have already alluded to, that suggest themselves to account for this defence. Not least of these are the 'supposed' implications for already over-tight budgets if mechanisms to manage the stress the structure were to be improved as I briefly outlined above (I say 'supposed' because, self-evidently, some such structure would surely produce less sickness and better functioning of individuals and teams).

If stress is eventually identified, it is frequently viewed as something that has 'got in' from outside, an intruder that has to be removed. As in the Walker case, overwork is often the first suspect and there may be joint attempts to rectify this. When this 'intruder' hypothesis inevitably breaks down, a more appropriate search may be made on the 'inside', but this search, as I have said, seems predisposed to fail through polarisation.

The above process may be likened to that of parents who blame 'the school' for a child's delinquency, thereby avoiding their own responsibility. When that 'explanation' fails, the parents may blame each other (thus ignoring the child) in preference to the more painful task of trying to understand something together with the child.

Stress in the context of social work implies a certain kind of 'relationship', of something being done to somebody that is uncaring, harsh, unthinking and sadistic. One frequently hears of practitioners and managers alike complaining that they are treated as inanimate objects: 'I don't count', 'They are inhuman' or 'I am treated as an unthinking machine expected to do everything'. Several of the authors draw attention to this kind of treatment. However, this treatment is not simply something meted out by others. People also treat themselves in this way. Expecting themselves to be able to cope with the emotional demands placed on them, we may sometimes hear 'I'm immune' or 'I just switch off' to describe a practitioner's response to the impact of an overwhelming number of traumatising cases. More privately, they may resent their client's demanding phone calls and may also feel cold and hateful towards them. Managers may equally expect themselves to cope with impossible demands, say, of providing appropriate services to all on a paltry budget and they may resent their employers as well as their employees for failing to do the impossible. They may feel cold and sadistic, hence such increasingly heard expressions as 'I am going to kick ass' while sometimes, in a number of cases to my knowledge, privately harbouring suicidal thoughts. When eventually somebody is clearly observed to be 'mal-functioning', they may be disciplined, given sickness leave, sent for 'counselling' or ignored. The 'switched off' or mechanical defence has collapsed but the response, albeit sympathetic, may itself be 'mechanistic'. The real basis for the stress is unlikely to be explored in the context of the organisation and its work. Polarisation is maintained, with opposing 'explanations', often unstated, such as 'overwork' versus 'inherent weakness in the employee'.

In pursuit of some further understanding of the mechanistic elements that emerge, a reference to *Chambers Dictionary* will reveal 'Stress' as: 'A system of forces applied to a body'. The term, with origins in Physics, refers to the way different materials behave differently, *bend*, under a set amount of force. I think this way of conceptualising stress, reserved for inanimate objects, tends to be utilised by many people to describe feeling under pressure from other people. Furthermore, while the *internal* 'forces' in a human being tend to be ignored or denied in this process, so too is the idea that different people may respond differently under the same 'weight' of 'forces'; a luxury which, although afforded to inanimate objects, is not so easily allowed to, and by, humans, particularly in the context of an organisation. Differences between people, when they are acknowledged, tend to be pejorative with an implication of weakness. For example, 'X does twice as much work as Y but he/she never goes off sick'. In the case of Walker, it may be considered that both 'sides' differed as to the capacity of a 'human being'.

Some credence is given to the notion that a certain amount of stress is useful to maximise an individual's performance. While this might be regarded as yet another legitimate use of the term, more appropriate terms might be 'pressure', 'stimulation', 'deadlines' or 'encouragement'. Perhaps 'stress' is used in this way to differentiate between those who 'benefit' from being pushed and those who can't keep up. This 'whip them to see if they go faster' approach complies also with the mechanistic notion. To expand on the comparison with physics, a metal placed under a certain force will recover its former shape when the force is released – like a spring. If the force is exceeded, the metal will not recover, hence 'metal fatigue' often heard about in relation to unfliable aircraft. In relation to human beings, are we to accept this sadistic notion of deliberately pushing people to ascertain their breaking point?

There is much to give reinforcement to this notion of stress as one where 'forces' are applied to a passive, inanimate and, therefore, unthinking body. I recently heard a teacher on the radio say that 'stress levels in schools are high'. Does this mean there is something external to the person built into the fabric of a school that threatens anybody entering? We also hear people say that they are 'all stressed out', so is it, perhaps, something that emerges from the internal fabric of the body under certain conditions? We also hear people say that they are 'under stress', which again suggests something external but related specifically to one person, much like a private rain cloud. Is there something about the 'work' of social work that is responsible for the 'dehumanising' notions about stress?

Social work deals in chaos, poverty, hatred, child abuse, violence, criminality, delinquency, depression, debilitation, incompetence, vulnerability, deprivation and mental ill-health. Many of its clients will have experienced and internalised a sense of being dehumanised through being treated as 'inanimate' objects of violence or sexual abuse. In the constant attempt to respond 'professionally', the practitioner is open to be traumatised to some degree on a daily basis, however 'well trained'. To deny this with such retorts as 'I have become immune' or 'You should be able to cope' is to say that a way has been found that seems to prevent another's misery from making any impact', in other words to have also 'become' dehumanised. In consequence, the desperately desired defence against the primitive anxieties that are aroused becomes, by default, contempt. Forced to deal with many cases at a time, the social worker might easily succumb to the omnipotent idea that he/she should be able to be manage, emotionally if not practically. Their managers may also succumb to a need to acquire 'immunity' against their anxiety by attempting to meet the contradictory and high demands of the public and their elected representatives.

In the way individuals may behave to defend themselves against anxiety, organisations create structures for protecting themselves. The work of Isabel Menzies Lyth (1959), *The Functioning of Social Systems as a Defence Against Anxiety*, is well known in this area. The omnipotent wishes of society, which too wants to protect itself from anxiety, are projected into politicians, who, in turn, make unrealistic demands on social work organisations. The organisations, partly because of the way they have been structured historically, attempt to comply. The consequence is an inevitable split between the administrators and the practitioners.

The practitioners, who, responsible for enacting the central task of their organisation, in the attempt to comply make unrealistic demands on themselves and, in doing so, can begin to feel helpless and impotent. If they go 'against the grain', for example to engage in a more worthwhile professional alliance with a client than 'care management', an absence of support and supervision would mean that they risk the same feelings of impotence through exposure to projections for which there may be no understanding container. They may then have to try and defend themselves from the anxiety arising from these feelings in ways such as I have discussed above. Several authors here draw attention to the demise of casework and casework supervision.

The administrators also seek ways to manage their anxiety arising from the financial restriction and other unrealistic demands that I have mentioned above. Many social work organisations, to achieve an illusion of control and thus allay their anxiety, have put themselves through constant re-organisation, in one case twice in three years. Whatever gains are expected by such manoeuvres, they must also be met by uncertainty and insecurity among staff to the detriment of their clientele. Some organisations have introduced computers for some social workers and probation officers to record actions to confirm procedures are being followed. In having to type their own records, and gradually replacing typists with staff who were trained to work with people, they are also being encouraged to communicate with each other by 'E-Mail'. It seems evident that there is an unconscious and 'dehumanising' attempt to create a 'safe' distance between the organisation and the people it is there to serve, that is to defend against the source of anxiety.

Social work organisations differ from many others in which the responsibility is forced upwards into the management structure, for example medicine, police, law and banking. The profession is, perhaps, unique in that the central task of the organisation is almost entirely the responsibility of the most junior. It is not surprising, therefore, that, given the demands of the work in relation to practitioner status, many social workers become administrative managers at the first opportunity. Often, for reasons I have discussed, this hoped-for 'escape' with a little extra salary and status is found to offer no refuge.

At the public interface, enquiries, into child death tragedies for instance, in the way they are set up, provide an example, how the polarising defence is strengthened. Many of these enquiries are chaired by lawyers whose professional milieu is adversarial and whose professional purpose is apportionment of blame. Each enquiry finds its scapegoats and makes the same trite recommendations for more procedures to 'ensure that this never happens again' – which, of course, it does, repeatedly. Why lawyers? Why not professionals trained to understand organisational processes and with experience of working with psychic and physical injury and deprivation? This is not to say that recommendations of better liaison, training, supervision and management are not laudable and often vitally necessary but these risk being mechanistically applied through the wish to defend against recognition of anxiety of the task.

Conclusion

Unlike many other professions, the practice of social work offers little potential for obvious rewards, as, for instance, the winning of a case offers to a barrister or an operation offers to the surgeon. Because they deal in actual and emotional injustice, and actual and psychic injury, the reality for social workers much of the time is that while they may bring about some relief or improvement, the most that they may hope for is some damage limitation, particularly in areas such as child abuse and criminality. While many social workers will take issue with that statement, I think that an unrealistic expectation, or 'omnipotent' wish, is hard to avoid when it is considered that social workers are given the burden of the unrealistic demands of society, politicians, press and their own organisations to some degree but, most importantly, their internal demands. While it is very difficult to face constantly the occupationally expected reproach of others, it is much more difficult to face the more pernicious 'internal' critic that may not allow damage to go unrepaired.

While the experience of disappointment and apparent professional 'failure' is commonplace, much professional satisfaction is also reported. There are obvious rewards, say, in the satisfactory adoption placement of a child. Similarly, if 'allowed', sustained work with an emotionally impoverished, damaged child or delinquent adult can be enriching, more so in an environment where realistic and achievable objectives can be accepted by all concerned. I have discussed how I think such an environment cannot properly exist unless the impact of the task upon the providers of social work is properly understood, and thus managed, in a way that recognises institutional defences when they arise.

To draw my main conclusion into a workable statement, anxiety is an intrinsic part of social work, which, when it is not recognised and understood, is likely to lead to stress.

CHAPTER 1

Public Pressure: Private Stress

Chris Wilmot

Introduction

In November 1994 the case of *Walker* v. *Northumberland County Council* put the issue of stress in the workplace firmly on employers' agendas. More specifically, since John Walker was a team manager responsible for child protection cases, it raised particular issues for local authority social services departments.

Briefly, the facts are these. In February 1988 John Walker was dismissed on the grounds of permanent ill-health following his second nervous breakdown in just over a year. With the support of his union, he sued the council for breach of its duty of care implied to him under common law. He won his case. Damages were agreed in an out of court settlement in April 1996.

The basis of the case was that Mr Walker, quite simply, had too much work, which, combined with the stressful nature of his work (managing a child protection team), led to his illness. Because the council was aware of his excessive workload and of his previous illness, it was judged to have failed in its duty of care. The first breakdown should have alerted his employers to his vulnerability and adequate support provided to alleviate the pressures on him. Although some extra support had been given to Mr Walker, it was not felt by the court to have been sufficient and hence the second breakdown. The employer was thus negligent.

The case has prompted many local authorities to take various measures to help identify areas of stress and develop awareness among staff of it's causes and symptoms. These, primarily, take the form of training courses, especially for managers, but may also include employee development schemes, access to counselling and the monitoring of absence through sickness – the last more through reasons of economy. These measures are necessary because, as the Walker case showed, once employers are aware of problems caused to workers through stress, they have a duty to respond appropriately.

What is stress?

Everybody will have experienced stress at some time in their lives. It should not be confused with pressure, although, to some, the terms are interchangeable. Rather, stress can be defined as an individual's reaction to too much pressure. The situation creating the pressure does not seem to be avoidable. The reaction will be negative, professionally and personally.

Consequences and causes

Individuals react to stress in different ways. They may feel undermined, lose confidence, develop a heightened sense of vulnerability or suffer from anxiety, depression or apathy. Stress can also manifest itself in more externally identifiable ways. These may include irritability, loss of concentration, cynicism or avoidance rituals. The stressed individual may also develop patterns of heavy drinking or smoking, compulsive eating or absence from work.

Most people would understand that simply having too much work is a major cause of stress. While this is undoubtedly true, other stress-inducing factors will become apparent in my consideration of the job of a local authority social worker. There will be pressure from clients, managers and from the organisation as a whole. Moreover, because social work is 'publicly owned', every social worker, especially those working with children, will know that their work is subject to regular scrutiny by press, politicians and public. These pressures lead to stress-inducing factors that include role conflict or uncertainty, dealing with anger and hostility and the mismatch between need and resources.

The local authority worker in a children and families team

In this chapter I will be focusing on potential sources of stress in the job of social worker in a local authority children and families team. I will assume that the social worker is working in a typically under-funded department, with existing and anticipated financial constraints and their consequent impact on workload and resources. The following themes will be addressed:

- ◦ The effect on the individual of working in the public sector, with the concomitant local procedures, accountability and auditing mechanisms

- ◦ The increasing variance between the social worker's perception of her role and the expectations not only of the public but of her own department

- ◦ The necessity to be conversant with the wide-ranging statutory powers and duties, primarily under the Children Act 1989, and the impact of working within this framework.

The Children Act introduces the concept of a 'child in need'. It requires each local authority to provide services to each child who has been identified as being 'in need' in their area. Although the definition of a child in need can encompass a wide range of children, in reality the social worker's caseload will consist almost entirely of children who come under two categories: child protection and children in care, or 'looked after' as it is termed in the Act. These two categories will provide the focus for my discussion.

Child protection

This is the area that many people might imagine induces most stress in a social worker. Posters of battered and neglected children and newspaper accounts of severe physical, sexual and emotional abuse do indeed prompt distress and anger in the public, and social workers are not immune to these responses.

In addition, the social worker is aware of the possibility of publicity in the field of child protection if a child dies or is seriously injured. There is a realistic fear that this eventuality could lead to an internal or public inquiry, exposing the individual worker, her supervisor and her manager to detailed and painful scrutiny. When this arises, the resultant publicity is invariably negative for the worker and the authority. The potential for anxiety and stress in the worker in such a context is considerable, as one might expect.

There are, however, two important moderating factors in this area of work that should, in theory, effectively reduce anxiety in the worker.

The first is that there are very clear procedures governing the appropriate action on child protection cases. From the moment a child protection referral is made, the social worker has to follow a specific set of procedures. These involve consultation at the outset with a senior practitioner, information gathering and then action. Other agencies become key players in the investigation, in particular the police child protection team and a medical practitioner.

The second moderating influence follows on from the first. Other agencies are not simply involved at the initial stages of an investigation. Recommendations of public enquiries, government guidance and indeed the Children Act require a local area child protection committee to oversee inter-agency co-operation in cases of child protection. Relevant agencies, including the police, education and health service professionals, are invited to every child protection conference and have a key role in monitoring children on the child protection register. Although the social worker is usually nominated as the keyworker, other statutory agencies have equal responsibility. However, because each agency approaches a case from a different professional perspective, there can be disagreements, often only in emphasis, but sometimes about the nature of approach or action. Moreover, in the event of serious injury to, or death of, a child it is the perceived inadequacies of the social work input which will be highlighted by press and public.

Procedures and guidelines may provide the social worker with a framework within which to practice in this field but she also recognises that as the keyworker, she will be viewed as the person holding prime responsibility for a child at risk. She has to try to learn to live with risk and uncertainty.

Hostility and violence

The threat to the *status quo* of a family, which child protection investigations pose, unsurprisingly produces a reluctance on behalf of parents to co-operate with the social worker. This reluctance will sometimes develop into hostility directed to the worker. This situation is exacerbated when the parents assemble an array of supporters, who may include relatives, lawyers or local councillors. The social worker can sometimes feel under siege. This circumstance is an inevitable consequence of the powers invested in a social worker that are designed to protect the child. Almost always it is the parent or step-parent from whom the children are to be protected.

Hostility may often develop into threats or actual violence against the worker. A survey commissioned by the National Institute of Social Work during 1993 and 1994 found that almost a quarter of field social workers had been physically assaulted at work, nearly half threatened with violence and over three-quarters shouted at or insulted (Balloch *et al.* 1995).

In my recent experience, two staff have received counselling – one following a serious physical assault and the other following threats and racist abuse. Nor are managers immune. As a manager myself, I have been physically assaulted at least four times by people as diverse as a female parent and an eight-year-old boy. The NISW report indicates that more than one in five fieldwork managers have been physically attacked.

Most local authorities now define violence to staff as including not only physical assault but also verbal abuse, racist and sexist abuse, threats of violence and intimidating behaviour. Abuse may also come in the form of telephone calls and letters. As research and experience have indicated, it is rare for a social worker not to have been subjected to any of the above and, as a consequence, have suffered some psychological effect.

Accommodating children

The second main area of work is with children and young people coming into the care system. They come into care either through a voluntary arrangement (accommodation) or through the courts.

A local authority has a duty to provide accommodation for a child in their area who may be abandoned or where there is an absence of a responsible parental figure. The most common reason for accommodating a child is because of a perceived breakdown in the relationship between a child and the parent. If, at the outset, the parent, child and social worker all agree that it would not be safe for the child to remain at home, and there are no relatives who could take over the care, the decision to accommodate is relatively straightforward.

However, such consensus is rare. More commonly, when presented with a request from a parent (or more usually a demand) to accommodate a child, the social worker attempts to identify the causes of the difficulties and to offer a package of support. This may include a referral to child guidance or other community resource, which typically have long waiting lists. However, since the referral has been borne of crisis, the parent or child will usually want an instant 'solution'.

The social worker becomes pressurised:

PARENT: If you don't take him away I'll leave him here. I can't be responsible for my actions.

CHILD: I'll only run away again.

Presented with these options, she discusses the case with her manager:

MANAGER: Have you offered community support, such as it is?

SOCIAL WORKER: She won't accept anything. Just wants him out.

MANAGER: Child Guidance?

SOCIAL WORKER: Six months waiting list. Doubtful they'd accept anyway.

MANAGER: Call her bluff. Say we won't accommodate.

SOCIAL WORKER: She's left the office. The boy's still here. Says she's had enough. He won't go anyway.

MANAGER: Relatives?

SOCIAL WORKER: Father not seen for years, Grandmother doesn't want to know. Anyway, she's too ill.

They both know the manager is under extreme pressure to reduce the number of children in care in the team due to the escalating cost of placements, especially for children's homes:

MANAGER: Friends? Neighbours? We'll pay them.

SOCIAL
WORKER: I've explained that. She won't agree, nor will the boy. I
            think they do need a cooling off period. We've got no
            option.

MANAGER: OK then. But only for two weeks maximum, and draw
            up a tight contract. Foster home?

SOCIAL
WORKER: Just one available, who only take under-fives. He's twelve.

The manager agrees to a local private children's home for two weeks. It is three
times the cost of a foster home:

MANAGER: We'll have to allocate the case tomorrow. There's a lot of
            work to be done quickly.

SOCIAL
WORKER: You know I haven't got the space. Nor has anyone else.

The case is allocated three weeks later. The boy remains in care for five months
before returning home.

This typical scenario has costs:

- *to the child*: the emotional cost of knowing his family were unwilling
  or unable to persevere with him through a turbulent period. Their
  solution was rejection

- *to the manager*: the cost of this period of care was the equivalent of
  one year's salary for a full-time social worker

- *to the social worker*: the frustration of once again being forced to
  simply react to a situation rather than use her skills in working
  constructively with the family to help them tackle their difficulties.

Care proceedings

Another route into care is through the courts and, therefore, takes longer. In
spite of the principle of minimal delay enshrined in the Children Act, care
proceedings often continue for several months.

If a child is found to be suffering 'significant harm', a social worker may
apply to the court for an emergency protection order to remove that child to a
safe place for a maximum of eight days. If, during this period, it is still felt that
the child would be at risk if returned home, the social worker will return to

court and apply for an interim care order. Further interim care orders are likely to be made and a date for a final hearing will be set. More commonly, care proceedings will be instituted without the prior making of an emergency protection order. The court may make specific directions, such as frequency of contact between parent and child or a psychiatric assessment on child/family. A *guardian-ad-litem* will be appointed as an independent representative of the best interests of the child.

Care proceedings can take up a significant proportion of a social worker's time. Pressure builds up from a number of sources. These will include deadlines for producing written statements, cross-examination by lawyers representing the parents, the child and other interested parties and making arrangements for contact between child and parent. The social worker may also have to deal with the hostility of the parents, the confusion of the child and the possibility that the *guardian-ad-litem* or a psychiatrist may have a different point of view. Meanwhile, her other cases, comparatively neglected, continue their relentless demands.

Preparing a case for court and undergoing cross-examination will be an expected and naturally-occurring experience for any social worker in this field. Even a competent worker is likely to feel anxious, sometimes almost paralysed before giving evidence. However, a degree of professional satisfaction may be obtained in the process if the task is successfully completed.

Nevertheless, especially in contested cases, which are the majority, most social workers will acknowledge that care proceedings are among the most stressful aspects of their work. Their professional judgement is subject to detailed and open scrutiny by lawyers, a different profession operating on its own familiar territory.

Placement

One of the most problematic and stressful areas of work with looked after children is that of identifying and then successfully maintaining an appropriate placement. It is generally accepted that for most children, especially younger ones, a home within a family is preferable to a residential establishment. Foster carers are in short supply. A foster carer who can meet the needs of a particular child will be in even shorter supply. Children's homes are generally less satisfactory, the quality often questionable and they are expensive. It will frequently be the case that the social worker takes what is offered, especially when an immediate placement is needed.

Placement breakdowns are a regular occurrence. Recent publicity has highlighted a number of cases where children have had as many as a dozen placements. One child experienced twelve fostering and four residential break-downs between the ages of ten and fifteen. When this happens, it can be distressing for the social worker who has established a good constructive relationship with a child. It is demoralising for the social worker if the placement has been carefully prepared with the hope that it will be long term. A typical example:

> An abused and very damaged eleven-year-old girl, on a care order; three fostering breakdowns, now in a barely adequate children's home. The social worker and psychiatrist recommended a long-term residential therapeutic community with education. Only three were identified. One turned her down – it was felt by the home that she would not fit into the current group. Another was not seen as suitable since it was too far away from her most significant relative. The third seemed appropriate but she would have to wait six months. There was also a dispute about funding between the social services and education departments. The child remained in an inappropriate placement.

The work is a struggle to match the assessment of need with available, appropriate and affordable resources. The task of attempting to work in these circumstances constantly produces feelings of frustration, powerlessness and hopelessness in the worker. Provision of appropriate resources is a central function of social service departments and such feelings are thus common to all social workers working in this field.

Contrary to popular belief, the social worker has little control over resources. She does not work alone but plays a small part in a publicly accountable, organisational structure. Each section of the organisation controls a resource that may be accessed only by adhering to specific bureaucratic procedures. Moreover, the organisation itself is linked to other organisations, both statutory and otherwise, each with their own bureaucratic procedures that may conflict with one another. In relation to resource provision, since social services are funded through local taxation, the nature and availability of resources depends to a large extent on the preferences and ideologies of the political party that holds power locally. Thus, to understand further the nature and causes of stress in local authority social work, it is important to examine the context within which the core task, as I have described it, is carried out.

The context

The Local Authority Social Services Act 1970 states that each local authority must have a social services committee and must have a person who undertakes the duties of director of social services. These duties are enshrined in relevant legislation. The key Act for the social worker in a children and families team is the Children Act 1989. The Children Act attempted to bring together fragmented laws covering children. It is founded on the belief that children are generally best looked after in their families and it introduced the concept of parental responsibility. The Act also outlines the duties of a local authority to give support to children and their families and provides a number of court orders designed to protect and encourage the welfare of the child.

In 1995–96 the total number of social services departments in England and Wales was 118, with a staff of 350,000. There are, therefore, an average of 3000 staff in each social services department. The annual budget of each department will be between 40 and 70 million pounds, largely made up from central government funding and local council taxes.

Central government imposes a number of duties and powers on a local authority, in the form of legislation, regulatory and statutory instruments and circulars. Moreover, and importantly, performance is monitored through the Social Services Inspectorate and the District Auditor, and, in complaints cases, the Local Government Ombudsmen may be approached to investigate specific issues. This scrutiny from central government, allied with an increasing expectation of a quality service by members of the public, has meant that local authorities have become more aware of their own accountability.

Local councillors, especially, appear to have become more sensitive to their accountability. As elected members, they have always been accountable to their electorate. However, it is only since the early 1980s that they have become more involved in decision making and initial appointments of officers. They no longer allow their employees – the professionals – the autonomy they formerly enjoyed. Similarly, chief officers have become more politicised and less disposed to challenging the customary division of responsibility between members and officers. Also, since councillors are themselves drawn from varying sections of the community, many, even those on social services committees, share the public's scepticism of social workers. Alongside this shift in member involvement and the decreasing autonomy of the 'professional' chief officer, has come the necessity for severe financial restraint in all local authority departments.

Consequently, the priorities of the directors and senior managers of all local government departments will reflect this finance-led approach to service delivery. The run-up to the end of each financial year will see a scramble by the various departments for a sizeable slice of the authority's diminishing financial cake. And along will come a blueprint for another reorganisation, the rationale for which will, almost certainly, be economic rather than improved service delivery. The social worker (and, to a greater extent, the middle manager) thus finds herself monitored on two fronts: quality and cost. She is confronted with volumes of forms issued by the Department of Health concerning 'looked after children'. There is increased regulation, standardised procedures and more centralised control over social services work with children and families. This has meant that costly placements have to be justified, often scrutinised by a panel, and constantly reviewed. Many departments will establish advisory posts – a misnomer because, in effect, this group of staff will be concerned with monitoring, setting up meetings, sitting on gate-keeping panels and devising procedures – largely to control expenditure.

A complaints unit will produce leaflets publicising the customer/client/council taxpayer's right to complain. Clients, now customers, also have the right of access to their files. These rights, although laudable, place extra pressure on the front-line social worker, who will frequently feel criticised, undermined and put in a position of defendant on trial.

In addition, she becomes subject to various organisational initiatives, such as staff appraisals, absence monitoring, excellence awards and regular restructuring. She also becomes aware that her employing organisation talks about a vision or mission statement or a set of core values and that her manager appears to be preoccupied with quality standards, performance indicators and service plans.

In short, the local authority social worker in the 1990s has become very much an 'organisation person'.

Role conflict

This role, however, does not sit comfortably on her for two inter-related reasons: the erosion of her professionalism and her doubtful commitment to the values of her department. The National Institute of Social Work's survey revealed that about half of field social workers felt that a source of stress for them was that they were expected to do things that were not part of the job (Balloch *et al.* 1995).

Even more important, they felt they were unable to attend to matters they see as central to the job. The areas of work for which the social worker has been trained and which afford satisfaction – assessing need and obtaining resources, interacting directly with clients and using interpersonal skills – are increasingly becoming swamped in a sea of bureaucracy and organisational demands. The literature on the subject of organisations has long recognised that 'role conflict' at work can be a major source of stress in individuals (McKenna 1987; Vecchio 1995; Khan *et al.* 1964). This can be defined as the incompatibility between ones own values and beliefs and the values and expectations of the role senders within the organisation. In a practical sense, it means having to do tasks which you do not feel should be part of the job or, perhaps, undertaking tasks which conflict with your values and beliefs. In 1990 I conducted a survey of social workers in the local authority where I worked at the time. This revealed that 93 per cent saw themselves as professional social workers rather than local government officers. Not one respondent felt that the council's core values were more important than social work principles.

The social worker is a professional who, through working in a bureaucratic organisation, participates in two systems: the profession and the organisation. Within this scenario it would not be surprising to discover areas of frustration, stress and even conflict. Scott (1966) highlighted four possible such areas that the professional in a bureaucracy would experience: resistance to bureaucratic rules, rejection of bureaucratic standards, resistance to bureaucratic supervision and the professional's conditional loyalty to the organisation. He comments that a worker with a developed professional self-image tends to take an 'instrumental' view of the organisation for which she works. In other words, if the employing organisation seems unable to fulfil fundamental work needs, the professional will look elsewhere for employment.

An equally important fact shared by these professionals is that they work for human service organisations in the public sector. They, and the organisations they work for, are publicly accountable. Yet, within these organisations, there exist three separate, yet interlocked, spheres of influences, or domains, each with its own set of values and success measures. These are, briefly, the policy domain (centrally and locally elected representatives), the management domain (manager) and the service domain (in this case, social workers) (Kouzes and Mico 1979). The success measures of those in the policy domain will be concerned with public satisfaction and equity, those in the management domain with cost efficiency and 'effectiveness' and those in the service domain with meeting perceived client need. The conflicts inherent in this system have, in the past, tended to be tolerated and accepted as inevitable and, on occasions, have contributed positively to a developing organisation. However, over recent years there has been a blurring of the boundaries between the separate domains, which has upset the previous equilibrium.

As I mentioned earlier in this chapter, local councillors have become more 'hands on' and have adopted the principles formerly owned by managers: those of economy, efficiency and effectiveness. At the same time, managers, themselves mostly former social workers, have tried to refine and develop their management skills. Management consultants are engaged to work on specific projects. Suddenly, 'management speak' has become as common and, to the 'untrained ear', as meaningless, as 'social work speak' was a decade or so earlier. The duty to provide a service within increasingly severe budgetary restrictions results in regular dilemmas for managers at all levels but most especially for the middle manager, who is more closely involved with the day-to-day work of the social workers. Moreover, it is the middle manager who has to persuade the social workers of the necessity of carrying out the many organisational and extra-organisational demands, even though he or she may question the value of some of them.

Front-line social workers, understandably, have been more reluctant to adapt. The emphasis on regulation, standard setting, performance monitoring, value for money and quantitative and qualitative appraisal is hard to reconcile. Although they will have been trained to hold the same values and have the same skills as social workers of a decade earlier, they are now in an 'organisational world' that has quite different expectations of them.

Summary

The very nature of the social work task can be stressful, but it can also be stimulating and afford considerable job satisfaction. It offers relative job security, some degree of autonomy and flexibility and colleagues who are likely to be supportive – all important stress moderators. It is also, however, a job firmly set in the public sector. The social worker will experience pressures common to many other public sector workers, including the consequences of scarce resources, the sense of feeling overwhelmed with forms and procedures, the erosion of professional skills and the demand for ancillary skills such as computer technology. She is also increasingly accountable for her work, not only to her employer and external regulatory bodies but also to her client, who has the right of access to records and recourse to a complaints procedure and the local government ombudsman.

The demands of the role – the expectations others have of ones behaviour – have become greater than the demands of the core task itself. It is expected that the organisational success criteria become the individuals success criteria. This situation of qualitative underload – not being given adequate opportunity to use acquired skills – can lead to frustration, depression, and job dissatisfaction.

The increasing awareness of the cost, human and financial, of stress in the workplace and, as in the Walker case, the possibility of litigation, has led to many employers introducing stress management programmes, health promotion schemes and, in some cases, individual counselling. These have their place, but they tend to focus on how the individual can better cope with stress rather than on the factors within the workplace that cause stress.

The focus should additionally be on the interface between the individual and the organisation, and the structure, policies, procedures and priorities of the organisation. If these issues are not addressed, social workers, the people responsible for the protection of some of the most vulnerable members of our society, will continue to become depleted and demoralised.

CHAPTER 2

No Health, No Service…

Ann Kutek

At the time of writing (May 1996), the world of work is seeing unprecedented transformations. The purpose of this chapter is to show that with retrenchment in resources and changes in work practices, there is an attendant risky mismatch between service demands on the one hand and the responsiveness of the workforce on the other (Pink 1995). It is proposed that an analysis of this mismatch needs to focus on organisational as well as personal aspects and would further benefit from being informed by a body of paradigms from a psychodynamic perspective in order to accommodate the complexities thrown up and to increase the effectiveness of interventions.

Setting the scene

At this point we probably cannot comprehend fully the shifts that are affecting all professions in general and the helping professions in particular. Major changes have been in evidence for a decade or so and seem to be accelerating. Here are just some of them: large corporations, like extensive bureaucracies, are contracting; in this country, at least, manufacturing industries have been eclipsed by the service sector. Previously enduring command and control structures are giving way to flatter management processes and to a proliferation of time-limited project teams.

Developments in information technology make distance working an increasing practice; the working day merges with all night facilities, as in food supplies and financial services. Careers no longer follow a straight nor upward path. Part-timers are swelling the ranks of the employed, either because that is all that is available to them or because that is how they can balance home and earning responsibilities. Indeed, portability and re-skilling are in prospect for growing numbers of workers who are likely to see retirement in their forties or fifties.

National welfare costs are no longer sustainable at the rate they once were. The introduction of a market economy into social and health care is an attempt to control demand. As purchaser-provider arrangements come into force, so have fragmentation and remoteness. Another feature is that of managerialism and audit brought in to drive and cope with these reforms.

It is clear, therefore, that in a maelstrom of this kind, uncertainty and anxiety will be expected to grow. In the absence of predictability there will be individuals who will fall victim to pressures they neither envisaged nor were prepared for. Cumulatively, some organisations will see their primary task put at risk or will have to adapt in ways that may be less than humane (Menzies-Lyth 1988). At its most basic, anxiety, often redefined as 'stress', is a hallmark of our time. It can be described as code for attacks on certainty and on meaning combined with a sense of shame.

Some definitions of stress

Hans Selye (1975), an early writer on the subject, characterised stress as 'the non-specific response of the body to any demand made upon it' (p.13). The non-specificity means that a demand requires adaptation to a challenge, irrespective what it may be. He explains that in addition to specific actions, all agents to which we are exposed also produce a non-specific increase in the need to perform adaptive functions to re-establish normality. This non-specific demand is the essence of stress. He argues, and it is generally accepted, that stress is a necessary factor in life and that many positive outcomes ensue from it. Only when it reaches excessive proportions does it affect individuals in their ability to perform.

Cournoyer (1988) defines this state as 'when the perceived causes of stress are so extreme, occur so frequently and for such a duration that a person becomes overwhelmed or exhausted, when their ability to function becomes impaired or when their coping skills become inadequate, or when external resources are not available or are not sufficient to deal with it' (p.260). What then can we say about the working environment as a whole?

Health in the workplace

There is nothing new about the notion that work carries with it risks to health. By law, employers must provide a safe place in which to work, safe equipment, a safe system of work and competent colleagues. Under the 1974 Health and Safety at Work Act there is a duty to ensure the welfare at work of all employees. However, much of the legislation was enacted at a time when many in the workforce were engaged in the old smoke-stack industries. Since they have been replaced in large measure by service industries that are, on the whole, physically cleaner and less obviously dangerous, a new nomenclature of complaints has appeared: repetitive strain injuries, back problems and a range of stress-related illness. Until the 1990s most occupational health was seen in predominantly physical terms and was clearly tied to a dominant medical model. The emergence of 'stress' fills a vacuum of understanding in the face of a visible decline and failure in performance among workers that cannot be accounted for merely in terms of injury. It coincides with the confluence of change, inadequate management and the intrusions of life events, all of which bring low morale and the foothills of mental and physical ill-health. Recent research findings have indicated that adverse life events, including prolonged stress, are linked to the development of breast cancer (Chen *et al.* 1995).

In December 1995 *The Sunday Times* reported that although most companies are insured against stress-induced illness under their employers' liability policies, cover for stress claims was free because the level of claims was low and insurers believed it would remain so. This attitude is set to change in the light of the Walker case that was resolved in April 1996 in an out-of-court settlement of £175,000 in compensation to a Northumberland Council social services manager who suffered a breakdown attributed to a relentless workload (McGowan 1996).

If the visible bill for stress is still very small, it is the invisible bill that is potentially more insidious. Aside from the estimated 90 million working days lost each year computed by the Health and Safety Executive, which is said to cost the country around £4 billion, there is the human toll on people's health, relationships and, significantly, on the decisions they make or fail to make – with possibly far-reaching results.

The extent of stress and its consequences are partially obscured by people's reluctance to come forward and register their suffering, even when they have been able to identify it for themselves. This may be due to a fear of being targeted as a suitable candidate for future down-sizing or to a powerful sense of shame in a culture of 'presenteeism' that translates as putting in long hours means impressing employers with hard work and loyalty. That long hours bring diminishing returns is nowhere better documented than in the case of thousands of junior hospital doctors who have long pushed the claim that their working conditions put lives at risk. One such, a Dr Johnstone, reported in *The Sunday Times* piece, won £5600 from his former employing health authority, after six years' battle, in another out-of-court settlement. Also during 1995, a trade union representing professional employees published the results of a survey that showed that as many as 60 per cent of skilled and professional respondents had suffered excessive stress at some time in the previous year (Manufacturing Science and Finance Union Survey 1995).

Perceived causes of stress

The last Government responded slowly to the onslaught in the press about spiralling stress statistics and the cost to the exchequer and employers. The publication of the HMSO employers' guide to mental health and stress in the workplace (Cooper and Cartwright 1996), sponsored by the Department of Health, was delayed for months, due, it is thought, to the fact that it had specifically linked coronary heart disease to excessive stress. It lists a range of physical mental symptoms of stress and suggests as typical causes:

- factors intrinsic to the job
- role in the organisation
- relationships at work
- career development
- organisational structure and culture
- home/work interface.

Jose Pottinger (1995), a contributor to the stress debate from the perspective of a leading human resources professional, has divided causes of stress, or stressors, into two distinct categories:

Environmental stressors:

- increased competition
- rapidly accelerating change in technology and IT
- organisational restructuring
- increase in dual earning homes
- greater insecurity.

Psychosocial stressors:

- erroneous value systems – overwork is admired
- poor organisational culture
- role ambiguity
- lack of career prospects
- control and command systems
- difficult inter-personal relationships at work
- conflict between home and work
- task design

- ○ workload and pace

- ○ work schedule.

While undoubtedly helpful as general pointers to the origins of some stress, such lists, on their own, eschew the complexity of the human factors and remain isolated in much current personnel and management thinking. Arguably, unless inter-personal aspects can be more fully unpacked and understood, there remains the risk that other responses to stress stand to be themselves over-whelmed.

Pressures on the social services

The Walker case may yet prove to be a watershed for employer liability. However, social and health service employees, whether in the statutory or independent sectors, have long expressed concerns in terms that ask 'who cares for the carers?' This has been highlighted whenever attacks, some tragically fatal, have taken place against residential workers, social workers, GPs and probation officers.

The issues are not only related to personal safety but to those causes that lie at the root of demoralisation and burnout. Social work (and health care) as a profession can draw on a distinguished tradition of 'psycho-social' work and writing to inform its understanding, structures and working relationships (Balint 1954; Bion 1961; Emery and Trist 1972; Menzies-Lyth 1988; Mattinson 1975; Temperley and Himmel 1979).

More recently, Jack Nathan (1993) has written about the arduous task of the 'battered social worker' at a time of substantial legislative and structural change. Social workers, or commonly now 'care managers', in local authorities have to take into account the demands of a bureaucracy that includes devolved budgets, targets and legally defined procedures guided by local policies. He writes: 'the social worker comes with an agenda that is complex, loaded with meaning and riven with anxiety — has the child been abused, are the parents lying, are the children safe, what are the possibilities of physical or perhaps emotional violence against me?' (p.74). He asks further: 'Could you imagine anything further from the social worker's mind than undertaking an assessment without memory or desire in a state of uncertainty where doubt can be tolerated?...the social worker's primary focus is on the external life situation of the client for which he or she has to take responsibility if there is for example a child at risk.' (p.74). This situation is parallelled when a person, within the ambit of community care, 'blocks' a hospital bed having suffered a broken hip and can no longer contemplate returning to a life alone while, at the same time, the financial year decrees that budgets for home care, let alone residential care, are running out. We can multiply such instances across the country's departments and only speculate about the net effects on the clients and their workers. So what has happened to the nurturing framework of social work training and practice that apparently helped to see it through the Kilbrandon and Seebohm reforms 25 years ago?

A service audit

The topic of stress has undoubtedly been assisted by the plight of John Walker and has fuelled discussions in numerous professional forums, legal and other. Addressing a conference on 'Stress at Work in the Social Services', Robin SeQueira (1995), past President of the Association of Directors of Social Services (ADSS), identified among sources of prevailing stress, conflicting demands for all work types and the introduction of legislation across all areas of work that had forced staff to grapple with new procedures and skills while under government scrutiny and media attention. Even if the recent reforms in child care and community care were welcome in principle and implementation achieved more or less adequately, tensions in the system were evident. One of the main difficulties was the pace of change, another was strict cash limits. In one authority he quoted there was a 15 per cent increase in all referrals, with a 28 per cent growth in work with older people. In England and Wales there was a reported 36 per cent growth rate in assessment activity. A further new pressure was the duty to publicise services and entitlements alongside the reforms in the health service, driven by its Patients' Charter targets.

A recent ADSS survey showed that among 75 per cent of the respondents, departments were facing budgetary cuts of up to 10 per cent. This had inevitably led to the shuffling of priorities between sectors and the introduction of ever tighter eligibility criteria for services. Care managers were increasingly having to refuse help to any but the most needy cases. A survey by *Community Care Magazine*, cited by SeQueira, indicated that one-third of care managers suffered heightened levels of stress attributable to cash limits. In addition to having to develop financial skills, workers were spending more time on form filling. This raised a common complaint that social workers had neither entered the profession nor received the requisite training for the tasks they were now obliged to carry out.

Consonant with a receding welfare state is the mounting frustration and rage experienced by some clients of social care agencies. This has created fertile ground for acting out feelings in abuse and violence against employees. Although anxiety about attacks could be related more often to perceived vulnerability than to the actual frequency of attacks, it was a signal to protect staff and help them cope. The pervasive need to do more with fewer resources affected all levels in organisations. For example, in child care, chronic under-staffing meant that experienced staff were at a premium. They, in turn, were obliged to concentrate on child protection, fraught as it is with the possibility of mistakes and condemnation by the informed and the ill-informed. There appeared to be decreasing scope for the most rewarding aspects of child and family work. Practitioners were finding themselves challenged and criticised and this eventually gave rise to a sense of inadequacy and helplessness. This was a dangerous condition in which to undertake assessments and contribute to far-reaching decisions.

Although apparently shielded from the worst onslaughts through status and remuneration, senior managers were not immune to stressors of their own. They were trying to implement reforms while often exposed to government censure for inefficiency. The Local Government Review has imposed new boundaries for operation, for new alliances and networks and the inevitable doubts about job security – all to be managed while trying to stay within financial limits and acting as a motivator and support for an anxious workforce.

As a departmental head himself, SeQueira was advocating 'appropriate coping mechanisms' in answer to the overwhelming challenges. He asserted, optimistically, that there were things that could be done to make stress in the workplace more tolerable; one was the improvement of the professional profile of social work as might follow from the establishment of a Social Work Council. He concluded with a *cri de cœur* that staff should not be allowed to remain society's scapegoats, soaking up all the societal problems associated with unemployment, homelessness, family pressures and poverty. He pointed out that social services staff wearied of 'the repetitive, seemingly relentless projection of negative images with the resultant detrimental effect on their self-image and worth'.

Detailed findings

Evidence for some of the foregoing broad-brush analysis is becoming available through a number of studies currently under way. The National Institute for Social Work (NISW) is carrying out a national longitudinal survey of 1276 social services staff in England on behalf of the Department of Health. Although the brief is wider than just looking at the effects of stress on six categories of postholders, a preliminary report highlighted some pertinent indicators (Balloch *et al.* 1995). One of the co-authors, McLean, reporting findings to the Stress at Work Conference, concluded that in the social services field, extreme levels of stress could badly affect the ability of individuals and departments to deliver services effectively.

Stress levels in the study were measured in two ways, by means of an interview about known sources of stress and by scoring a self-completed standard questionnaire for detecting psychiatric disorder in the general population, GHQ12, (Goldberg 1972). The study isolated three groups of stressors, out of a list of a possible twelve, to analyse with the indirect measure of the self-test. They were: unclear boundaries, role conflict and ambiguity and an unpleasant or unsafe physical working environment. The job types included in the study were: home care workers, social work assistants, social workers, non-residential managers, residential workers and residential managers.

It was recognised that stress was a highly complex issue for social services staff. Representatives of each job type experienced stress but it was not a necessary feature of any particular job. While work stress was associated with all job types to a degree, it mostly affected residential managers, non-residential managers and social workers in that order. Neither were stress levels associated with any particular client group, even in the case of residential managers. However, stress levels were higher for those fieldworkers and their managers who were responsible for the provision of services to older people than for other fieldworkers. Levels were also high for field and residential workers who were involved in work with clients who had mental health problems or severe learning disabilities.

In regard to the stressor from an unsafe working environment, two-thirds of residential workers and managers, almost a third of social workers and over a fifth of non-residential managers and home care workers had reported physical attacks or threats of violence in their current jobs. No job type was thus immune to this source of stress, although it was especially high for residential staff and social workers.

In terms of the age distribution of those most prone to stress in the sample, it was associated with younger age on the whole but it was also a particular problem for older fieldwork managers and workers.

The NISW Workforce Survey also looked at the stressors connected with balancing employment and home life, to what extent they might be in conflict and give rise to heightened stress and whether there was a gender difference. Three-quarters of the people surveyed were married or cohabiting. One-fifth of staff had a child of under 12 at home but only 2 per cent were lone parents of such a child. A quarter of staff provided informal care for an elderly, sick or disabled person. This was found to be a higher proportion than among employed people in general, of whom only 16 per cent were informal carers. Conflict between home and work roles was likely to be greater where there was a dependency relationship but the way responsibilities might be reconciled with work could differ.

One aspect of adaptation was to compare the amount of time spent in work. 10 per cent of the men and nearly 50 per cent of the women surveyed worked part-time and the latter's choice was associated with having a dependent child. It was found that those who were part-time had more onerous commitments than full-time counterparts and overall demands on them in work were not necessarily less.

Three conceptually distinct potential stressors were used: job stress – arising out of factors such as excessive workload and responsibility not matched by power, with a lack of support from managers and colleagues; home stress – arising out of problems and pressure at home, such as insufficient time to cope with child care, family illness or care for a frail elder; role conflict – arising from the interaction of job and family, for example having to leave work promptly to collect a child from a minder could make the limit placed on shifting the workload a source of more stress.

The findings in this part of the survey showed that staff were far more likely to report feeling pressure from their job than from home. Thus a quarter felt emotionally or physically drained after work most or all of the time and 41 per cent said they frequently had to rush to get things done, whereas less than 2 per cent of staff reported frequently arriving in work feeling drained due to family pressure. However, in this group, those with caring responsibilities were far more likely than those without to report such stress. The majority of staff reported a good balance between their two roles, although 9 per cent felt the job kept them from their family too much and a quarter frequently wished they had more time with their family.

The conclusions in this part of the study were that parenthood and informal care exceeding 20 hours a week gave rise to increased stress in reconciling job and family and within each home situation men reported more stress than women. Stress from combining paid and unpaid roles may be experienced as due to problems in the job – such as having too much to do, rather than from demands in the home.

Work scheduling, therefore, is a key task for managers in social services to address.

Is there a crisis in social work?

A more recent survey conducted across the whole UK and Northern Ireland by the publication *Professional Social Work* in association with the University of Central Lancashire (Crompton 1996) found that of 1391 social workers who responded to the questionnaire, 687 said they had considered leaving the profession in the last three years and 400 quoted stress as a major factor. Frustration at the lack of resources was named by 387, too much paperwork by 329, erosion of the job they were trained for by 304 and too much work by 210. Violence was mentioned by 72. Seventy per cent of respondents thought that stress was getting worse and almost a fifth stated they had had to take time off work because of symptoms of stress. Those groups most affected by stress were workers in health authorities or health boards (66%), followed by those specialising in drugs and alcohol work (61.8%), and health care provision (61.3%). The sample represented 15 per cent of BASW members, of whom 97.1 per cent held a social work qualification and the mean experience in social work was 17.9 years, 64 per cent of respondents were female and only 2 per cent described themselves as non-white.

The survey also looked at social workers' experience as consumers of social services: 5 per cent had been clients themselves with a further 20 per cent having been clients with a relative, 40 per cent had a close relative who was a client. A majority found services satisfactory, but this depended on the type of service used. The lowest satisfaction ratio was in the area of learning disabilities: 58 per cent of those with client experience said that it had influenced their own work and had underlined the importance of the client-worker relationship.

Given this last indicator, the emphasis now emerging on targets, rationing and paperwork lends weight to the view that the individual relationship with the client, other than as a unit for service delivery, is no longer the primary tool in social work. The publishers of the survey saw the results as a sign that there was a crisis in social work morale and they would form the basis of a campaign by the main professional association, BASW, for better staff care and to promote good staff support among employers in social work.

Potential remedies

Given that the social services sector is not alone in contending with the problems of stress, there are likely to be useful exchanges with industry in sharing ideas about stress and its management. These will be examined here and in the following section. Some coherence of conceptualisation and language is desirable in the first instance.

Pottinger (1995) is representative of some current thinking in industry and proposes responses on several levels – beginning with identification of the hazards, followed by risk assessment and by the implementation of effective control strategies. A summary of the important specifics would be:

- employee assistance and stress management programmes
- employee involvement
- appropriate job design
- compatibility of employee and role
- defined roles and responsibilities
- training and development
- robust communication systems
- appropriate leadership skills
- flexible working patterns.

In contrast, the government's 'Health of the Nation' initiative uses somewhat more militaristic terminology in the 'Defeat Depression' campaign led by the Royal College of Psychiatrists. Cooper and Cartwright (1996) adopt a language more redolent of organisational psychology. They propose a strategy composed of a number of options to combat stress through 'prevention' at a series of levels.

Primary prevention is concerned with taking action to reduce or eliminate stressors and positively promoting a supportive and healthy working environment. It involves changes in policy, improving communication systems, redesigning jobs and enhancing autonomy at all levels. It relies on a prior diagnosis and, or stress audit to identify what the stressors are and whom they affect.

Another step is to create the opportunity for employee discussion groups on sources of stress. This can be achieved in an organisational climate where stress is recognised as a feature of modern work life and not interpreted as a sign of weakness or incompetence. Explicit steps need to be taken to remove the stigma of emotional problems. This is possible through occupational health programmes, incorporating self-development in appraisal systems and extending the people skills of managers to convey a supportive attitude. Crucial in this is to demonstrate commitment to the issues of stress and mental health at work from senior management and unions. This may require more open communication and the dismantling of certain cultural norms (one could add here that these norms include racism, bullying and glass ceilings.) Employee involvement and communication at times of change have a key role in reducing stress.

Secondary prevention initiatives focus on education and training. It is particularly important for managers to be able to recognise stress in themselves, the cascade effect it can have and the stress in their team members. The effects of management style can have profound effects on others.

Tertiary prevention is concerned with the recovery and rehabilitation process of those individuals who have suffered, or are suffering from, ill-health as a result of stress. It requires the implementation of support programmes. They may include a form of internal or, for reasons of confidentiality, external 'employee assistance programme' (EAP). This may be composed of a number of services such as a telephone helpline, access to personal legal and financial expertise and, sometimes, childcare advice. Confidential counselling is commonly offered by EAPs and thought to be particularly effective when the stressors are of a type that cannot be changed – for example restructuring, job loss, bereavement – but which are likely to intrude into work and home life. Some brief focused counselling can be shown to be dramatically effective in the short term and inform organisations about hidden traps caused by stress (see Pink 1995). Counselling is sometimes 'covertly' offered in the form of mentoring, especially at executive levels.

Cooper and Cartwright are clear that to develop an effective and comprehensive organisational policy on stress, employers need to integrate all three approaches. Getting started on the path to more humane and, therefore, more productive organisations as outlined requires sustained commitment at key points in the structure from the board room down. It requires mind shifts away from 'molly coddling' and redefinitions of relationships and boundaries of jobs and tasks. Current practices, even when benign, tend to isolate and pick off individual casualties of stress.

Inevitably, policy creation of this type assumes a redistribution of authority, time and other resources. Scepticism about this kind of implementation may be only partially allayed by the threat of litigation or poor employee relations. Sometimes, it takes a shock in the organisation, such as the suicide of a senior manager, to bring about positive action.

Containment and the facilitating environment

Were social work not so beset with the split between the 'cared for' and the 'caring', were it not embracing so exclusively a market model and had the currency of social work not travelled so far from the concern with the dynamics of relating, social services departments and social work educators might be able still to call upon a rich seam of understanding fostered for years in its psychodynamic thinking and practice (Brearley 1991). It is predicated on the variety of relationships common to us all and uses a language and formulations that speak of containment, attachment, holding and reflection as well as threat, anxiety and attack. It is based on the premise that service delivery always involves a set of triangles – for instance the organisation, the worker and the client, where the left-overs of very early unresolved three-person conflicts are liable to come into play and may become intrusive by isolating, say, one of the three parties involved.

It is a paradigm employed in supervision, so lucidly exposed by Mattinson (1975) and by Mattinson and Sinclair (1979) and much favoured in dynamic consultation to groups and organisations (Brearley 1985). Nathan (1993) gives an example of how the conflict between managerial demands and the increasingly violent responses of the client could be reflected and mediated in the safety of a consultation group. Hypothesis generation about what was happening between and inside people lay at the heart of this activity aimed at learning from each encounter and situation.

Another version of the paradigm is elicited from the work with couples at the Tavistock Marital Studies Institute (TMSI), where an action research project involved the creation of learning systems to unpick the complexities of relationships between professionals striving to work together and couples coming for help. It enabled understanding and monitoring of the mutual impacts that occurred through and in the personalities of the workers, their institutions and the clients. The role of anxiety in this work is often definitive and the value of these research findings is applicable to the present discussion. Two TMSI therapists, Woodhouse and Pengelly (1991), have described their experiences in a volume entitled *Anxiety and the Dynamics of Collaboration*. Their formulation of the undermining effects of anxiety uncovers how this major stressor operates among service providers:

> There is ample evidence to show that the painful impact of anxiety on the human psyche and the measures taken to ward it off can inhibit individuals' capacity to think with all their minds, leading at times to what can only be considered as a kind of madness. Practitioners and managers in the caring professions, in their work with and on behalf of clients and patients, are bound to find themselves in situations where events external to themselves seek out and speak to raw sense data from the past. As is now clear, they will use their respective groups and institutions in an effort to avoid the impact. Collaboration is impeded by these powerful and largely unconscious psychodynamic factors. They are necessarily resistant to change since change threatens established ways of perceiving and understanding and, more fundamentally, it also threatens the identities practitioners and their agencies have found themselves impelled to assume. Personal, professional and institutional boundaries are employed to protect them (p. 235).

There are, of course, other theoretical approaches available to the helping professions to explain and deal with such phenomena, most notably systems thinking. As two of its exponents (McCaughan and Palmer 1994) have said in a recent book, 'No theory has an exclusive claim on the truth, because what is said, in language, can never be equated with what is' (p. 106). The important point is that consultants, workers or managers should remain within one discourse and attempt to communicate about what they think they are doing and what is happening without seeking to impose causalities, if they are not shared. A level of linguistic consensus needs to be developed in any 'raids on the inarticulate'.

The difficulties in helping organisations are compounded when there is no shared language to describe what their primary task is and how to analyse and deal with problems. There is also a disinclination to grapple with complexity and perplexity. Nathan (1993) draws attention to the fact that whereas analytic psychotherapists are specifically trained to tolerate what Bion (1961) calls 'negative capability' to remain in doubt, to stay with the anxiety of not knowing, their main concern is with the client's inner world. Social workers and their managers, as we have observed, have to grapple with the hazards and inequities of the outer world. What, then, have therapists and consultants to convey to those who neither have the orientation nor the inclination to delve into intra-psychic issues?

Analytic therapists (among other schools of therapy) have, perhaps perversely, withdrawn to the margins of work life or have been isolated there between the client and the organisation. Nevertheless, workplace issues reach them in the consulting room and many of them are specifically detailed by EAPs to help people cope with stress. They are not only the recipients and containers of the effects of anxiety but witnesses to some of the emotional and psychological congestion that cumulatively afflicts organisations, which presumably they 'think' about. Yet the fruits of that thinking remains isolated from employing organisations and they mostly surrender to them what invariably remains at the level of lists and statistical trends and colludes with the avoidance of examining where the pain, or dysfunctions, might be located and how organisational relationships might be challenged. Since many client organisations of EAPs resist organisationally oriented interventions, this probably accounts for the lack of published research in this area and the reluctance to undertake what Cooper and Cartwright (1996) have called primary and secondary prevention of stress.

In this regard, social services organisations might be better placed and motivated than most to undertake enquiries into how they are falling short in service delivery, beyond financial considerations, towards creating a facilitating environment. They could also reclaim their professional roots to inform their management and supervision systems to sustain and release the thinking of a frequently demoralised workforce. The complexity of the task is already faced by them daily, only mostly at a procedural and political level.

CHAPTER 3

Pass the Parcel: Dynamics of Stress in Management

Linda King

Over the last few years concern about crime has risen. Crime is a frequent media topic, either as fact or fiction, and has become a major political issue. It affects most people's lives and is frequently the subject of debate in the media. Most people have opinions about its causes and how it should be addressed. The government is under pressure to be seen to be in control of crime. This responsibility lies with the Home Office and, ultimately, the Home Secretary. With particular reference to the probation service, I intend to discuss how the potential for stress, arising from unclear or unrealistic policies, seems to be relocated within the criminal justice system through its management structures down to those who attempt to enact those policies. The seeming lack of capacity, at policy level, to recognise the reality of dealing with offenders has serious implications for the police, the courts, the prison service and the probation service. The stress that would arise at policy and legislative level becomes passed around like an unwanted parcel, seemingly, with no one able to open it, unpack it, face it honestly and make the best of it.

Media coverage of crime tends to be fairly simplistic. Politicians wish to be seen to respond to demands from an apparently media-led public. There have been outcries over dangerous dogs, the Jamie Bulger case and knife attacks. All of these have resulted in rapid, barely thought out responses from the Home Office. These have been piecemeal in nature and appear not to be part of an overall strategy. Successive governments choose to treat crime as if it were a simple and not a highly complex matter. Perhaps administrations behave in this way out of a sense of fear that there will be spiralling crime and public disorder.

Governments seek quick results in the attempt to gain popularity and to convey the impression of being effective and in control. In this way the government avoids the stress of trying to face a problem that appears intractable. The stress is 'passed' to its employees – the police, prison officers, judges and probation officers – who not only have to deal with the primary problem but also have now to contend with trying to implement political 'solutions'. They may also suffer from the implications of failure to achieve this. This also impacts on any attempt at a longer term strategy for attempting to reduce crime. The Home Office seems to co-operate little with other government departments on measures such as increasing nursery education or after-school clubs, whose effects on crime will take many years to show results. Genuine support for parents in relation to child development is not considered to be important even though this could both reduce crime and have a beneficial effect upon other problems, such as under achievement in school and mental health, in later life. Such measures would also require investment and a considerable time lag before a return on this would become evident. In some cases government departments may work against each other, increasing frustration amongst individuals throughout the departments. This is reflected at all levels of the probation service. The Home Office, for example, requires probation services to have an employment strategy and encourages them to develop training opportunities for clients. However, training programmes that interfere with the Department for Education and Employment's 16-hour rule mean that participants will be ineligible for benefits if the training exceeds 16 hours per week. As the goal is to gain employment and thus to reduce claims on state benefits, it does not seem sensible to have this barrier. The political demand for quick solutions, to show that 'something is being done', is transmitted to the probation service. An urgency for 'action' prevails over serious considerations of efficacy. The notion that quick solutions are possible seems to be contagious. For example, groupwork programmes of a session a week, lasting a few weeks, are invested with the potential to make a major impact on a person's offending that may have continued for several years. Moreover, the many possible causes of offending are ignored while the offender is 'treated' with simplistic blanket modalities underpinned by political belief systems rather than the hard-won understanding of professionals in the field. Working in this political arena is a struggle for staff at all levels in the probation service.

Inherent stresses

Before going on to examine the kinds of stresses that are 'passed around' the organisation and how staff attempt to defend themselves from these, I want to consider first the inherent stresses in the job of probation officers and probation managers.

To an outsider, the potential for stress in a probation officer's working life is probably obvious. The kinds of people that the probation service deal with are difficult, unmotivated, hostile, unrewarding and, sometimes, dangerous and their crimes can be disturbing even for those with considerable experience of this work. Listening to their life histories and descriptions of their current circumstances can be horrifying and traumatic. In working primarily with the offender, rather than the victim or communities affected by the crime, probation officers are often seen by other criminal justice agencies and by the public of identifying with and defending the offender. Probation officers are not generally well regarded by the public nor are they seen as doing a worthwhile or legitimate job in the same way as other public servants, for example nurses and firefighters. Probation officers also deal with trauma and despair, but this is little understood.

The potential for stress for probation managers is, arguably, even greater. Even though they do not work directly with probation clients themselves, they have to trust their staff for whose mistakes they are responsible – staff who may be ill-prepared, poorly resourced and already under pressure. Stringent budget cuts in recent years have seriously affected the probation service to the detriment of good practice and it is the manager who has to bear the responsibility for the implications of these cuts while at the same witnessing their damaging impact.

Furthermore, the work itself has no certainties and, reflecting this, individual professionals espouse a variety of ideologies and philosophies about offending and how it should be treated. Sometimes, people of different 'persuasions' can work creatively together but such a situation may also be a source of tension or stress, particularly if the views of one individual are neither shared nor respected by colleagues. Currently, cognitive behavioural approaches are popular and psychodynamic work tends to be viewed as old fashioned and irrelevant.

Another source of stress can be having to implement poorly crafted policies while at the same time having to work to systems that are designed to show that these policies are being adhered to. It is accepted that sound professional standards are needed but where the government has responded impulsively to the media with 'popular' legislation, the professional task can become more difficult and sometimes stressful. Professional judgement does not always sit well with the government's desire to be popular. I shall discuss how policies and systems that require rigid adherence can produce stress but also how they may be used by practitioners as an insurance policy or defence against the fear of professional judgement being questioned.

The role of the probation service

The work of the probation service is little known by the public. It is given little attention in the media, whether it be through fiction or current affairs. Until comparatively recently, the profession seemed to avoid the economic scrutiny that many other public services endured. It is in any case a much smaller organisation than those agencies from whom it derives its clients, that is the police, courts or prison services. It deals with a comparatively small number of people. In 1994, of those offenders who were prosecuted (many crimes are not reported, go undetected or are dealt with by a caution), about 34 per cent were supervised by the probation service – either on probation or community service orders or on licence after serving a prison sentence. In England and Wales this amounted to approximately 162,000 people. The service is unlikely to make a substantial impact on reducing crime nationally. There are, however, opportunities to reduce the offending of some of the people that the probation service supervises, particularly young people. For this group, prison is likely to have the most negative influence on continued offending and it is, therefore, important to attempt diversion. By the time the probation service gets to work with a young person (in most areas this is 17 or 18 years of age), many will have appeared in court several times already and they are likely to have a greater involvement with crime than their convictions suggest. The difficulties such young people face in becoming settled, stable and law-abiding are often enormous. They are likely to have little or inconsistent family support, a poor school and employment record, involvement with drugs and/or alcohol and be part of a peer group with similar problems and who are also offending. The probation service becomes involved too late in many cases and the likelihood of failure is high. Probation officers may protect themselves against the feelings of failure by having low expectations of their clients and anticipating reoffending. When this happens, the probation officer will not have to feel surprised or disappointed. There is a tendency to 'blame' the client-offender for behaving like one rather than examine whether the intervention offered was appropriate or timely.

Time and role management

Probation staff are largely grouped into specialisations within the whole field. Some will concentrate on preparing reports for court (usually with a three-week deadline) and then supervising those people placed on probation. The work is pressured because of the court deadlines and because of the restrictions the Home Office, through its 'National Standards', places on these probation officers on how they are required to conduct probation orders. The National Standards are clearly and simply defined by the Home Office (1995a). They outline how quickly someone should be seen after the court has made a probation order, how frequently they should be interviewed thereafter, the issues that should be discussed, the ways in which work arising from this could be done and how it should be described and recorded. There is little opportunity for flexibility in the timing of court reports and in the frequency of appointments for those under supervision. Staff often find it difficult to manage their workload within the time allotted. Newly trained staff tend to join units engaged in this time-pressured task. Trainee probation officers have intensive support and supervision and a protected workload. Post-training probation officers can find their jobs much more pressured and less rewarding than they anticipated. The more experienced staff are likely to have opted for work in 'throughcare' units or in other specialisations where concern about meeting deadlines is less than that faced by the inexperienced. Those probation officers remaining in 'community supervision' (preparing reports and having responsibility for probation orders) may complain to their manager of overwork, 'too many' reports, 'too many' difficult people. They place pressure on their manager by demanding more staff and time off in lieu for the additional hours they say they are forced to work to get the job done.

As well as the above, the manager has a number of other pressures with which to contend. The allocation of court reports and arranging cover for court can be complicated, particularly when staff are on leave, off sick or working part-time. There is usually little possibility of delaying this type of work, so time pressures are often keenly felt. Additional staff is generally not a possibility. Staffing levels in the probation service are beginning to be reduced in response to budget cuts and this trend is expected to continue. The middle manager is likely to be under pressure both from team members and their line management; the work needs to be done within existing staffing levels but there is frequently too much work. The middle manager may react by blaming the team for under-functioning or blaming managers for their unrealistic expectations. Senior managers may lose patience with their middle managers and probation officers may feel their line manager is unreasonable and is not putting their case sufficiently strongly to upper management. Middle managers may seek a way out of this situation by turning to posts that do not have the same pace as community supervision teams. The tendency is, therefore, for these teams to contain the least experienced probation officers and the least experienced middle managers. This is unfortunate because community supervision teams are probably best placed to work with people, especially young ones, to prevent reoffending. Once staff have found posts elsewhere in the organisation, many are reluctant to return to community supervision. This may reduce the opportunities for a career move to relieve the pressure for those in community supervision, particularly in a small service or one where distance may also be a factor to be considered in changing jobs. Some areas have tried to resolve this by having a mobility policy that requires staff to change jobs after so many years. For some, this may bring respite, but for others, resentment and antagonism.

Stresses inherent in the job are added to by these structural problems that are not easily solved. Time and emotional energy are spent on trying to cope with stress to the detriment of service delivery. There will be little inclination to seek refuge in work with the client group where rewards and progress are limited.

Values

Earlier, some of the inherent stresses in probation work were discussed. This section looks at some of the tensions that arise when the government's paradoxes and struggles have not been resolved prior to legislation. This lack of resolution thus becomes encapsulated in the legislation and its dilemmas become embodied in subsequent policy development. The probation officer is then often faced with the problem of having to enact conflicting roles or demands at the same time.

The current three-year plan for the probation service (The Home Office 1996) describes the statement of purpose, goals, values and responsibilities of the service. The statement of purpose outlines the tasks of the probation service and the goals are concerned with effectively supervising offenders, reducing crime, providing high quality work and value for money. It is unlikely that the statement will be viewed as being contentious and most probation staff would subscribe to the Home Office's outline. Generally, people will have joined the probation service sharing the same broad values described by the Home Office plan. Yet, surprisingly, there is much tension and division between the Home Office and its probation areas. These tensions seem to be manifest between two levels of management: the senior managers and the middle managers and between the middle managers and the main grade staff (probation officers). The probation service is a hierarchical organisation and although presently most managers are recruited through promotion, the culture is often one of distance and unease between the tiers. The strains between the layers can engender stress in individuals as difficulties are passed around from layer to layer, sometimes without recognition of the impact. Individuals are forced to try and reconcile conflicting ideas or statements within themselves. As an example, probation services are currently urged to spend a minimum of 5 per cent of their budgets with partner organisations. Areas vary in the extent that they have achieved it. There has been little discussion cross-grade about the merits and anxiety associated with this (fear of probation officer's skills being lost and the service being increasingly contracted out) or whether appropriate agencies or pieces of work are being funded. Nevertheless, probation officers are expected to refer to those agencies or schemes.

The Home Office document lists the values of the probation service. It includes: 'that the service is committed to treating all people fairly, openly and with respect' and to 'working at all times to bring out the best in people'. The document also outlines the Home Secretary's priorities for the probation service over the three-year period. The first of these is to 'ensure that community sentences and supervision after release from custody are effective as punishments, through the implementation of the 1995 National Standards and improved enforcement'. The emphasis on punishment as a response to criminal behaviour was marked under the former Home Secretary and was exemplified by his slogan 'prison works'. The conflict between the views of the Home Secretary and his ministry seems evident here.

The probation order was not, originally, a sentence but a contract whereby the offender agreed to be supervised by the probation service and not reoffend during the period of the order. The probation order became part of the 'punishment philosophy' under the Criminal Justice Act 1991. The notion of punishment seems to conflict with the values that the Home Office has described for the probation service. Few probation officers would see punishing someone as a good way of 'bringing out the best in people'. Indeed, 'punishment' has often been a central feature of their development. Furthermore, while the 1991 Act changed the emphasis of the probation order to punishment, the Home Office did not require the nature of the work to change. The work is concerned with identifying factors that are likely to contribute to further offending and then working with the client on these. Examples of the work might be to examine relationships with others, to explore the function of alcohol misuse or to look at the issue of unemployment. There are two sources of tension here for probation officers. First, they are required to punish offenders, which they are unlikely to regard as an effective method of rehabilitation for the kinds of people with whom they are working. Second, they are required to describe their work as 'punishment' for their clients when they may feel, say, that work to improve the client's self-esteem may obviate their need to offend but is unlikely to be framed as, or perceived as, 'punishment'.

Front-line managers (the middle managers) usually have the task of convincing local magistrates that it is sensible and worthwhile to place offenders on probation. However since the Home Office wants probation to be viewed as punishment, middle managers may find themselves in a dilemma. They may not understand 'punishment' as a means of achieving the probation services' purposes and may struggle to comprehend what is required when someone is given a probation order as punishment. Magistrates are likely to hold a range of views on crime and punishment. The middle manager's task is to try and convince them that they should put (more) people on probation with the consequence of being left to try and manage unreconcilable demands. Similar problems will exist for chief probation officers in their discussions with the Home Office, judges and members of committees who employ probation staff.

The Home Office has made attempts to define the punishment aspects of supervising offenders in the community. For example, in relation to community service, they prescribed the number of hours an offender had to spend working in a group and considered the idea of banning smoking on community service.

However, the former was revoked and the latter reconsidered before it was implemented. The Home Office currently says that community sentences are punishments because of 'the implementation of National Standards and improved enforcement'.

A requirement of being on probation is to attend all appointments arranged with the probation officer. Before the introduction of National Standards, it was possible, and common practice, to space the appointments at wider intervals for those who did not appear to be benefiting from them, thus freeing up time for those in crisis or those who might gain by seeing their probation officer more frequently. The Home Office now defines frequency of appointments. This relates to how much time on the order that has transpired, rather than to need or progress. The Standards also define what should happen when appointments are missed. Three 'unacceptable failures to attend' would normally result in the offender being returned to court for infringing the terms of their order. Thus these rules, uniformly applied, allow politicians to talk about the toughness and consistency of probation and other community sentences. They are also a means for probation managers to report to the Home Office, and they, in turn, to their masters, that 'work' is being carried out.

The Standards are described as requirements and any departure from them must be exceptional. Authorisation must be obtained from the relevant line manager and the reasons explained in the case record. The intention of the Standards was to ensure consistency and equity as well as punishment. Probation officers find them difficult to apply in some of the complex situations they experience and this is exacerbated with additional paperwork for monitoring compliance.

National standards – whose standards?

Probation services are required to monitor how well their staff adhere to National Standards. Senior managers pass on this responsibility to middle managers, who, in turn, produce figures relating to individual members of staff as well as their team's overall performance. There is pressure on probation officers to do well within this frame of reference and for middle managers to be able to say that their team is performing as required. Much effort goes into meeting National Standards as well as a commensurate effort to demonstrate that they are being met. Those concerned may feel that much of this effort detracts from the professional task for which they were trained: to work with offenders productively. Each layer of line management experiences itself as being tightly controlled. The probation officer as the final 'controller' (and 'controlled') in the chain experiences his or her professional discretion to be compromised by the requirement to execute a policy that largely disregards the individuality of the offender and the uniqueness of his offences. The pressure to comply finally lands on the offender, who has already demonstrated through his offence that compliance and conformity are perhaps the least of his attributes and, therefore, the least likely to emerge in response.

At first glance, the National Standards appear to be straightforward. However, adherence to National Standards does not necessarily mean good practice is occurring. Probation officers can get credit from their managers for fulfilling National Standards whilst being aware that the content or substance of their work amounts to very little. An offender may be given monthly appointments because, according to National Standards, they have reached that stage in the order, yet their needs and risk of reoffending may continue to be high. An officer may find it hard to argue in favour of good practice in such cases when, under pressure from new probation orders that require weekly contact, he or she will also wish to keep some control over their workload. National Standards are met, but risk management may be compromised. Another rule concerns the failure to attend appointments. Three missed appointments with unacceptable explanation means a return to court for breach of probation order. When someone misses an appointment this should be dealt with within two working days and where breach becomes necessary, proceedings should be started within ten working days. The intention of these rules is to ensure consistency and effective punishment. However, in practice, they are not so easy to apply. While open to some local interpretation as to what is an acceptable explanation for non-attendance, they demand an unthinking application by a professional who has been trained to think about and with the client. Furthermore, requirement of proof of an 'acceptable' explanation conveys distrust in a relationship where the attempt to establish trust is paramount.

Middle managers' levels of tolerance naturally vary as to the degree of professional discretion they will allow in those they manage and the extent to which they ally themselves with policy directives that oppose discretion. Monitoring compliance with National Standards is often all that seems possible. This can be unrewarding and anxiety provoking if the clients are hostile to this process. Systems have to be devised which ensure that staff are available to see clients on this basis and if morale falls or tempers fray, the middle manager is required to deal with this and defend policies about which they may feel ambivalent.

Defensive strategies for individuals

To protect themselves from the anxiety generated in their staff in their attempt to comply with mechanistic policies such as National Standards, managers may distance themselves from the day-to-day work of probation officers. They may engage in bureaucratic tasks gratefully and welcome the relief of frequent meetings at 'headquarters'. Managers are not expected to work with clients.

Most were practitioners before National Standards were introduced and have not experienced for themselves the pressures of coping with the high volume of work imposed by National Standards. It is easy for managers to minimise the experiences of their staff since they, of necessity, have to engross themselves in their attempt to satisfy their managers. Supervision of probation officers by middle managers (and by senior managers of middle managers) could be an opportunity for each to be aware of the working situation of the other. However, it is easy for supervision to become predominantly that of checking and monitoring rather than a process of trying to identify and work on obstacles to good practice. The important task of assisting staff to manage the stress and tensions as they progress from trainee to experienced officer is given low priority or even ignored. Instead, the difficulties that occur in the probation officer-client relationship through the National Standards requirement for enforcement and adherence to punishment may be reflected and replicated between middle manager and probation officer. As I have said, the supervisor can avoid becoming involved in the complexities of the work or the supervisee's day-to-day situation and, therefore, can choose to see it as a less complex task than it is in practice. There have also been significant changes to the physical work environment for probation staff over recent years. Pressure on office space and financial restrictions has resulted in a move towards buildings that see probation officers in open-plan settings for doing paperwork and the use of interview rooms for seeing clients. Concern for safety of employees has led to alterations such that visitors and clients have restricted access. This provides another opportunity for managers to distance themselves from the essential purpose of the organisation in which there is an enhancement of bureaucratic culture rather than the *raison d'être* of the organisation to address human conflict and distress.

Senior managers are often physically based away from probation officers and are able to perform many of their duties without immediate supervision of their staff. Workload pressures and 'higher' priorities may be given as reasons for being unable to provide an adequate level of supervision. Persistent avoidance, by managers, of this vital task may be understood in terms of the anxiety (and the concomitant wish to defend against it) that becomes generated in the proximity of the stress of others 'at the coal face'.

Managers' knowledge of clients and the work that is undertaken comes increasingly from written material. This is largely in the form of reports for courts and agency records of contact with clients. Managers require these documents for inspection or monitoring purposes, a function delegated to them by the Home Office. A full account of work with a client is unlikely to be present in the case record and, in any case, is not a proper substitute for regular discussion and supervision. Managers thus become more distanced from the real task and 'forget' the feelings of resistance, ambivalence, fear, anxiety and being deskilled which are all part of the experience of the probation officer. In short, I am saying that managers may, by default, ally themselves with the perspective of the policy makers that I have described above.

The probation officer, in turn, can become frustrated by the manager's apparently unreasonable demands, such as reallocating work in a colleague's absence, that appear to show a lack of understanding of their working situation. As a group, probation officers may complain about abandonment by their 'uncaring' managers and in so doing reinforce their feelings of helplessness, neglect and impotent anger. Unable to feel their professional concerns can be properly addressed, they may 'give up' to some extent. The unrecognised stress that develops as a result may lead, in many cases, to 'burn out' or, more generally, to under-functioning (while feeling over-burdened) and frequent sickness. In some cases resentment is transmitted unconsciously to their clients, for example through neglected visits or vindictive court reports. Thus they may unwittingly treat their clients in the way they feel they have been treated. The parcel has been finally passed to the end of the line.

Managers have undergone a similar process, reinforcing each other to protect themselves and their group. They may resent the way in which they are asked to operate unrealistic policies by their masters and unconsciously transmit their resentment to their staff. In this way, each group defends itself against the anxiety of conflict with another and what it is feared such conflict may produce. Senior managers, like the middle managers, occupy themselves as a group in tasks that are felt by those below to have little relevance to their tasks.

Many probation staff are intelligent, hard working, enthusiastic and committed to their undertaking of a difficult, arguably, impossible job. Whilst they may see themselves as possessing expertise and human resource skills to help their clients, they often behave as though they are dispossessed of these attributes through a seeming lack of capacity to recognise or manage stress in themselves or their colleagues. Entrenched in their defensive positions, the component groups experience difficulty in working together and instead maintain a culture of 'them and us' between each layer of management. An atmosphere may develop where it is not possible for colleagues to treat each other 'fairly, openly and with respect' in order to 'bring out the best in people'.

Managers need to bring out the best in people to be successful in their role. However, they can all too easily succumb to competitive behaviour with other managers, fighting for limited resources or trumpeting good team statistics. Far from producing co-operation, this leads to isolation from, and mistrust by, colleagues. The lack of an environment conducive to mutual support can only enhance conditions in which stress can prevail.

In relation to National Standards, for example, the difficulties that they present have, generally, not been acknowledged and discussed within probation areas. It seems that senior management has taken them as an edict from the

Home Office that cannot be questioned. There is, therefore, no open discussion about the pros and cons, the difficulties of implementation and the consequences for professional practice. It is as if none of these issues arise. There may be no choice but to try and conform with these National Standards. Nevertheless, greater recognition within the organisation about the impact of such measures might lead to a reduction in stress through an understanding of what practitioners are attempting to implement.

Thus, in attempts to control crime, it can sometimes feel as if probation managers and probation staff are being controlled. The work is more prescribed and there is less encouragement and less opportunity for professional discretion judgement, creativity and spontaneity.

Defensive strategies for the organisation

Over the years the Home Office has put pressure on the probation service to prove that it is able to work with difficult people who are at a risk of re-offending, possibly in serious ways. In response to this there has been a growth in the number of strategies, policies and guidelines within the probation services. These are there primarily to demonstrate to the Home Office that the work is taken seriously, that clear expectations are laid down for staff and that systems have been put in place to check that the staff are doing as required by Home Office directives. All probation areas will have a policy on child protection, for example, and most have one in relation to 'dangerous offenders'. Home Office inspections are now 'thematic' and a recent one was titled *Dealing with Dangerous People: The Probation Service and Public Protection* (The Home Office 1995b).

So, having a policy is a 'good thing' and demonstrating that it is being implemented becomes a priority. The bureaucracy can be highly time consuming as well as anxiety inducing since this is the activity perceived to be the central task required by the organisation for its survival. However, the focus on systems, statistics and adherence to guidelines creates a false sense of safety. The chances of things being overlooked or mishandled that relate to the actual task of the organisation increase as more and more emphasis is placed on administrative procedures. The need for the organisation to 'protect' itself in this way becomes paramount. The consequence of this is that, at the same time, the organisation may not be contributing significantly to public protection, helping the offender to change and facilitating staff development, even though these are the fundamental aims of the various laws, guidelines and policies that the probation service is required to administer.

A recent example illustrates how the paramountcy of adhering to policy overrides good practice. A murderer was released on licence into the community. Initially he managed well but was unable to secure work. He was offered employment by someone he knew in another part of the country and where he had already spent a successful home leave during his sentence. Whilst the usual enquiries were being made before his move, a potentially dangerous incident occurred which intensified the need for him to move quickly to minimise the risks. However, a number of procedures were instituted by various agencies in the new area that delayed the transfer at a highly critical point. Procedures took precedence over risk, perhaps employed as a way of avoiding the anxiety of coping with somebody who was dangerous. Such incidents may also result in lengthy complaints between organisations, taking up time and energy that also serve to avoid anxiety.

Since 1995 the Home Office has required probation areas to provide information on offenders being supervised who are accused of a serious offence so that it will be briefed to respond to adverse publicity if necessary. Again the objective is alleviation of organisational anxiety. In the process, professional practice may again be compromised and the anxiety and stress shunted to the individual probation officer.

An example where practice may be compromised concerns the supervision of offenders on their release from prison. Regardless of how dangerous the offender and whatever risks they pose, they will be released from a prison sentence (provided it was for four years or less) on supervision to the probation service. They may be inappropriately housed in a voluntary hostel, with no facility for supervision, because there is no better alternative. The probation officer may not have been a party to any such decisions but now has to accept this unacceptable risk. If things go wrong, the probation officer may feel or be held accountable. The obvious individual defence to this is to be certain that policies and procedures have been followed exactly. This may mean returning an unco-operative client to court, even when it is clear that the court has no remedy and time will be wasted. If the officer wants to pursue a more professional avenue, which would require departure from The Standards, the approval of the line manager may be sought. However, if practice is questioned by the Home Office, individuals may worry about whether they will be supported by managers.

In summary, it is important to state one simple truth: the offender is an offender because he or she cannot, for whatever reason, comply with standards, laws, systems and policies. The wish to make probation officers apply rules and standards universally in an unthinking manner does not recognise the nature of the task at the heart of probation practice. National Standards are simply the current attempt to try and enforce control and to reassure those in power that they are in control.

As I have said, the work of the probation service is, by its nature, potentially stressful. However, if occupational stress and the way its sources permeate an organisation are not understood and addressed, difficulties are only going to be further exacerbated as professional and managerial groups adopt defensive positions and, instead of communicating, simply continue to 'pass the parcel'.

CHAPTER 4

The Eyes and Ears of the Court
Tightrope Walking in a Strong Wind

Alison Jones and Brynna Kroll

> The litigation had seemed interminable and had in fact been complicated; but by the decision on appeal the judgement of the divorce court was confirmed as to the assignment of the child…and the little girl disposed of in a manner worthy of the judgement-seat of Solomon. She was divided in two and the portions tossed impartially to the disputants… She was abandoned to her fate. What was clear to any spectator was that the only link binding her to either parent was this lamentable fact of her being a ready vessel for bitterness, a deep little porcelain cup in which biting acids could be mixed. (*What Maisie Knew*, James 1897, reprinted 1984, p.17.)

If anyone had ever been in need of a welfare report, it must surely have been poor Maisie, although one would have had the deepest sympathy for the unfortunate family court welfare officer allocated to the case of *Farange* v. *Farange*. In Maisie we have the epitome of all that is most distressing in the predicament of the child of divorce – the sense that she is a parcel to be 'assigned', 'disposed of' and 'divided in two', with neither parent considering her needs due to their more pressing preoccupation with hurting and punishing each another. Bitterness and 'biting acids' are, sadly, all too often the stuff of acrimonious separations and, rather like the child, the court welfare officer is also a receptacle for these. In the picture as a whole we get a glimpse too of all that is most distressing about becoming entangled in the wreckage of someone else's relationship. While, indeed, a 'spectator' of sorts, the role of the court welfare officer is more complex and it is the stresses, tensions and contradictions inherent in this role that we will be addressing. As Wallerstein and Blakeslee (1989) observe: 'Divorce is unique in that it unleashes our most primitive and profound human passions – love, hate and jealousy' (p.35). It is by such emotions that the welfare officer is constantly assailed.

In this chapter we will be arguing that an analysis of the personal, professional and organisational stresses that characterise this area of social work practice is not only long overdue but, indeed, central to the provision of a good service and to the survival of the species. How can personal/professional boundaries be maintained in an area of work that can touch private lives in tender places to an intense and, often, paralysing degree? How compatible are speed – in accordance with the 'no delay' principle laid down by the Children Act – and the realities of the disintegration of relationships? How are workers trained, sustained and supported to deal with children in a way that enables their wishes and feelings to be established? Is the Family Court Welfare Service's 'parent' agency – the Probation Service – adhering to the 'welfare checklist' in relation to its workers by meeting their needs so that stresses can be contained, or have they been waiting for 'adoptive parents' for this 'problem child' for so long that they have lost interest? These are some of the questions that we will be touching on.

Part of the Probation Service, the Family Court Welfare Service – formerly known as the Divorce Court Welfare Service – was established in 1959. Historically, the location of this area of practice in the Probation Service was due to its expertise in the preparation of court reports and its familiarity with court processes. This relationship between the 'parent' agency and its offspring, however, is not without its tensions and has been the subject of much debate (Murch 1980; Parkinson 1987; Foden and Wells 1990; Jackson 1992).

The major task of the family court welfare officer is to provide reports to the Family Proceedings, County and High Courts in private law matters where the adults are in dispute about arrangements for the children. These are usually, but not always, cases where the parents are separated or divorcing (Children Act, s.7).

The initiation of court proceedings in the context of separation or divorce has manifold consequences. Writers on the subject have underlined the significance of public intervention into the private domain of the family (Murch 1980; Clulow and Vincent 1987; Parkinson 1987; Eekelaar 1991) with the attendant consequence of being placed, to a lesser or greater degree, 'under the microscope'. A private matter becomes horribly public when parents are unable to reach agreement about their children. There are complex cultural issues which flow from this and which raise additional tensions and issues for practice. We will be addressing these later in the chapter.

The organisational setting – an unwanted child?

Many family court welfare officers feel that they do not belong within the probation service. Their feeling was reinforced by the determination of the previous government to rid the service of any last vestiges of social work. This makes their position increasingly peripheral and has serious implications when it comes to the distribution of scarce resources and the response of higher management to competing needs. The debate about what to do with a child about whom the parent probation service has mixed feelings has been going on, to a greater or lesser degree, for many years. The placing of family court welfare work with the probation service is something of an historical accident, associated with the role of probation officers as 'officers of the court'. The ambivalence of some probation service managers towards the service is related to the fact that, while it is undoubtedly quite a prestigious section of the probation service much valued by the judiciary and magistracy, it is also expensive to maintain. The family court welfare service is only a small part of the service as a whole but frequently has to be subsidised from other more mainstream areas of probation activity as its staff tend to be very experienced and the Home Office funding formula tends to discriminate against it. Such ambivalence on the part of the wider probation service and the long-standing debate about the future of the family court welfare service has, over the years, caused some uncertainty amongst officers who also view their individual futures with a degree of anxiety.

All probation services have a policy of reassignment whereby, after a certain length of time in post (usually five years), officers must move on. This may mean returning to work with offenders, against one's will, and they may feel out of touch with both policy and practice in the criminal field. The prospect is rarely an attractive one for officers. It is frequently viewed with considerable reluctance and anxiety, particularly by those who may have entered directly from other areas of social work and have no previous experience of working with offenders. One of the ironies of such reassignment policies is that it generally takes two to three years to develop knowledge and expertise in this complex area of social work, by which time the next move is on the agenda. The consequence is often a service staffed by the less experienced, while those who have built up considerable specialist skills may be forced to transfer to settings where they have little opportunity to use them.

There is no doubt that if the powers that be were setting out with a blank sheet of paper today, they would not place family court welfare officers within the probation service. Notwithstanding, the future remains uncertain and there seems no immediately obvious alternative. Despite most governments' stated commitment to the family, it seems there are few votes to be had in this area, in contrast to the enduring attraction of crime as an electoral Trojan Horse.

The role of the family court welfare officer: 'Solomon's Servants'

First dubbed 'Solomon's Servants' by Clulow and Vincent (1987), who saw welfare officers in the unenviable position of having to try and prevent parents from pulling their children in half and advising the courts about seemingly insoluble problems, this epithet also reflects the role played by these workers in relation to that of the Judge. Surrounded, and often engulfed, by the rubble of a disintegrating relationship, the family court welfare officer must find a pathway through the wreckage in order to engage with the issues at hand. With the steady increase of mediation services over the last few years, those families who reach the doors of the family court welfare service are likely to be those with the most severe and intractable difficulties, since those for whom compromise or resolution have been possible are likely to have been assisted by intervention at an earlier stage. Here one is faced with the formidable task of either attempting to succeed where others, such as mediators and legal representatives, may have failed or providing a full assessment of the family's situation and what is likely to be in the child's best interests in order to assist the court with decision making. Under these circumstances, what is the potential for successful intervention? What is the task and how can one circumnavigate the hazards?

There has been much consideration of the role of the family court welfare officer. In particular, debate and confusion over the primary task and the identity of the principal client has long featured within the service. As Foden and Wells (1990) observe: '…welfare officers have adopted or been attributed the roles of investigator, court reporter, conciliator, settlement seeker, family therapist, agent of the court, child protector, divorce counsellor, upholder of society's traditional values, and agent of social control and state intervention – to name but a few!' (p.189)

The officers interviewed in a recent research project (Kroll 1994) were further able to add to the list of potential roles: 'the eyes and ears of the court', 'the court's independent assessor and witness' and, more evocatively, 'we are bandaging wounds, we can stop the flow of blood, emotion, further damage'. 'I think we walk a tightrope', said one very experienced senior officer, 'it's a minefield'.

All the officers saw their main task as working with parents, supporting and encouraging them to make their own decisions about their children and resolve their conflicts. The main client was seen, by the majority, as either the couple or the family. What emerged from talking to these professionals was a sense of continual struggle to reconcile the various conflicting demands to which they felt subject – demands from the courts, parents, children and the service. Establishing a clear role, therefore, was often problematic, since although clear in theory, once subjected to the various forces it became much harder in practice.

Additional dilemmas sprang from the preparation of reports for the court. To recommend or not to recommend? Where did the welfare officers responsibility end and the court's begin? Some specialist units made decisions to adopt a particular style of intervention in which recommendations played no part.

Others felt strongly that to recommend a course of action in the best interests of the child was a clear part of their brief (James and Hay 1992; Kroll 1994). Judges issued practice directions in response to both extremes of approach (Stone 1991), reflecting the degree to which boundaries had been blurred and making clear their expectations of a service that was still fundamentally trying to find its way.

The provision of the Home Office National Standards for Family Court Welfare Work (1994) finally addressed many of these issues and set out a clear definition of the court welfare officer's role. Such standards were already extant for the probation service's work with offenders (Home Office 1992) and, despite some criticism of specific content, were seen as a helpful way of standardising practice so that clients could be assured of the same quality of service throughout England and Wales. For the family court welfare officer the task was: '…to inquire professionally and impartially into the circumstances of the case in order to discover information to assist the court and to report clearly and concisely to the court… The authority of the court welfare officer, to act, is derived from the court in the exercise of its powers under the Children Act 1989' (Home Office 1994, p.16). Within this framework was the acknowledgement that there might be opportunities for the welfare officer to help the parties reach agreement but the resolution of disputes was not the primary task when preparing a welfare report.

The way in which the officer should pursue the task was left flexible but emphasis was placed on seeing the child or children 'unless there are strong grounds for not doing so' and adhering to the welfare checklist. Parents could be seen together, separately or a mixture of the two; there could be family meetings, meetings between each child and each parent and with the children individually or with brothers and sisters. Other significant family members, new partners or other professionals may also be interviewed if appropriate. Interpreters should be involved where there are communication difficulties and awareness of cultural differences in relation to family breakdown should be at the heart of all enquiries.

Attempts have similarly been made to achieve national coherence regarding the management of family court welfare services. The three-year plan published by the Home Office lists a set of Key Performance Indicators (KPIs) and Supporting Management Information Needs (SMINs) including:

- number of reports completed

- number of reports completed within twelve weeks of order

- number of reports completed within ten weeks of receipt of referral

- average number of weeks to produce a report.

Setting aside the questionable logic of measuring the efficacy of people-centred services in this over simplistic yet ever popular fashion, it does convey the relentless pressure under which officers have to work. Family court welfare officers are now each expected to produce around sixty reports each year. Many would argue that to complete such a complex and significant assessment in the case of a family with entrenched difficulties is often unrealistic in such a short space of time. Indeed, such a time scale can sometimes be counter-productive. Separation is not a single event but an emotional process involving a number of stages and the time necessary to complete the process will depend on a variety of factors, both internal and external (Wallerstein and Blakeslee 1989). Given time, family members may go some way toward re-establishing their ability to negotiate with one another without the court having to impose a solution. In private law matters there is rarely a neat fit between the Children Act principles of minimum delay, minimum intervention and the paramountcy of the child's welfare. It is not easy for the worker to assess their relative significance and withstand pressure from lawyers, courts and service managers to finalise the report.

The practice: working with power and difference

The families with whom the family court welfare service works are a true cross-section of society, representing every group and a huge diversity of race, culture and religion. The potential for discrimination in family work is immense. The risks are particularly acute in two areas.

First, there is the risk of making assumptions, for instance about the implications of a particular disability for parenting skills, the position of women in a family from a particular religious background or the attitudes of parents from a certain culture towards the disciplining of children. Such assumptions may be the result of stereotyping, lack of knowledge, prejudice or the particular world view or cultural perspective of the worker and could result in a fundamental misunderstanding of what is happening within the family.

Second, there is the risk of failing to pay sufficient regard to the significance of race, gender, sexual orientation, language, disability, religion and culture. These factors may be of significance on several levels. They will have a bearing on the future needs and identity of the child. They may affect the daily experience of the family members, both within the family and in the wider social context, resulting in oppression and disadvantage to some individuals or to the family as a whole. Differences between family members will affect the power dynamics within the family and differences between the family members and the worker will also have an effect on the power differential.

The family court welfare service is predominantly white and is likely to be experienced by black families as yet another part of the powerful, white and oppressive authority of the wider court system. Much of the research relating to the effects on children of divorce and separation has been in respect of white children born and brought up in the West. There is an urgent need for more work in this area, so that practice can be informed by a wider knowledge base.

In recent years family court welfare officers have paid increasing attention to the power imbalances within some families. This issue is brought into sharp relief in the family where there has been domestic violence. National Standards (Home Office 1994) require that all parties must be informed that they have a free choice concerning joint or individual interviews and 'a joint interview must not be convened if it can be reasonably foreseen that the safety or well-being of either party might be jeopardised' (p.18). It is increasingly recognised that the welfare of children and that of their primary carer are inextricably linked and cannot be treated separately. Recent studies suggest that there is a history of domestic violence in at least one in three marriages which end in divorce (Borkowski, Murch and Walker 1985) and in up to 90 per cent of these cases violence continues after separation (Radford and Woodfield 1994). Frequently, contact between the child and the non-resident parent provides the forum in which the continuing violence occurs (Hester and Radford 1996). Violence may not always be physical; it often takes the form of threats, intimidation or the belittling of one parent – usually the mother – in front of the children. Given the extent of domestic violence, many family court welfare officers would argue that, rather than assuming it is not an issue unless raised by one of the parties, there should be a presumption in favour of violence that should be tested through appropriate questioning. If the presence of domestic violence has been established, it is then possible to explore the effects upon the children and the potential and preparedness of the perpetrator to effect a change in behaviour. This is, of course, no easy task for the family court welfare officer: retaining an essential degree of neutrality whilst making it clear that violence and abuse is not condoned; working with the perpetrator's denial without appearing to persecute; exploring an individual's violence whilst feeling, in all likelihood, intimidated, frightened, angry or disgusted.

Being faced with denial is an extremely common experience for family court welfare officers – not only in the case of alleged domestic violence – where there is frequently no substantiating evidence such as police involvement or convictions, but also in the case of alleged sexual abuse, where there may have been insufficient evidence to proceed. The welfare officer may be confronted by one person's word against another but have a strong suspicion about whose account is the more accurate:

> Bella is almost three. Her parents separated eighteen months ago and since then her father has been trying to have contact with her. The court welfare officer has prepared reports on three occasions, each time

suggesting ways in which contact might be started. Despite this, contact has still not been established. Not only has Bella not seen her father, she seems to have little idea of what a father is or that she herself has one. Her mother is receiving treatment for an anxiety disorder that is thought to be related to her violent relationship with Bella's father. She tells the court welfare officer that her last memory of him was of a violent attack and she recalls her blood dripping onto Bella, who was sitting on her knee at the time. The court has made various orders, including one that required Bella to be taken to a contact centre and one ordering her mother to take her to the court welfare office to see her father. Each time panic attacks prevented her from complying with the court's direction. Bella's father has appeared to behave in an exemplary fashion throughout. He has waited patiently and his apparent commitment to his daughter has not wavered. He denies the allegations of violence and tells the welfare officer that he knows Bella's mother of old and that she is 'putting it on'. The court has now attached a penal notice to the order for contact. If Bella's mother does not comply, she will go to prison. Mother, father and Judge are all at a loss and look to the court welfare officer to solve the problem. The court welfare officer must consider Bella's welfare. In the longer term she needs to know her father and develop a real sense of identity. However, in the short term, she may have a mother who breaks down completely or is imprisoned. The resultant stress is enormous.

The practice: working with separation and loss

For many years divorce was referred to as a 'life event' – something that happened, like marriage, birth and death and then was over. It was supposed to take between two and five years to recover from the experience of divorce, and yet divorce often featured in lists of stressful life events, including moving house and losing a job, implying that it was simply a transition from one state to another (Wallerstein and Blakeslee 1989). Others liken divorce to bereavement and in a study carried out in the 1960s among American Servicemen (Rahe, McKean and Arthur 1967) divorce came second only to the death of a partner in terms of traumatic experiences. Wallerstein and Blakeslee poignantly reflect this dichotomy: 'Divorce is deceptive. Legally it is a single event but psychologically it is a chain – a sometimes never ending chain – of events, relocations and radically shifting relationships strung through time, a process that forever changes the lives of the people involved' (p.18).

Wallerstein and Blakeslee make a persuasive case. In *Second Chances* both children and parents talk evocatively about the impact of the experience ten, fifteen years after it has happened, sometimes with such passion that it is hard to believe that it happened so long ago. Clulow and Vincent (1987) liken the experience of divorce to the process of bereavement, where definite stages are passed through, ranging from denial to the realisation that the loved one is dead or that the ex-partner is indeed 'ex'. The fundamental difference between death and divorce, however, is, of course, the lack of a body to mourn.

Somewhere there is the continued existence of the 'lost' person, who may be deeply mourned, intensely hated or a cause of sorrow, resentment or bitterness for whatever reason. Separation is rarely experienced with indifference; loss, whether one initiated the separation or not, leaves us lost, too, at least for a while. Continued contact with the lost partner, for the sake of the children, can, as a consequence, be fraught with pain and littered with emotional land-mines.

Why did it happen? How did it happen? What went wrong? Divorce and separation, of course, rarely happen out of the blue. Prior to the actual separation there is inevitably a period where it is apparent that things are problematic. There may be acrimony, arguments, violence or distress, all or some of which may be witnessed or simply sensed by the children. The process leading up to the separation becomes increasingly significant since prolonged conflict and uncertainty can be particularly damaging to everyone, particularly children (Richards 1990; Kroll 1994). To ignore this is to over-simplify the whole phenomenon.

Equally important is the fact that the process takes different forms and moves at different speeds depending on the people concerned. Our capacities to deal with painful situations vary depending on all the factors that make us different from one another. The time scale for recovery cannot be dictated by anyone – courts, lawyers, court welfare officers, parents or children.

Stress and the court welfare officer

It is in this emotional climate, then, that the welfare officer must operate: engaging with, managing and containing, rage, despair, depression, distress, feelings of loss and grief, revenge and bitterness. In short, working with people expressing very primitive reactions to pain, disappointment and fear. Encountering such emotions is a test for any one – the sense of powerlessness, sadness, anxiety, not to mention irritation, frustration, and 'stuckness' almost appear to be contagious. There is competition for attention since the adults are as needy as the children and it is sometimes difficult to resist concentrating on the former – who are more able to articulate their needs – to the detriment of the latter. It is not only essential to know something about how individuals might behave under such circumstances but also to have a grasp of marital and family dynamics. Becoming entangled in other people's lives can be a very taxing business.

As we have already indicated, the clients of the family court welfare service are those for whom other remedies such as mediation or counselling have proved ineffective or they are families where there have been allegations that make a full enquiry essential to safeguard the welfare of the children. It can, therefore, be safely assumed at the outset that the level of conflict and /or mistrust between the parents will be high and that the adults at least, if not the children, bring with them hopes, fears, expectations and assumptions about what social work professionals should, can or ought to do.

What most divorcing or separating adults also want is to be able to tell their story (Clulow and Vincent 1987). There is a ferocious need to go through the details of the other partner's wrongs and failings and to relive happier times and it is essential to mourn or 'rage, rage against the dying of the light'. The understanding family court welfare officer is expected to be sympathetic but there is also a deep-seated hope on the part of individuals that their side will be taken. Separating parents are often adept at getting others to take sides – friends, relatives, solicitors, etc. To take sides is, of course, fatal as neutrality is of the essence and one of the key sources of stress is retaining one's position on the tightrope. An inadvertent nod of agreement to a negative statement about the other partner can have solicitors' letters flying through the air like confetti.

The pressures on the welfare officer to take sides are, of course, not all external. Remaining impartial is no easy task when a set of circumstances has resonance and touches us personally. On becoming a grandfather and delight-ing in daily contact with the new baby, a particular court welfare officer found it difficult to avoid feeling and demonstrating anger towards a mother who appeared to be 'intractably hostile', resisting contact for no other reason than to punish her ex-partner. Another welfare officer whose own relationship had ended in similar circumstances had to work very hard to remain even-handed and to see both sides in the case of a father who had left his wife and children for another woman. Such collisions of circumstance take their toll and make it difficult to avoid over-identification and to stay upright on the tightrope.

The adult

Separation does not bring out the best in anyone, however much of a relief it may be, at least in theory. The range of emotions, so similar to those associated with other losses – denial, anger and depression – often deactivate the coping adult parent part of the self. What the family court welfare officer is then faced with is an adult in a very childlike state who is unable to see or respond to the needs of the real children in the family. It is their needs that must be met and there is often strong pressure on the family court welfare officer to intervene on a therapeutic level to a more intense degree than may be appropriate. 'What about me?', one mother was heard to cry, 'all I hear is "what about the children?". Well, I'm a thirty-five-year-old child. When is anybody going to listen to me?' This sums up one of the central dilemmas in this work: how much can be offered to parents to support them sufficiently to reactivate their adult, coping mechanisms? After all, it is only by this means that they will be able to support their children through the experience of loss. How realistic a goal is this? Where on earth can one find the time?

> Sandy was thirteen. Following a stormy row with his father, his mother had gone to stay with a friend. When she returned a couple of days later, her husband refused to let her back into the house. Both parents applied for residence orders in respect of their son and the court welfare officer was asked to report. She discovered a very sad situation and could not avoid being touched by the mother's desperate plight. It is not unusual for adolescents to cope with parental separation by taking sides and Sandy was closely allied to his father, refusing to see or speak to his mother, whom he blamed for the years of conflict at home. He was angry not only that she had listened to tales about his father from other people but also that she had talked to him about her husband's misdeeds and had attempted to use him as a go-between. Sandy's mother felt badly wronged by a violent, unfaithful husband whom she said she had always loved. She had now lost everything. She was isolated and shunned within her community, being seen to have left her husband. She pleaded desperately with the court welfare officer to persuade her husband to take her back as her only child was all she had in the world. For the court welfare officer to retain a cool and analytical focus on Sandy's welfare was quite a challenge.

One of the consequences that flows from the abdication of the parent/adult role is that this becomes available to be taken up by the children in the family. The family court welfare officer may find him or herself in a roomful of adult children and childlike parents, all muddled up in one another's worlds. Even very small children may adopt an adult persona in order to create the illusion that someone around the place knows how many beans make five. It is not uncommon to hear a four-year-old express concerns about maintenance, unpaid gas bills and unhoovered carpets. Adults, meanwhile, often retreat to earlier stages of development resulting in unusual behaviour that puzzles and discomposes their offspring. The parent may appear to retreat to a state akin to adolescence with its 'attendant battle between identity and role confusion' (Erikson 1965), 'vulnerability of the personality' and 'inadequacy of the psychological defences to cope with inner conflicts and tensions' (Coleman 1974). This may be demonstrated by mood swings, emotions very close to the surface and non-conformity – a series of new relationships or a sudden sartorial transformation from sober business suit to jeans and earring. Everyone is finding their way, wondering what has hit them, puzzled about where and who they are. Family court welfare officers are supposed know who they are, what they are there for. In a strong wind they must attempt to hang on to the boundaries (and ideally their wardrobe) amidst this confusion.

In such a context it is easy to absorb the pain, confusion and rage that is flying through the air. Feelings of depression, desolation, hopelessness and despair can seem contagious. Yet for the worker to understand what is happening in the life of the parent – to gain some insight into what life might be like for the child – he/she must be accessible to these feelings and yet not be so overwhelmed that the professional self ceases to function. Salzberger-Wittenberg (1970) uses the term 'counter-transference' to refer to the reaction experienced by the worker as a response to the client's transferred feelings. Working with counter-transference reactions such as feelings of anxiety and anger can provide valuable insight into the dynamics of the family but can leave the worker feeling drained and impotent. Denial of this dimension, however, is a tempting means of avoiding additional stress for the welfare officer but is likely to detract from the quality of the assessment that has to be made.

In view of the contentious and highly charged nature of the work, and the fact that the 'loser' frequently feels a sense of grave injustice if matters have proceeded to a courtroom battle, it is not, perhaps, surprising that the number of complaints received about family court welfare officers is disproportionately high. However skilled, experienced and supported a practitioner might be, to have one's practice and integrity questioned and examined is inevitably un-pleasant and likely to undermine one's confidence to some degree. In extreme cases family court welfare officers have been subjected both to media intrusion when parents have gone to the press with their grievances and have had police protection as a result of threats made against them.

The child

From managing the feelings generated by the adult clients we now turn to managing the feelings generated by the children. Research makes it clear that most children want their parents to stay together, however awful things may be (Wallerstein and Kelly 1980; Walczac and Burns 1984; Mitchell 1985; Wallerstein and Blakeslee 1989; Tugendhat 1990; Kroll 1994). Research also indicates that children are rarely told what is happening or helped to talk about their feelings. Typically, they feel they have nobody to turn to at what is, invariably, a difficult time. The family court welfare officer, therefore, occupies a unique position in being able to intervene to ensure that the children's wishes and feelings are attended to – a clear expectation enshrined in the Children Act. This in itself can prove stressful, however, as the time available for court welfare officers to talk to children is inevitably short and if it is the first opportunity the child has had to express their wishes and feelings, the need may be enormous.

Establishing the wishes and feelings of children and, in the course of this, being exposed to the realities of their lives, their feelings and their sorrow is, however, far from simple and can be very harrowing. Children have many unanswered questions that they hope a friendly family court welfare officer might answer: what is going to happen to me? Why did they split up? Why can't they stay together? Why can't we live with them both? Will my daddy still be my daddy when he moves out? Some children can and will talk about their pain and rage, some will just show it – whether this be by rocking and keening with a blank expression in their eyes, by destroying the contents of the office or by moving anxiously from one parent to the other bearing toys or trying to drag reluctant parents across the room to sit beside one another.

How can such experiences be managed? Witnessing such scenes is extremely painful however skilled and hard-boiled the worker may feel him or herself to be. The temptation to make things better, rescue, bandage and reassure is strong. The dangers of becoming the ideal parent, the only one who understands, are real. The child who asks if they can move in to the office, come back the following day or go home with the worker is saying something powerful and important about their plight. While essential for assessment purposes, this type of communication pulls at heartstrings to what can feel like an unbearable degree.

Children also get used as pawns and weapons during the process of divorce. They are primed, prompted, brainwashed, bribed, over-indulged, castigated and rejected depending on the requirements of the adults. While looking longingly at the toys her father had bought for her, Jane, aged five, told the welfare officer that she could not accept them as, if she did, her mother would not take her to the zoo tomorrow. Mark, aged three, who had been living with his father and paternal grandparents who adored him, was not returned by his mother and her new boyfriend after a contact visit. He had not seen them since and, several weeks later, told the welfare officer, in subdued and expressionless tones, that neither he nor his mother liked them. Children, one of the largest oppressed groups at the best of times, can, in this context, be exposed to domination, manipulation and emotional abuse on a grand scale. To witness this as a professional can engender feelings of powerlessness and rage that are hard to manage.

Balancing on the tightrope: the safety net

The child's pain, the distress of parents, domestic violence, different kinds of abuse, working with loss, working with difference, organisational pressures, uncertainty about the future and an awareness of the far-reaching effects of a court's decision based upon one's own recommendation – this is the milieu in which the family court welfare officer operates and these are the sources of stress and tension that must be managed if they are not to become either persecutory or overwhelming.

How are workers sustained and supported to deal with such stress? In many areas the importance of a team approach and of co-working has been recognised and this does much to alleviate anxieties through mutual support and a sharing of expertise, skills and decision making. However good a team may be, there is still no substitute for effective individual supervision which pays attention not only to the immediate practice issues but also to the personal impact that the work may have. If practitioners are not to be daunted by the realities of working on a daily basis with tortuous family dynamics, child protection, domestic violence and the complexities of establishing the wishes and feelings of children, the provision of a comprehensive programme of induction and ongoing training is also essential.

If it does come to pass that the family court welfare service is adopted at some stage in the future, perhaps by the Lord Chancellor's department or the *Guardian ad Litem* Panel, for instance, the 'adoptive parent' will have the good fortune to have an addition to the family who is experienced, committed and highly professional – if a little weary. There will be many rewards, but only if it is nurtured, treated with respect and encouraged to reach its full developmental potential!

CHAPTER 5

In the Place of the Parents: Stress in Residential Social Work with Children and Adolescents

Paul Van Heeswyk

There is, sometimes, a sad discrepancy between the needs of those children who come to live in residential establishments and the actual provision of care they receive, despite the best efforts and intentions of all the individual people concerned. Many young people will arrive at children's homes following a breakdown, or series of breakdowns, in their families of origin or foster families. Perhaps they have lived with parents or carers who have felt themselves to be under extreme pressures of stress – the consequence of racism, unemployment or poverty. Perhaps the children were born into families where the parents themselves have had little or no experience of good parenting when they were young and have struggled, in lonely isolation, to find ways to look after and understand their own children without the support of extended family, neighbourhood communities or accessible, professional services.

All parents try to do their best. We know, however, that the sometimes bewildering complexity of infants and small children, in combination with their relentless, insistent neediness, can leave already vulnerable people feeling that they are confirmed as worthless failures. Isolated parents may have genuinely unrealistic expectations of the capacities and abilities of their young. They may then feel both persecuted and accused by what seems to them to be an apparent wilful refusal of their children to behave and comply or by the persistent cries of distress of their infants.

The later consequences for those children who begin their lives with neglectful, depriving or abusing parents are well known. In terms of recovery, it is clear that an urgent need of such children is for a sustained period of reliable and attentive care from a small group of committed adults. In these benign circumstances the grown ups can get to know each child in his or her own right and are able to remain alongside the young person, with appropriate levels of pre-occupation. Disadvantaged children will then have the opportunity to come to terms with whatever previous bad experiences they may have had and, more importantly, can have the chance to see that other kinds of relationship and experience are possible.

We are in danger, however, of re-creating certain aspects of inadequate provision in our residential settings when we fail to give sufficient thought, resources and commitment to such places. Where professional carers are poorly rewarded and are not trained, supervised and supported to understand and cope with the impact of their stressful exposure to the behaviour and despair of troubled young people, there may arise a culture of frequent staff change, or of distracted and demoralised carers, whose main pre-occupation may be their own needs and their own survival, much as it probably was for the children's own parents in their families of origin. They 'become' the disadvantaged 'children'.

Young people who live in residential settings are, for a variety of reasons, unable to live with one or both of their parents and some or all of their siblings. Clearly, the circumstances felt by the young people and their carers to have brought about this state of affairs will influence the feelings and attitudes of both clients and workers in regard to the new situation in which they all find themselves. However, the ideas about their own lives that the young people bring with them and display may not correspond in any obvious way with the real experiences that the social workers understand them to have had. Nor may the residential workers easily recognise themselves from the picture that the young people seem to have of them, a picture that can be inferred from the manner in which the young people regard and treat their workers.

The ideas we have about ourselves derive from the complex interaction between our dispositions and the responses that we encounter, or think we encounter, in the emotional attitudes of those on whom we are dependent in our earliest years. If a child is badly treated by her natural parents, either through physical abuse or neglect, she may not simply conclude that she was, in innocence and misfortune, born to bad parents. Instead, the child is likely to believe that there is essentially something wrong or bad about *her*. 'If my father does not love me, I am unlovable'. 'If my mother does not want me, I am unwantable'. Such traumatic early experiences are clearly shattering to a child's identity and leave a deep residue of feelings of low self-esteem and self-loathing.

A child from such a background may understand her removal to a residential setting as a punishment for having been bad. She may then see the workers as some sort of prison guards or as stern and frightening figures who are charged with exacting retribution. The workers may represent in the child's mind the abusing or neglectful parents of her early years. This, of course, will be in marked contrast to how the workers initially think of her – possibly as the innocent victim of cruel or inadequate parents – and will deeply offend the view that the workers have of themselves as caring and forgiving rescuers.

The forceful tendency for us all to see new people as replicas of those we have known before may lead the child to be wary, distrustful and suspicious or defiant, angry and aggressive, either as an expression of revenge or in antici-patory self-defence. The workers may be shocked to find themselves ignored, retreated from or attacked and, worse still, may be horrified to find themselves experiencing hostile and violent feelings and thoughts towards the children. Workers may worry that they are, in fact, no better than the children's parents, of whom they were, hitherto, so critical.

It is alarming and disturbing of one's composure and self-esteem to be put in touch with a violent and uncaring part of oneself and this significant concomitant of work with rejected, abused and deprived young people is a major source of stress for residential staff. The feelings aroused by working in close proximity with young people who have been sexually abused can be even more troubling. Something of the nature of the perverse and inappropriately sexualised relationships that young people may have been subjected to by previous carers is often re-created. Workers can be dismayed to find themselves uneasy and confused about the feelings and meanings they discover in the ordinary, but intimate, encounters that inevitably occur in situations where people live together.

Carers can withdraw from young people and become cool, distant, harsh or rejecting when feeling threatened at moments of potential contact, emotional or physical. This can take the form of a terror at discovering themselves thinking, for the first time, of the sexual interpretations that may seem, suddenly, to suggest themselves in everyday situations of the care of abused children. Or, alternatively, workers may begin to worry compulsively about their vulnerability to accusations that they fear the young people may make. Such anxieties can cohere into almost paranoid delusions that colleagues or members of the public are regarding them with suspicion. Extended moods of generalised guilt and unworthiness may follow and can result in an impover-ished relationship with the young people and collusion and scapegoating in the staff group. Where these pressures are not acknowledged, staff are vulner-able to feelings of demoralisation, lack of appreciation and exploitation. Since such emotions in the staff group are likely to mirror those felt by the deprived and abused young people themselves, there is a further danger that a vicious circle will ensue in which the workers pass on to their managers their own version of the troubled complaints and states of mind that they have been experiencing from those in their care. Deprived people can put us in touch with our own feelings or phantasies of deprivation. In these circumstances it can be easy to hold supervisors and employers responsible for our discontent, those whose task, we feel, is to protect and provide for ourselves.

To some extent these latter problems are also, it must be said, a real consequence of the poor commitment we have shown in our society to the needs and welfare of deprived young people in places of residential care. It is only in recent years that we have insisted on the importance of proper screening and supervisory procedures for those adults who wish to undertake this extremely responsible and important work. Many settings have, of course, always been aware of the dangers of employing paedophiles who seek positions of access to, and power over, the most vulnerable in our community and such places have taken steps to prevent this kind of occurrence. But, unfortunately, there are also examples of appalling and widespread negligence in these areas that have led to cases of individual, and even systematic, abuse within Children's Homes. The whole society must carry the shameful responsibility for these cases of the abuse and betrayal of a trust that the young clients were entitled to assume in regard to those selected to care for them, but residential workers may feel the continuing legacy in more direct ways, as indicated above.

It is not only the children, of course, who will have pre-conceived ideas, based on their previous relationships, about the new people they meet in the residential setting. The workers will have to counter an inclination in themselves to regard each child as just another example of a particular type, shorn of any individual difference, and reducible to a particular trauma or syndrome. We may talk of 'abused children' and young people with 'conduct' or 'attention-deficit disorder', for example, and assume that because we have the labels, there must, indeed, be objects that correspond exactly to them. A casual institutional reliance on these terms of convenience and shorthand may cause us to assume that all the young people so described will be the same. We may then subject those in our care to a two-dimensional caring style that fails to take the trouble to listen to and get to know each person as an individual in his or her own right. This is likely to have been exactly the treatment which the young people will have previously known only too well in the homes or placements from which they have come.

It is essential that workers in residential institutions are supported to understand, through individual and ·group supervision, that the situations in which the young people will try to put them, and the feelings that the workers themselves will have about the young people, are important clues to an understanding of the personal histories of those young people. These moments of understanding are the stepping-stones that can lead towards recovery and health and it is vital to promote a culture in which thoughts and feelings about the children can be shared and discussed by workers, in a professional manner, in team meetings and supervision. Not only does such a culture facilitate greater understanding of the children, it also reduces the likelihood or dangers of staff acting out their moods.

All of us are, at all times, living out our ideas and feelings about ourselves, other people and our relationships. In this way, the young people in residential care will unconsciously try to make their carers behave in a way that is familiar to them from their past. The work process will be for the staff to be able to receive sometimes powerful and painful feelings that the young people may themselves have felt, or have been unable to let themselves feel, if they are to believe that they have been heard and understood.

From the young peoples' point of view, the developmental need is to meet a new kind of person who acts and responds differently from the significant figures of their past when exposed to familiar stresses in familiar situations. The new response will need to be receptive and thoughtful without impulsive discharge of unprocessed feelings or flight into acting out, which would merely constitute the workers' own unintegrated conduct disorders.

Children who have been beaten or cruelly treated in other ways, for example, may behave in such a provocative way that their carers themselves feel like behaving in violent or punitive ways towards the children. Or the staff may feel abused and cruelly victimised because of the treatment they receive from the children on a constant daily basis. The evocation of our own feelings in others – making other people feel how we feel, without the use of words – is a primitive method of communication and is often the only way such children are able to let adults know what has happened to them and how they have felt about it. The children will sense from the demeanour of their carers that their communications have been received. They look, then, to see what the adults will do. Will they beat, abuse or otherwise humiliate the children, as other adults have done before? Will they sink into hopeless despair and suddenly leave, unable to cope a moment longer with the stress, leaving the children to feel guilty about the damage they may think they have done? Or will they try to hold onto the feelings and not simply act them out; decline to play the role that has been forced on them and continue to provide reliable care?

A different and unexpected outcome to these exchanges and interactions presents the young people with the possibility of identifying with adults who can contain and recognise their own feelings and offers those young people the opportunity to reclaim parts of themselves that they have felt, in the past, were unsafe to acknowledge. I am thinking here of those feelings of suffering, vulnerability, dependency and need that may formerly have been exploited by adults and may, therefore, be associated only with unbearable pain but which are, in fact, the essential pre-requisites of the capacities to learn and to love.

For the workers concerned, however, it may be hard to hold on to this understanding when they may be feeling they are just a dumping ground for the evacuated and undigested emotions of angry, anti-social and ungrateful clients who are felt to persecute them by turning them into versions of themselves that they hate. It is hard to feel good about yourself and your work when you feel in constant danger of losing control and retaliating, seeming, thereby, to confirm the cynical view that the young people may express about adults. However, as we have seen, such feelings are probably close to those felt by abusing parents. Shirley Hoxter (1983) has written how children in residential settings can feel themselves to be the unwanted waste products and refuse that the society feels it must keep off its streets. This perception can be heightened when the children are moved far away from their own neighbourhoods owing to the lack of adequate local provision. Understandably, the children may then turn into rubbish the place where they live and the provision, personal and material, that they are offered. In these circumstances it will not be surprising if the workers feel like rubbish themselves or, at best, like 'rubbish collectors'.

The attitude towards residential child care held in the wider society probably reflects the ambivalence with which parenting, but especially mothering, is regarded. On the one hand there persists the idealised sentiment that care of the young is neither 'work' nor a 'career' but is, rather, a vocation or special calling, an instance of selfless and devoted dedication, of *noblesse oblige* (it is not something that people should expect to receive any or much money for). On the other hand there may be an opinion, held at the same time, that parenting (by which people usually mean 'mothering') and child care are tasks that anyone can do because they can be, and are, done by women.

However, external social prejudices will be carried internally by the workers in residential care and will generate their own sources of stress. It is likely that carers will themselves be ambivalent, with greater or lesser degrees of consciousness, in regard to the kind of parenting that they feel they have experienced in their own lives. In this respect the workers may try to use their relationships with the child or young person to work out unresolved grievances with their own parents. Rivalry with one or both parents could then lead to a compulsive drive to be the perfect mother or father, or a combination of both. Apart from colluding unhelpfully with something anti-developmental in the children, who may, for their own reasons, be looking for an idealised parent when they need to be helped to bear disappointment and accept what is possible and real in relationships, this project will lead to enervation and distress, whether as the consequence of triumphant guilt or the more likely (and potentially productive) despair of failure.

Mr B was keen, from the outset, to be liked by the children in his care. This understandable wish, however, took extreme forms for him as he behaved in a seductive and collusive way with the young people. It seemed he wanted to be their favourite, preferred to all the other staff members, and he created a culture of high excitement around him. Whenever he worked, all the children wanted to be with him and the other staff felt redundant, dull and discounted. When he was off-duty, there was a vacuum. It was as though everyone was waiting, only, for his return. He appeared to have little or no discipline problems with the children – they would do whatever he asked – whereas his colleagues lacked authority and could exert no leadership. They never felt in charge.

Gradually this state of affairs began to break down. Mr B had always been prone to a kind of sulking when things did not immediately proceed according to his wishes – it was one of his weapons of control over others – and these moods became deeper and more extended. He conveyed a kind of hurt disapproval that began to make the children wary of him. They continued to be polite and concerned around him but were increasingly wary and fearful. They acted as though they needed to make him feel better, as though it were their fault that he was permanently upset. Finally, in a staff meeting, Mr B exploded in tearful rage. He accused his colleagues of subtly undermining him, of failing to support his ideas and initiatives, of exploiting his good-will. He felt, he said, like a discarded old shoe.

Fortunately, the almost delusional quality of the outburst made it possible for his colleagues to feel empathy for him, rather than a fury of their own at this attack, and their sympathetic response enabled Mr B to break down in tears. From within his sadness he spoke of his discovery that his belief in his own perfect and happy childhood was without foundation. He had needed to believe his childhood had been wonderful to cover over the forgotten memories of loneliness and despair. His father had left home when he was three years old and he had been brought up by his hurt and bitter mother, who continued, right through his childhood, to play out the role of the abandoned wife. Mr B had always thought she was self-obsessed. She expected pity from him, without giving attention to his own needs.

In growing up, Mr B had constructed a compensating picture of a perfect father who would deliver him from this misery and it was this idealised figure that he tried to become in his work. The children in his care represented the unhappy memories of his own childhood. His project was to rescue the poor children, to make them happy. Disappointments and difficulties in the performance of this task, however, forced Mr B to the new realisation of how much he had hated his father for his absence.

It was a fortunate and productive breakdown of the false and brittle ideals that he thought had sustained him and Mr B was able to re-evaluate, also, his view of his mother. He came to understand that his idealised picture of his absent father was sustained by an equally unrealistic picture of his mother as totally bad. He became more forgiving and accepting of her difficulties and more appreciative of what she had managed to give him in the difficult circumstances of her life. This had profound consequences for his professional work. He could now be a good-enough parental figure. He did not need the children in his care to be grateful to him for his sake. He could allow them to come to their own view of him in their own time.

The existentialists used to say that it is in an emergency that a person finds out who she is. Living with deprived and disturbed young people could be described as being in a constant 'state of emergency'. Much of what residential social workers begin to find out about themselves in the course of their inadvertent journey of personal discovery may be things they feel they would rather not have known. Perhaps they will begin to wonder whether their motives for this kind of work are as clear and straightforward as they thought. The wish to help others may be an alibi when the unacknowledged project is to compensate, vicariously, for one's own unmet needs and deprivations (if acknowledged and worked on, this may be no bad thing since it offers the possibility of empathy and is probably, anyway, an important part of altruism).

Alternatively, a worker may feel resentful of the commitment to the lives of others inevitably involved in residential work but may begin to wonder whether this is not a self-imposed restriction on his or her own freedom of desire. Sometimes it can feel safer to day-dream about what one would like to do and then blame clients or employers for not allowing oneself the time and opportunity to do it, rather than confront the fact that one could, with appropriate planning, try to live out and make real those dreams. Such an acknowledgement exposes us, of course, to our deepest personal fears of failure and success. We all know how fears of disappointment can inhibit us from making changes or taking risks. But we know, also, that we must be careful of what we wish for, because we may get it!.

It is, unfortunately, a general truth that in our society the most vital jobs are the ones which are most badly paid (one thinks of posts in nurseries, primary and secondary schools, residential homes, hospitals, etc). People are the most important resources that a society has and those whose primary task is to help others with the impact of past traumas on their present lives are undertaking essential work on behalf of us all. An appropriate evaluation of the full significance of this work would be reflected in higher salaries for the staff but it will equally be demonstrated in those residential settings that recognise and meet the need for high levels of staff supervision, training and support. If workers are left to feel that the inevitable stresses of residential work are simply evidence of their own weakness, the result will be increased stress. Workers will feel bad about feeling bad. If, however, staff can be given the time and space to share the difficult and painful feelings that they will always have if they are working well, and are encouraged to understand their responses as potentially useful therapeutic tools, there is the opportunity for greater insight and self-knowledge and for increased job satisfaction.

CHAPTER 6

Being Different: A Black Perspective

Sonia Appleby

This chapter will discuss, using anecdotal experiences, stress felt by some black professionals within social work. The duality of being different, reinforced by societal mechanisms of alienation (Littlewood *et al.* 1981), be they manifest or latent, are forceful factors which may evoke stress in black professionals. The focus of this chapter will consider some variables within organisations which illuminate difference and its consequences as a *de facto* reality. Inner world images of ourselves and others enables an understanding of who we are and how others see us. The dyadic of 'self and other' will be illustrated by an experience which helped me to visualise myself and the external world. The second section considers the working environment as a potential stressor. The treatment process of a long-term patient provides an opportunity to unmask the pleasantries which often camouflage racist and prejudicial thinking. It is my contention that being different and, more importantly, the context which illuminates difference, increases vulnerability and provokes stress as a response. It should be borne in mind that attention given to black workers within social work does not negate the potency of 'cultural' stress as a dynamic factor in the lives of white professionals. Indeed, I hope this chapter can be read to facilitate an understanding that difference, as a cultural phenomenon, however it manifests in our lives, is compounded by an inability to think and feel as though we are the 'other' (Klein 1987). I will refer to the 'other' fairly often in this chapter – meaning anyone, whomever they may be. The concluding section briefly considers some strategies for detaching and coping with stress in the working environment

A personal account

The apparent tranquillity of my life changed when I was nearly four years of age. The event was simple enough, an everyday occurrence. Walking into a room does not in itself yield profound experiences. A room is a space contained by walls which separates it from other spaces. There was nothing special or significant about the room, except something was about to happen that would change my life. In this sense the space became the conduit for me to discern a presence which thereafter shaped my early, internal and external worlds.

The room represented my external self, which enabled me to make a profound discovery. It was also a compelling encounter which revealed an alchemy of perceptions; the process by which some of us come to know ourselves and, thereafter, others. At the time, I, of course, knew none of this; the outer world had not impinged upon me. I felt – when I was with my family – a degree of mastery in my world that allowed me to be free enough not to have puzzled who I was, nor what would become of me. In the room I saw a little girl I did not recognise. I moved closer and, much to my surprise, so did the girl, who seemed shorter than me. She was silent, but her eyes, which were small and piercing, stared at me with still wonderment. Then, in a moment when time feels as though it has arrested itself to facilitate the comprehension of a paradox, I realised the little, awkward girl was me. The girl was my image, my reflection, my outer self. I had never seen my composite mirror counterpart, which revealed an anterior perspective of my body.

My mirror self was a lesser reflection of me in almost every respect. The person I thought was on the inside was not the person imitated by the mirror. She was too short and not as pretty as the posed impressions I had become reliant upon as an accurate image of my facial self. Beyond the room I reappraised my parents, siblings, friends, relatives and neighbours, accumulating ideas that every one in my world was different. Slowly I began to comprehend what was happening around me. I absorbed more about myself within and beyond the ambit of my familial environment, realising that the colour of my skin was the means by which decisions and assumptions could be made. People who were hostile to me, based on nothing I had done or could remember doing, must have responded to something related to my outer persona: my skin and its blackness.

The subtleties of the world, including people who have poor social skills with limited regard for other people's feelings or that I was not a likeable child in everyone's eyes, were remote concepts. For some people, relating to others dissimilar to themselves is a fundamental challenge. They may never have created a consciousness in themselves to adapt in the presence of others. Such people may define safety as never venturing from their world into a place where they can permit themselves to be influenced beyond the boundaries of their existence. Being black, and the positive and negative impressions which had began to seep into my psyche became the salient medium for me to learn and decipher my outer world interactions.

This early or late awakening was pacified by attending an excellent Infants School with imaginative and loving teachers and children who had the capacity to be kind. In my eighth year, seated in the dining room at primary school, a child said: 'Guess who's the odd one out'. I considered my clothes compared to the others, the colour of the crockery (in those days school dinners were served on pastel-coloured plates), the food selected and our teachers. However, a racist perspective did not require such depth of thought. I looked into the eyes of my young persecutor, which twinkled with a triumphant glimmer. I felt the 'game' was constructed as a means of humiliating me and pointing out that I was black. I was the only 'nigger' seated at the table. The child knew calling me a nigger was abusive but she had artfully constructed a means in which she could exercise her duplicitous aim. In retrospect, the child, Lara, increased my understanding of covert, hateful communications and consolidated my suspicion and guardedness amongst people who were different from me.

As a child I learnt that the most primitive forms of evil require the individual to be cognisant of what is to be inflicted upon them. If there is any comfort that can be distilled from such encounters, it is the lack of stealth practised by some protagonists, serving as a reminder of how provocative differences can be and, in this context, ensuring that we should never lose consciousness of this reality. These experiences, whilst distressing, enable children – who are affected by being different – to know, adjust and cope with the vagaries of the external world. Tragically, negative, individual and societal expressions based upon being different have a profound and deleterious effect, particularly if it erodes the inner self.

There is a much perpetuated cliché that black children fantasise about being white (Dominelli 1988). The ideas which appear to support this belief are that the black child envies his/her white counterpart's blonde hair and blue eyes, having inculcated such negativity about his/her own body. Concurrent to the introjection of a bad black self is the counterbalancing introjection of the idealised other: a good white self. Yet if we cast around, we can see this 'so-called' body ideal is sought by many white people. Therefore, to use it as a prism to discuss the complexity of the black psyche fails to illuminate this dynamic as a societal projection rather than a distinct manifestation of the collective black unconscious. Undoubtedly, there are black children and adults who strive to adapt themselves away from the stereotypical tacist images of being black. It is arguable as to whether they wish to emulate white people, as neither adaptation nor all that is invested in such adjustments are the prerogative of white people. The paradox is that both white and black people are encouraged to conform, using positive (for whites) and negative (for blacks) images, to the belief that one race is more superior and vital than another.

Case one

A young black girl was subject to care proceedings and was placed with Black foster carers. She had a number of problems and was being assessed by a child psychiatrist. The child's mother, because of the circumstances of the case, had a poor relationship with her social worker, the line manager who was supervising the case and the psychiatrist. As a result, she had become marginalised as a valuable person in her daughter's life. The child disclosed to her white social worker that she wanted to have straight, long hair. This was immediately understood by her social worker as the child's desire to be white. Further exploratory work revealed that the foster carer had mentioned, whilst combing the child's hair, that it was 'tough' – an expression denoting coarse, difficult to manage hair. It is possible the child's disclosure was a covert communication that a part of her self – her hair – had come under the unwitting attack of the foster carer. Furthermore, a desire for long, straight hair could have been an expression for her mother, who, by perming her hair, had acquired the child's idealised hair type. Fortunately, because the foster carer acknowledged her interaction whilst grooming the child's hair, the social worker's assumptions were not pursued to the exclusion of other possibilities.

Beliefs predicated by values which inform notions that Black people want to be white because their skin connotes as being less worthy than their White counterpart's is detrimental – even more so when agencies are populated by workers who have beliefs and assumptions which obstruct positive experiences of being Black and, therefore, different. The following section will address social work organisations, the relationships between black workers and their agencies and between black and white professionals.

Organisations and the black professional

A colleague once told me it was commonplace for black social workers to enter the profession by the back door of residential work. As a newly qualified social worker, I began my career as a trainee residential worker. I felt the skilled task of caring for distressed children separated from their families and the people caring for them was minimised by this pernicious remark. Notwithstanding, this statement, which could also be seen within the context of the low value given to caring within our society, also served as a barometer to measure the profile of black professionals within social work.

In the early 1980s during my first years as a generic social worker in a London local authority, there were no black workers beyond the level of senior social worker, although there were many Heads of residential units. Black social workers were encouraged towards posts which were specialist when, in fact, the specialism was in skills related to their race – being non-white. The term 'race' is used advisedly since there are many workers within social work and allied disciplines whose intellectual and subjective experiences lead them to a perceptual awareness that race is synonymous with being non-white .

Case two

During a cultural awareness training session the course participants were asked to identify their ethnicity. Several white members of the group were puzzled and asked for the question to be clarified. It emerged that some of the group had never previously considered themselves within the constructs of race and ethnicity.

They had internalised the reality of racial identity as a being something not about them and their lives. Race was a term applied within the context of non-white groups because it had become fused with 'difference' juxtaposed to being white. If an understanding of race can be diluted in its relevance to one group and concentrated in relation to another, the ability to understand how we interact with our differences can be so polarised we suspend the capacity to think. In this case, the members of the group were able to re-evaluate their assumptions by exploring their racial and ethnic identity.

Some black workers are positively sought by social work agencies to provide specialist services for black clients. Black workers can, in most circumstances, facilitate and help their clients without compromising issues regarding race or ethnicity, which allows organisations to overlook black clients and their issues by making black professionals responsible for black clients. Professionals who work within social work agencies where there is a palpable awareness of the complexity of clients' needs will recognise that allocating workers where difference can be minimised is but only one component. Consequently, there are limitations for black workers who are absorbed within organisations as the 'black specialist'. This process propagates the mythology that black specialism is the only viable and truly legitimate role available for black professionals. It can be a source of irritation for some black workers, who may only be asked to make contributions regarding skills related to their ethnicity.

And yet it is inescapable that organisations who want, and need, to respond to their clients in a culturally sensitive manner will wish to consult and utilise Black workers. It is my contention that workers may be saturated with a sense of being exploited by organisations who perceive their worthiness solely on the basis of ethnicity. Organisations which only acknowledge black workers from a fixed perspective can undermine the personal and professional attributes of these workers. Many organisations, because of numerous constraints or lack of interest, are unable to pursue facilitating their workers to their full potential, despite this objective being in everyone's interests.

The practice of black social workers in these conditions can be compounded because the organisation has covertly exported the complexity of working with diversity. It is a sophisticated means of alienating clients *vis-à-vis* their workers and the workers from the managerial structures within the organisation. Agencies which merely graft workers into the working culture without training and monitoring working practices in the management structures are more likely to perpetuate institutional isolation experienced by workers who are different.

Case three

A black female social worker was almost exclusively referred black clients. This was convenient for her and her managers. She worked with the issues stemming from ethnicity with good effect. The unspoken quid pro quo enabled the social worker to have far more independence than her role warranted, giving rise to an aspect of her personality which was very idiosyncratic and occasionally bordered on being highly inappropriate. This intensified the belief amongst the worker's peer group and immediate supervisors that she was unmanageable. No one advised this worker that her behaviour was becoming a cause for concern until her conduct became reprehensible and led to disciplinary procedures.

Clearly, the worker could, and should, have monitored her behaviour. However, isolation provides opportunities for autonomous functioning but deprives the practitioner of adequate supervisory and managerial input. Similarly, organisations which allow workers to perceive themselves as separate from the wider working culture merely reinforce the experience of being different. Furthermore, it is wholly negligent for managers to conveniently leave specialist workers to function within a void. It reinforces the experience that the only skill needed for non-white clients is the provision of a professional who is black. a mono-based ethnicity specialism prevents social work organisations acknowledging alternative skills held by black professionals. Black social workers may feel, by the nature of their work, removed from their line managers and the wider working culture of the organisation. Professional distance between workers and managers, perhaps, reflects a more fundamental split. In general, we like and attract people who are similar to ourselves. Unconsciously we will find ourselves pulled towards or against this primary means of relatedness. Organisations magnify this dynamic defensively, by leaving specialists to contain and manage what cannot be held by the agency. Earlier I discussed how the innate capacity to be imaginative is tested by being considerate towards people who are different. Hence obviating the need to think and feel beyond one's own pattern of relatedness is a mechanism which many organisations deploy through recruitment policies and practice procedures.

We should also ponder whether our propensity to gravitate towards people who are similar affects the depth and nature of our ability to identity with people who represent difference. The potency of social, emotional and intellectual conditioning influences our perceptions, distorting or denying reality to ensure conformity with our internal and external image of the world. The next example demonstrates the responses of two managers. The conduct of the social workers provides the focus but, as will be seen, the perceptual ability of the managers is pivotal.

Case four

A white worker was competent in her case management but had a very unstable personal life which occasionally impinged upon her work. Her managers, both of whom were white, seemed unable or reluctant to commence disciplinary procedures, despite a litany of warnings. The organisational procrastination was contrasted by the response to a black worker in similar circumstances to the white worker. One of the managers noticed the imbalance in the black worker's case, which was being processed much more quickly towards disciplinary procedures. A suggestion was made that perhaps the managers had a greater identification with the white worker and this had probably affected the level of their responses. The managers realised that their perceptual views of these individual social workers were based on a primary, unprocessed response. They had differentiated between people like and unlike themselves without modifying this in their managerial style and work.

It was not the bad practice of these workers which was crucial to the outcome but the subjective responses of their managers. Some workers are compromised by managerial practices which stimulate and maintain imbalance, giving room for unchecked bias and prejudice to flourish. This can be generated by workers or their managers or the more wider environment of the workplace. Managers and workers must be cognisant of their work performance, which should be supported by a lucid awareness of how they incorporate their personalities, assumptions, values and beliefs. The diversity of difference within organisations militates for responsibility to be taken to ensure policies and procedures incorporate monitoring managers to ensure their decision making in relation to staff issues is always balanced. Equality is a high ideal within a reality which can be deceptive. Therefore, equality procedures should ensure and endorse the organisation's commitment to pursue evidence of inequality.

Thus far it has been argued that agencies, which categorise potential and worth measured in terms of the ability to utilise ethnicity as the only marker of competence, profoundly underestimate the value of black professionals and perpetuate stereotypical images of black workers and clients. I have suggested on several occasions that organisations act (juxtaposed to the genuine effort to modify adverse practices) as a collective and primary conductor, processing and maintaining unconscious and unspoken values and beliefs. These are most likely to be felt in the smaller environment of teams and the interface between managers and their supervisees. Alternatively, black workers may be highly sensitised about their ethnicity, assuming all negativity about them and their work arises from their blackness (Fryer 1984). Any criticism is felt to have a racist sub-text, which may affect their ability to hear feedback or criticism objectively.

Case five

A young black male social worker was referred to me by his agency. He was upset with his line manager, who constantly criticised his work, culminating in a serious argument which was witnessed by several people. He complained that he felt his manager took great satisfaction in humiliating him; she was contradictory and made him feel inadequate. He finally accused her of being racist, which she denied.

During the course of our work together he realised that his heightened stress level had made him less contained. As the weeks passed, being able to verbalise his feelings and perceptions, his equilibrium was restored. He was still convinced his manager was racist but observed that her social and professional skills were lacking in relation to other, white, team members. Eventually he was able to instigate a meeting which resolved some of their difficulties, enabling him to resume his role within the team. This worker's manager had, by her lack of insight, reactivated her supervisee's vulnerability about being black within a white institution. The fear of being made to feel different in the workplace acted as a recapitulation of previous negative interactions related to his ethnicity.

During my work I have observed, or it has been brought to my attention by others, that black workers and the problems arising from their work are, or become, 'unmanageable'. In almost all of these circumstances the complexity of difference – who holds the expertise, who is responsible for the client and the case – becomes submerged by the primary resurgence of relating to difference. How we interrelate with others is completely dependent on our inner beliefs and any adaptations made in the course of our life experience. Conversely, in my work as a social worker I seldom encountered overt racism from clients and I am reviewing whether this is a valid belief or whether the effects of racism were mitigated by the power relationship between client and worker.

Clinical work

During my analytical training and subsequent clinical work I have learnt to understand (and am still learning) about my lack of tolerance and that of my patients. The treatment of a young woman confirmed a hidden truth which belies the social politeness conveyed by education, upbringing and political correctness.

Whenever I meet a patient for the first time, as well as listening to the details motivating them to seek psychotherapy, I also observe references regarding the patient's narrative about what is happening in the room, here and now. Such was the frequency of patients stating, for example, 'my life has become so black' or 'I feel as though I'm in a dark tunnel' or 'this black cloud follows me everywhere' that I formulated, with the help of my therapist, an approach to express any cultural differences between my patient and myself during the assessment session. Holding onto the patient's metaphors enabled me to interpret their coded references in a safe and meaningful manner without undermining their original significance.

The young woman I mentioned earlier arrived for her first session – an evening appointment in mid-winter – and said: 'I didn't expect it to be so dark' – a paradoxical statement given the time of year. The real communication she acknowledged later was a turbid reference to my blackness. At the time, she was so overwhelmed by her problems that my ethnicity was of little or no importance, and so it remained for several years of her treatment. During one session she said: 'When I first started seeing you, I was glad that you weren't white because I would have felt so inferior…I felt because you were black, you would do what I wanted you to do…you would be my black mammy' (not mother but slave). She blushed: 'I felt I could bully you and you'd have to take it because I'm white'. It was painful, and yet moving, listening to a patient whose racist antecedents were plainly spoken without falsehood. She was embarrassed, her cognitive processes were alarmed at the bluntness of her disclosures. She related a truth reflected by her inner world, which had been cultibvated to enable her to think, feel and 'be' superior.

Much later she acknowledged the unthinkable: she was envious of a Black woman but she could not easily reconcile a cultural gulf which made me a worthy object, at least when her inner world was dominated by thoughts and feelings which obliged her to believe superiority was bestowed by her race. This clinical material helped me to understand the dichotomy between intellectual and emotional views regarding racism. Some clients are placated unconsciously and consciously by fantasies that the black worker exists to provide services and resources for them, fulfilling their racist beliefs that the role of a black worker is to service the needs of his or her white counterpart.

General coping strategies

Social work is a demanding task which necessitates being professional, imaginative and challenging of ourselves, our colleagues and our clients. We should also consider what we bring to our work: our personalities; our past and some of our less integrated experiences. The nature of social work enhances the likelihood of being exposed to stress and stressful situations. Therefore, accepting the need for reliable, safe and consistent support is vital. Personal support may be given during supervision but this may not always be appropriate or possible. Establishing needs and differentiating between the professional and personal should enhance the ability to understand the genesis of stress. It is injudicious to confuse supervision with support. Supervision is the process whereby the work in the presence of the client is determined, assessed, ameliorated and monitored.

Stress may be felt in relation to the organisation, clients and/or a personal event. Some people are resilient and can cope with a multitude of stressors with seemingly little affect. Such people may be unconscious of their stress, which is usually noticed by others, causing no apparent damage to themselves, their colleagues or clients. Conversely, a stressed worker can become ill, overactive, passive or argumentative, a bully, demanding, abusing alcohol and drugs and anxious, depressed or phobic.

If an organisational variable is the trigger generating stress, discuss and record these issues with your colleagues and supervisor in a constructive manner. In these circumstances most agencies will seek to rectify problems. Equal opportunities policies, grievance procedures and mediation are useful structures to address and resolve concerns. Personal problems, particularly if they impinge upon effectiveness at work, should always be addressed. Again, most organisations will try to assist their workers and many have employee assistance programmes for this purpose.

The theme of this book is to promote the idiom of the internal and external world as cogent constructs in our lives. Stress affecting people who have already had a life-time of accrued experiences of feeling, and/or being made to feel, different presents a significant challenge. Should we be reliant on our previous coping strategies? And how can we be assured the way in which we have modified ourselves is adaptive? Working in organisations which reflect bias and prejudice may confound confidence, ability and ambition. Nonetheless, black workers are successful within social work, and we should share and crystallise our experiences which have enabled us to consolidate effective strategies to minimise the stress of being different within our working environments.

CHAPTER 7

Yes, and But, and Then Again, Maybe

Martin Ruddock

On the one and only occasion I argued that stress had negatively affected my work I was met by a response against which I could not argue. The response was: 'Yes, and but, and then again, maybe'.

Since this experience I have observed or talked to others who have suffered from stress and have been confronted by the same confusion of messages. It is almost as though there is fear that if people accept that someone has suffered from stress, we will have an epidemic, with everyone using the same argument either to avoid, or excuse, or attack. And anyway, 'it's a bit wimpish' and maybe it threatens the management styles imposed upon those, both in and out of the public sector, by numerous financial restraints. We are also probably poor at accepting our personal feeling because of our history in which sayings such as: 'Grin and bear it', 'a stiff upper lip' and 'if you can't stand the heat, get out of the kitchen', proliferate.

I was the Social Work Team Manager responsible for the care of Kimberley Carlile, who died on 8 June 1986 in circumstances that were horrific and disturbing. The press presented the events with indignation and blame. Society was once again confronted by the violence that happens behind too many doors in our society. The handling of the case was severely criticised in the media and by the inquiry team, led by Louis Blom Cooper, which was set up to learn from the events. It had been clearly evident to me from the moment I had heard of Kimberley's death that opportunities to act in ways that would probably have saved Kimberley's life had been missed. This was devastating, both personally and professionally, and, although I did not relish the process, I wanted to participate constructively to guarantee that learning from the event took place.

At its crudest, this chapter is about whether I was an excuse-giving, bumbling idiot or whether job pressure and its resulting stress undermined my ability, *and a services ability*, to intervene to save Kimberley Carlile. This simplified question is important because I consider the same question is asked every time someone draws the 'stress card' and listeners have to make a judgement as to whether it is authentic or an excuse.

In my evidence to the Inquiry I wanted the panel to understand that I was not a bumbling and incompetent social worker but someone whose functioning had been seriously diminished by levels of stress which were beyond the optimum I could handle. I felt tragedies were too easily brushed off with the basic assumption that the worker must be of poor calibre and could justifiably be scape-goated. This removed the responsibility to make a wider analysis and protected both organisations and other individuals.

Commenting on my submission to the Inquiry, the panel, in their report *A Child in Mind*, stated: 'It is not only an outstanding document of insight into a social worker's tasks. But it is also well written, movingly reflective and self critically analytical. It avoids casting blame on others, in circumstances where it might have been expected.' (London Borough of Greenwich 1987, p.199). In my submission, I evidenced the level of pressure and concluded:

> The level of pressure during those months became so intense that instead of being faced with a manageable number of tasks which required a major effort of me but which I was able to deal with to my satisfaction, I was faced with an overwhelming body of work which meant I could deal with none of it to anything approaching the degree of competence which I would normally demand of myself and was forced to adopt a method of working where by some tasks were not dealt with at all. (Ruddock 1987)

The Inquiry team recommended that my submission be published. This has never happened because others who gave evidence complained it would be unfair to publish only the submission of one participant.

The Inquiry team, responding to the stress argument, made the following comments:

- 'Stress, like hunger and thirst, is an inescapable part of life. It is difficult to judge when it goes beyond; "the monotonous moils of strained, hard run humanity" (from *In a Death Divided* by Thomas Hardy)' (p.199).

- 'It is the duty of professional people to have sufficient insight into their own condition to recognise if stress, in whatever form, is impairing their judgement and threatening their capacity to achieve a high standard of practice in their work' (p.199).

- 'It is the employer's responsibility to create an environment that does not in itself cause stress' (p.199).

These arguments seem to me typical of many responses made to people suffering from stress. They start by generalising and dismissing the specific experience and continue with a general statement about 'duty' and 'insight' and place the responsibility for doing something about having stress on to the individual. This is clearly an unrealistic expectation of someone whose functioning is impaired. Finally, they state a platitude that 'it is an employer's responsibility to create an environment that does not in itself cause stress.' Of course it is the duty of an organisation such as social services to recognise that high levels of stress are likely to exist and that every effort should be made to mitigate and alleviate the problem. However, it avoids the question as to whether this responsibility is actively taken on and, if so, whether it is taken on effectively.

The comments are, in my view, unrealistic and demonstrate the panel's inability to make a judgement. They left me angry then and, returning to the experience now, they still leave me angry. The response is 'Yes, and but, and then, maybe, and anyway, thank you and lets move on.'

In the angry environment that followed Kimberley Carlile's death, the desire to blame, hurt and punish was very understandable. It is not an easy time for learning and, in some ways, an inquiry becomes a needed cathartic process in which society's anger can be vented. From some of the letters sent to me at the time, it is quite clear that many would have felt happier if I was hung, drawn and quartered.

In the stressful experience of an inquiry, every action is placed under microscopic detail and personal, inter-personal and systemic conflict becomes public. At such a time of difference, defending a position, or attacking and blaming others, feels safer to participants than looking for understanding or learning or trying to understand behaviour. An inquiry, at these times, becomes an exercise of avoiding blame and little else.

Although my situation was high profile and in the public eye, I would guess that similar interactions take place at other times when the issue of an individuals functioning being impaired by stress is raised. As human beings, we have a natural instinct to defend ourselves and often our first line of defence is to attack.

In retrospect, I know that it would have been politically unacceptable for the panel to accept the stress argument and the 'Yes, but and maybe' response was better than 'bumbling fool'. Sadly, it diminished opportunities for learning and recognising the human and personal costs of working in a stressful profession where ones' emotions are constantly affected by the daily process of work.

Throughout the process of the Inquiry I was fortunate to receive support from Brian Raymond, a strong and sensitive solicitor, who assisted me to face my mistakes and their context and to learn from them. I also received therapeutic help that enabled me to understand and discard the incompetent script and regain the knowledge that I had something to offer. It also assisted me to avoid the temptation to become a powerless victim.

Looking back and reflecting about the events ten years later, I still feel much of the pain, hurt, sadness and anger, though I feel pleased to have rebuilt a career in social work management that I enjoy and to which I consider I make an important contribution. I think that the 'Yes, but and maybe' response was as good as I could have expected. I also think that my response to the panel was muddled between the 'stimulus', or what caused the stress and the 'stress reaction', or response.

Writers about stress have identified concern that contemporary science should tolerate a confustion about stimulus and response. This point is important because stress is difficult to define and, as such, is difficult to communicate, especially when different people have different personal experiences, responses and thresholds to it. Many of the personal experiences to it will have been unhappy and reactions to it may have been unhelpful.

On reflection, I consider that by using the concept of stress I became the focus of the inquiry and it became harder to define the external factors affecting my behaviour. I wonder how much this option was easier for me because it caused less friction with others involved in the inquiry and avoided the harder option of open conflict with senior management, who would, at a later stage, have a say on whether I worked again.

My response to the inquiry was also linked to a personal need to make sense of a horrendous experience and to learn to live with myself as an individual and as a parent of my own children. I also needed to make personal sense of my working life and whether I wanted to continue to practice as a social worker if I was allowed to. For me, the need to make personal sense of the events merged with the practical issue of dealing with the outside world and the inquiry.

Subsequently, I undertook management training and, as a result, if I was now asked to support someone in a similar situation I would try to use an approach that put the emphasis on *stimulus, cause and pressure* rather than *response, effect and stress*. Put differently, I would put emphasis on the *work environment and system rather than individual pathology*.

An alternative option

A possible model for looking at effective job performance might include looking at: the individual's competence; the job demands; the organisational environment (see Figure 7.1).

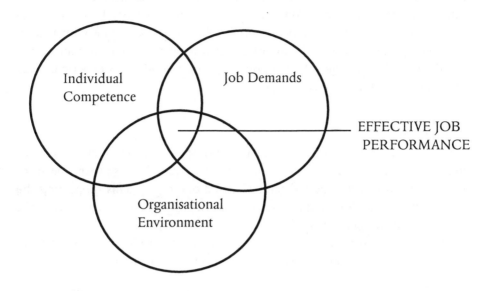

Individual Competence

Job Demands

EFFECTIVE JOB
PERFORMANCE

Organisational
Environment

Figure 7.1
Source: Open University

The individual's competence

The process of appointing people to jobs is to ensure that an individual has the right balance of skill, knowledge and experience to undertake specific job requirements. It is often the case that further training or mentoring is needed in post to bring an individual up to the standards required. It is an obvious requirement that this process is undertaken properly if the organisation is to provide a service of quality and workers are to be enabled to perform effectively, developing their skills and abilities.

At a time when organisations and their staff are having to change the way they think and provide services, managers need both quality training and ongoing support to assist them to deal with the difficult processes in effectively bringing about change. The competence to manage change, if the organisation is requiring change, is obviously essential.

When appointed to the post of Team Manager I had been working in the voluntary sector undertaking more community and therapeutic services. My day-to-day experience of dealing with child protection was rusty, as was my working knowledge of legal processes. These weaknesses were acknowledged at the time of appointment but systematic training to address them was not forthcoming.

I was also new to management and came to a team where two members had applied unsuccessfully for the post, team dynamics were dysfunctional and the workload excessive. The team was also in dispute with senior management about moving to a community location because of reasonable concerns that patch working would create additional pressures that the team did not have the capacity to handle. This combination of tasks needed someone with proven experience, competence and support systems to enable them to manage the conflict and change. The risk in appointing someone with less experience was not appropriate for this post.

The job demands

Job analysis needs to identify the demands of the post to ensure they are specific, attainable, realistic and can be done in the time required. This process needs to look at how the tasks required can be carried out, the systems supporting the process, the people involved in carrying out the tasks, the people receiving the service and other major players.

When I came into post, in addition to the normal tasks of a social work team manager, I faced a number of additional issues. These included:

- managing a dispute in which the team supported by the union was in conflict with senior management over a move to a joint localised office with housing department

- looking at building plans, negotiating the teams requirements and developing a marriage with housing without the commitment of either party

- addressing an unfair distribution of workloads between teams in the area.

As a result of my attempts to resolve these issues, I became an isolated outsider who had broken organisational culture. My attempts to find solutions through problem solving were unsuccessful.

These problems were compounded when, soon after I arrived, experienced team members resigned. I had also come into post just as the first large influx of referrals relating to sexual abuse occurred. These challenged us all but, additionally, heightened gender conflicts as people worked to address issues that left an enormous personal impact. The same conflicts were soon to become public as 'Cleveland' hit the news.

Either way, the additional job demands and their context were more than I could handle and, in my view, in excess of what should have been expected of any one person.

The organisational environment

The organisational environment relates to how the organisations' internal and external systems work and interrelate. The organisational environment in which

I functioned was one in which existed a mutual lack of confidence between local councillors and senior management. This was based in different perceptions of the role of councillors, different views about how social work should be carried out in the area and different value systems.

As team manager, I did my best to manage the conflict and relate to the different stakeholders and their objectives. In practice, I worked hard but failed to get to grips with the interactional processes and ended up feeling out of step with staff, senior management and councillors. I felt unsafe and like an innocent bystander caught up in a war.

The above examples illustrate that, during a short time in post, I was confronted by a range of tough issues whilst coming to terms with a new job and a heavy and complex social work caseload. This disrupted any positive learning process to address my weaknesses in the job. It also affected my motivation, confidence and emotional health that was undermined by having to manage systemic conflict and change while having minimal power or influence with any of the stakeholders.

Furthermore, I found my social work value base was undermined by lack of resources that left me no option other than to write 'NFA' (no further action) on numerous cases that I knew should be allocated to prevent further breakdown and future social work intervention. Of all the numerous pressures, this process made a mockery of my reasons for entering social work, conflicted with my value base and caused me the greatest anguish. It challenged me personally and devalued the struggle I was making to survive and get on top of a new post.

The above are examples that demonstrate the actual pressure of the job. They identify weaknesses in the organisational system and management of the department. They also identify the personal internal struggle that is essential and unavoidable for the individual if they are to use their own skills ability and knowledge in a job.

Reflecting back on the events has been a difficult process in which I have experienced myself moving against the use of the word 'stress' to define an experience. I have done so because people's understanding of what 'stress' means is so different. Maybe this is a defensive response to avoid fully understanding the other person's experience. Whatever the reasons, the 'Yes, and but and maybe' response was inevitable. It was also hurtful, rejecting and, in my view, unfair. Rejecting the word 'stress' is difficult because it defined my own mass of confused, stuck and muddled feelings that gave a language and label to that experience.

Unfortunately, the outside world that judges issues cannot relate to such unclear concepts of stress that are used in too many ways to have credibility for other than an expression of a range of personal experiences. It is difficult to judge whether the response would have been different if my submission had focused on good employment practices and the organisational system in which I worked. I fear that the choice I took, which felt authentic and right to me at the time, was possibly the wrong strategy for an outcome in which the *system failing the individual* was seen as more important than the *individual failing the system*.

CHAPTER 8

Professional Competence
Control and Confidence

Mili Mass

Introduction

In this chapter I intend to explore the effect of the accepted academic knowledge base of social work on the practitioner's sense of competence. I will submit that the dominant social work theory that still equates explanation with prediction leads to measure professional competence in terms of control – the ability to bring about a predicted outcome. Although control is conventionally conceived of as linked with confidence, I will advance the view that the employment of this notion of professional competence in social work practice undermines practitioners' confidence (Stevenson and Parsloe 1978) and will further claim that control as a measure of professional competence constitutes a stress factor. It is based on the notion that intervention proceeds in a linear direction defined by objectively set goals. These notions do not withstand the realities of social work practice and, therefore, place practitioners in subordinate positions. Their work is not valued by their observations and the nature of relationships which they establish with their clients but rather by some predefined goals which, under the disguise of objectivity, are arbitrarily imposed on their experience and judgement.

Instead, I will offer a view that considers explanation to be descriptive, not predictive, and will build on constructs derived from the professionals' experiences. Professionals' competence, according to my view, is defined by their ability to generate constructs that can be accessed by systematic observations and shared by the professional community. This shared experience, I propose, would enhance practitioners' confidence and thereby contributes to their professional competence.

Objectivity and the reification of the human event

In seeking to establish itself in the academic world, social work has allied with the social sciences, not with humanities or with the liberal arts. Manicas' (1987) description of academic social scientists may, therefore, have more than an essence of truth: 'They marked their territories, defined social science in positivistic and ahistorical terms, and adopted an unabashed technological stance' (p.216). Thus, although the basic tenet of social work has been that its subject matter – the 'human event' – consists of the constant interaction of person and situation and subjective and objective reality (Hamilton 1959), academic social work has been dominated by the division of the human experience into 'macro' and 'micro' elements and by a striving for objectivity. This split between macro (society) and micro (the person) is based on transforming what are essentially constructs, meanings and ideas into physical entities. It is as if the differences between the physical properties of a person and the physical properties of society in themselves determine differences in their innate essence. Thus the 'macro' part of the split has resulted in the demarcation of territories according to either geographical areas or to organisational frameworks and the 'micro' has led to defining the person within the boundaries of his/her physical existence (Kessen 1978) by focusing on personality theories or on fixed characteristics in people (particularly delimiting characteristics such as learning disability) and by categorising people according to the effects which might be achieved by ameliorating living situations – for example 'the homeless' and 'the poor'.

This reification of the human relationships into geographical-organisational territories and into fixed finite personal properties has led to the dominance in social work theory and practice of explanations based on deduction (Kaplan 1964). Explanation has become equated with the prediction of the effects of intervention on relationships among defined entities. The further leap into a linear concept of intervention directed toward preconceived goals was inevitable. This view of intervention was followed by an unabashed enthusiasm for technological skills accompanied by the hallmark of technology – control. Indeed, professional competence in social work has come to be judged by the worker's ability to master and achieve set, often tangible, goals.

This mechanistic notion of knowledge, however, is imposed on interpersonal events which are of a fundamentally different nature, being reciprocal and interactive. The ensuing search for control as a measure of professional competence seems, therefore, to undermine, not enhance, the confidence of the practitioner. The following example will illustrate my concerns.

The linear conception of intervention

In a study conducted by a social worker practising in a rural local authority in Israel (Lester-Levy 1992), the worker puzzled over the despair she experienced in working with one family. Her despair seemed inexplicable, particularly as she was then working with this family (family A) and another (family B) where she could discern very few differences between them. There was certainly not any difference in the lack of any improvement in the situation of either. Both families were classified as 'multi-problem families', both mothers suffered from poor health and were not working, both husbands barely provided for each family's economic needs. The housing conditions experienced by both families were very bad; each had been promised help with housing and, for both, this help had not been forthcoming. There were some differences in the 'properties' of the families. Family A was not very responsible in handling payments and money matters. The father in family A abused alcohol and drugs and there was some question as to whether the mother also took drugs. At the time that the worker was seeing the family, however, this was not an issue causing significant concern. Family B was different. No alcohol or drugs were used and better control was exercised in money matters. Nevertheless, the worker did not think that these differences explained the difference in her experience with each family. She realised that she did not always believe Mrs A, although she found her, at times, to be very engaging, witty and quite perceptive regarding her situation. At other times she would be evasive, bitter and accusatory. The worker could never tell whether the next appointment would be kept or not. Even when Mrs A did keep an appointment, it was never possible to continue discussion of the issues that had been raised in previous meetings. There would always be another new burning issue. As for Mrs B, although she too, at times, had attempted to manipulate the situation in devious ways, the worker's contact with her had followed an expected sequence: the worker knew that appointments would be kept and issues would be discussed in a predictable manner.

When the worker arrived at this point in describing her experience, she realised that she could explain the significant difference between her contact with Mrs A and her contact with Mrs B if she constructed her contacts with both families in terms of 'narratives lines', such as the ones proposed by social constructionism (Gergen and Gergen 1984). This proposal views social reality in terms of the direction patterns described in accounts of social events. Thus while the narrative of the worker's contacts with Mrs B took a steady even line, contacts were predictive and consistent and no improvement was noticed. The narrative recounted by the contacts with Mrs A did not give rise to any line at all. The worker's despair seemed to have arisen from the absence of an expected sequence of events. This revelation drew the worker's attention to how dominant the linear concept was when it came to assessing her own competence.

She decided to examine this construct – the significance of the effect of 'a line' on the worker's sense of confidence in his/her work. 'A line' was defined by her as in the dictionary (Even-Shoshan 1988) 'a thread stretched for measurement; a thin drawing between two distant points; the border of a uni-dimensional space – the length; the cutting edge of two surfaces; things arranged in a row; a border between two states; the front line; a fortifying line; a certain direction; a way of behaviour; a way of thinking; a way of executing a plan', etc.

With these meanings of the terms 'line' in mind, the worker interviewed 12 female and 4 male social workers. She told them about her despair with Mrs A and asked them to share with her any similar experiences. Although this was not meant to be a systematic examination, she did not share with them her explanation of her own despair, the absence of a 'line' which could be followed in her work. Four workers stated that they did not experience a sense of despair in their work, although they did relate some difficult and frustrating experiences. The others recounted despairing experiences. All workers, however, willingly shared their experiences with the worker. With the interviewees' permission, the worker wrote down the content of the interviews while conducting them. From these records she extracted all the terms which implied the workers' need for a 'line'. Those included:

> To try and create some continuity... To end a meeting with a thread for the next meeting... At every meeting I worry whether the discussion will lead somewhere... Things go around in a circle... And then I make a scale of one to ten and ask the client to grade the subjects he is stuck with on this scale...I am not willing to accept leaps... To know what the real boundaries are... He did not rebuild himself...I set goals which I want to reach... I thought after all this investment, I thought that he would turn out differently... After every input of help we still find ourselves at the same point we were at last year... To set limits, to write a work plan... Find one thing from which you can pull the rope and begin to unravel the situation... The image is that of being left at some junction with no route anywhere... We constantly chase our own tails... I would try to connect and create some sequence between meetings: where did we start from and did we move forward? nothing...going round in circles all the time... If she had understood me and followed my line... If I measure progress from 0 to 10 and their capacity is 4...

On reading these quotations, I wonder whether it is possible to find 'a line' at any given time in everybody's lives. Greenberg's statement about the line in painting (quoted by Benjamin 1994) seems quite pertinent: 'Line, which is one of the most abstract elements in paintings since it is never found in nature as the definition of contour, returns to oil paintings as the third colour between two other colour areas'(p.100). Indeed, these quotations indicate the workers' attempts to find 'a line in nature' and, by doing so, they introduce, at times, an artificiality – as of a line as a 'third colour area' – between themselves and their clients. As I suggested earlier, this was not a systematic study. It is, therefore, not known how dominant or pervasive these views are amongst social workers. There seemed, however, to be a link between this linear view of intervention and a defence against feelings of frustration for want of control over the outcome of their intervention, an expectation set partly by the social work theory. The introduction of an orderly sequence by the workers seems to serve *their* need to resolve their own stress, not necessarily their clients' needs.

There was a positive outcome from this study. The quest to discover the effect of the linear concept on the sense of professional competence in social workers stimulated the worker to surrender her expectations of a predictable sequence in her work with Mrs A. Every form of contact offered by Mrs A was accepted by the worker: telephone, urgently requested appointments and organised scheduled appointments which were sometimes kept. The worker remained relaxed throughout these contacts, no longer striving to achieve a set goal beyond the contact itself. Her ability to yield control, not to gain it, has paved the way for a more meaningful relationship with the client and has contributed to the worker's confidence. At this stage she could appreciate Mrs A's shrewd perception of the world, be amused by her wit and could also observe that Mrs A was less bitter or that she was able to share a more optimistic side with the worker. Mrs A's own reality, full of contradictions and one where chaos and order were both interwoven into the fabric of the different aspects of her life at different times, could unfold. The worker could comprehend that Mrs A's strengths rest with her ability to endure these contradictions and her ability to circumvent some of the obstacles which lay on her way. 'Manipulation' has lost its negative connotation in this context and the worker could convey to Mrs A her appreciation of her coping. In turn, the worker herself felt more confident of her ability to make a significant contribution to Mrs A's efforts to improve her life situation.

The contribution of knowledge base of social work to the worker's confidence will be further discussed in the following sections.

Knowledge and practice

My opening discussion has emphasised the tendency of the academic pursuit of social work to seek objectivity and a linear view of what is, essentially, a blend of objective and subjective realities and a reciprocal interactive process. This approach to the acquisition of knowledge has been brought about by following the 'psychology of universal rules' (Manicas 1987). People, according to this view, are conceived of in terms of their commonalties (Harré 1981) and

knowledge is acquired about certain groups because they seem to bear distin-
guishing characteristics. This assumption does not hold up in daily social work
practice. It is a constantly recurring experience that, as the worker comes to
know the client better, the situation is seen to become ever more complex and
fluid and the client does not fit neatly into whatever classification might have
seemed appropriate before a more meaningful worker–client relationship
evolved (Allsopp 1995). This leads to two possible consequences:

1.   When practitioners adhere to universal rules through which they
     perceive people as resembling one another, they are encouraged to
     keep at a distance from their clients and daily practice inevitably
     becomes routinised. This, however, is not a comfortable routine
     (although routines at times appear to be); this is a routine inundated
     by clients' distress – the 'bread and butter' of social work practice.
     The corollary is a growing sense of stress by social workers. Neither
     client's nor worker's experience is valued. Furthermore, the heavy
     emphasis on objectivity in itself often places workers in a
     professionally inferior position – their on-going relationships with
     their clients are taken to contaminate any truly objective view and
     external 'experts' are invited in when critical decisions have to be
     made. Thus the theoretical social work position of total objectivity is,
     in fact, one which is divorced from practice and, therefore,
     impossible to sustain. Many practitioners cope with the adverse
     effects of the adherence to universal rules by seeking administrative
     control, in lieu of the professional control which they could not gain,
     and move into managerial positions. In this way, the illusion of
     control is acquired through enforcement of the rules over their staff.

2.   Other practitioners attempt to ignore the guidance of universal rules
     and make a point of relating to the uniqueness of each client. This
     course, it seems, leaves no room for generalisations. These are the
     practitioners who, I believe, are so often blamed for not using
     research in their everyday practice. Such criticism is well worth
     heeding, especially in cases where workers have to take far-reaching
     decisions regarding their clients' life situations and where having
     some baseline assessments, such as reports of children's experiences
     of their separation from their parents, would help the worker in
     planning intervention. They might also be the practitioners who turn
     to psychotherapy, where attention to the individual and the unique
     privacy of the therapeutic relationship is cherished and considered to
     provide a valuable knowledge base.

Practitioners seem to be left with the choice of being alienated either from their clients, by adhering to the guidance of objectivity, or from the academic world, by keeping their knowledge within the privacy of the therapy room.

Towards alternative constructs of knowledge

This is not a 'radical choice', it is the corollary of defining knowledge in terms of the deduction of predictions from universally applied rules. This is not the only way in which knowledge can be constructed. An alternative would be to ally with the British school of the psychology of individual differences (Manicas 1987). Such a process attempts to decipher the rules underlying social behaviour, given the differences between people, on the basis of *induction* not on the basis of *deduction*. Induction can serve as a basis for systematic examination, provided it is derived from constructs and not simply from observed events (Bhaskar 1978). The myth that abused children become abusive parents, for example, is an inference based on observations of the incidence of early abuse found in abusing parents – predicting backwards, as Rutter (1987) described. Prospective studies have found that most abused children do not become abusive parents (Kaufman and Zigler 1987) and our encounters, mainly in clinical practice, with those who have become abusive in some fashion represent events, repeated as they may be, and not a construct.

The task involved in describing individual differences is, therefore, that of detecting the constructs which underlie social behaviour (Escalona and Heider 1959; Meehl 1973; Spence 1986). Inherent in this process are two assumptions:

1. Individual differences derive from the evolving relationships between people and their situations. These relationships are not rooted in inborn traits. Social behaviour is not determined by forces outside one's control, it is directed by personal preferences and beliefs regarding one's situation (Secord and Harré 1972).

2. Since individual differences between people are defined by the patterns formed by and within their situations, they cannot be described objectively from the outside. The social world is observed through our own constructs and shapes them. It is not the world out there that is being observed but our construct of individual differences (Mass 1994). The following example illustrates this process in action.

A Bedouin male social worker raised a recurrent dilemma in his practice (Mass and Alkrenawi 1994). By following the professional code and meeting in privacy with female clients he repeatedly encountered their seductive overtures. These seriously set at risk both the worker and the clients. If the nature of these encounters became disclosed, the Bedouin societal authorities would be bound to react severely to the violation of the Bedouin taboo on private encounters between a man and a woman whose relationship is not defined as primary. The worker thought that this behaviour might be provoked by the invitation implicit in the violation of societal taboo. It was specifically the 'neutral position', assumed by the worker as part of his professional stance, that, in this context, seemed to invite the seductive response of his female clients. Thinking that the prevalence of seduction in these meetings was unique to his minority culture, he had kept these observations to himself. Finally, he related his observations to a group of fellow Israeli graduate students who shared the same professional code. His understanding of the situation, in terms of the conflict between two codes of social conduct, was challenged in the group discussion by a competing view which saw transference as a powerful force operating within the helping relationships and these overtures as a manifestation of transference. Seduction is not an unfamiliar theme in treatment. This perception allowed him to explore his construct with his fellow Bedouin social workers of either sex. He found out that many of them had experienced these phenomena. It also seemed that they all had kept these occurrences to themselves, attempting to accommodate their professional code but, at the same time, struggling to keep seduction out of their professional work, either by severing their relationships with their clients or by limiting the help they had offered to practical services only.

The construct explored in this example is that proposed by the Bedouin social workers: that the seduction was provoked by the breaking of the societal taboo. Much the same view was apparently held by the clients who acted on what they perceived as an invitation by openly displaying what was commonly defined as dangerous behaviour. It is not altogether possible to differentiate the social worker's view from that of the clients. It was, however, possible to generate a construct based on interpersonal events as well as the interaction of objective-subjective realities once the worker examined the inference he had come to on the basis of his own experience.

Having proposed the construct of the conflict between these two cultural codes, the worker proposed a professional code for encounters between men and women within the Bedouin society. He would define professional relationships at the onset as analogous to primary relationships. When suggesting to a client of the opposite sex that they meet regularly, the worker would tell the client: you are like my sister/brother (to young clients) or you are like my uncle/aunt (to older clients). This solution was borrowed from the mental healers in the Bedouin society (Darwishes). This early definition of parameters would mitigate the invitation to seduction which seemed inherent in the privacy of professional meetings. Yet the definition of these relationships as analogous to primary relationships, which, theoretically, are considered to be the source of transference, would allow transference experiences to develop.

Knowledge acquired by this process is not finite, nor is there a clear demarcation between our constructs of the world and the constructs 'out there'. Objectivity is not the hallmark of this process of the construction of knowledge but accessibility.

Building reliability and validity into this approach

The task in this process of knowledge construction is to translate practice wisdom into systematic observation so as to detect underlying constructs of social behaviour. The wisdom arrived at in daily practice, usually kept in the privacy of the worker-client relationship, should be made public. The demand for systematic documentation to inform the construction given by the worker to observations is consonant with the empirical requirement for reliability. However, it is not the 'world' that is being examined in this process, it is the accessibility of the worker's construct to systematic examination. Validity, according to this approach, is measured not by objectivity but by allowing the correspondence between the worker's construct and empirical examination to serve as a base from which the constructs described may be applied beyond one discrete situation (Reason and Rowan 1981). The following example may serve to demonstrate what I mean by such measures of reliability and validity.

A social worker chose to pursue her 'practice wisdom' that the reminiscences of old people, which were experienced as a pleasant way to approach elderly clients as well as a rewarding activity for many of them, might be employed systematically in practice (Zernik 1994). In her practice in a convalescent hospice she therefore examined whether the stories told by a group of elderly people revealed information about the perceptions of choice experienced by these people at that particular stage of their lives. Taylor's (1977) proposition regarding 'second order' choices was used as a definition of 'choice' in this study – that is choices based on the consideration of value attributed to available options, not on considerations of utility. This proposal was tested for reliability – whether the classification proposed by the worker could be systematically employed by two observers. It could. The next stage – the test of the validity of this construction – was performed by linking the classified choices with the elderly people's experiences of needing to be helped by others – an inferior position in our society. Criteria for the classification of interviews regarding the elderly clients' experiences of being helped were devised and also tested for inter-observer reliability.

The data described a correspondence between elderly people's perception of choice and their experience of being helped. People who viewed their lives as determined by their own actions and decisions had a matter-of-fact approach to being helped – they would ask for it whenever it was needed. People who tended to perceive the resolutions of their life stories to be contingent on somebody else tended to avoid requests for help.

The worker's construct, that the reminiscences of the elderly are indicative of their attitude towards needing help, can contribute to daily practice. Instead of discussing their need of help, the worker can discuss their perceptions of choices as expressed in their reminiscences – a more dignified topic. Since the difference in perceptions amongst these elderly people was described in terms of tendencies and not as 'pure types', it would be easier to point out to them that it is possible to perceive choices in a variety of ways. Elderly people whose life stories tend to be portrayed as contingent on choices made by others may be helped to see the resolution of these stories differently and perceive the choices they made as determining their stories. This perception of choice and agency is more likely to be related to experiences of needing help that allow the elderly to ask for help whenever needed. The employment of second-order choices as an explanatory construct has already been applied in the area of parent–infant relationships, as I have described elsewhere (Mass 1983; Mass 1994; Mass 1997).

The search for constructs and practitioners' confidence

These examples are cited to help clarify the nature of the process of describing individual differences. They offer possible variants in individual differences, not any form of 'finite' knowledge. It therefore becomes possible to say that the subject matter of this process of knowledge construction is the construction of knowledge itself. No goals are predefined. Yet all three examples cited above carry with them practical applications. Placing the process of knowledge construction centre stage might mitigate the all too common tendency to reify abstract concepts into fixed entities. Knowledge acquired by a search for constructs, rather than through a definition of entities, renders the division between the 'micro' and the 'macro' obsolete. Constructs underlying societal norms cannot be conceived a priori to be distinct from the constructs underlying the social behaviour of the individual. People are at one and the same time the carriers of societal norms and the makers of these norms. Societal norms are not, therefore, set as a measure of social conduct, they are seen as part of the construction of social behaviour (Mass 1997). Whether the study concerns itself with social policy or with the level of direct practice does not determine the nature of the quest, it will determine with whom this quest is being conducted. One study describing individual differences in parent–infant relationships found that parental attributes which led them to focus on the infant's disposition (character and intentions) were linked to parental actions characterised by imposition and instrumentality rather than reciprocity (Mass 1983; Zilkha 1997). Similar constructs have been described in the analysis of court decisions regarding non-consensual adoptions in Israel. Despite declared intentions to the contrary, courts attribute character flaws and evil intentions to failing parents, such attribution frequently being followed by decisions to place children for adoption against their parents' wishes (Barkai and Mass in press). This parallel in observed constructs – whereby attributions as to fixed dispositions are linked to the absence of reciprocity in parental acts – reflects, and is reflected in, societal constructs whereby compulsory intervention in the parent–child relationships is related to attributed parental dispositions.

This alternative theoretical stance is propounded with the aim of enhancing the worker's confidence by building on the worker's construct of the world. It begins where the worker is. It does not dissect interpersonal events a priori according to what are assumed to be objective criteria. Whilst some workers do construct social behaviour in terms of (assumed) fixed characteristics of people and in terms of an a priori division between person and situation, this simply reflects one construct of the world and does not form an objectively reached statement of universal rules.

Competence, according to this approach, is assessed by the worker's ability to share constructs and examine how these constructs compare and correspond with observation. No adherence to universal rules is required from the worker, rather a deliberate choice. In the same vein, control and objectivity are not required but the ability, to share with colleagues and clients, is. This shift might, in addition, mitigate the sense of alienation often experienced by workers adhering to universal rules.

Process and outcome

The move from universal rules based on finite entities to the description of individual differences based on ideas, beliefs and values assumes this process to be infinite. Ideas, by their very nature, are not finite, unless, of course, they are taken as dogmas. This proposed approach to the acquisition of knowledge raises questions about process versus outcome. It is quite difficult to distinguish at what point process ends and outcome begins. Yet there is a sense in which outcome can be defined – the constructs formulated, examined and shared within the professional community and with clients. It is this shared activity which serves the consolidation of knowledge and professional competence. This view of outcome has been portrayed in the fable about the father of two lazy sons, who told them on his deathbed that treasure was buried in the garden of the house. Following his death the sons feverishly dug the garden, in the course of this cultivating and preparing it for sowing. While the treasure was never found, the garden became a source of prosperity.

Like the sons, social workers have not been lazy but they seem to have been promised treasure in theories which consider knowledge to be based on objectivity and professional competence to be equated with prediction and control. The concept presented allows to replace this image of treasure with one of the cultivation of understanding based on the practitioners' constructs of their daily practice – cultivation leading to treasure.

Public service organisation: accountability and responsibility

So far, the various approaches to the acquisition of knowledge have been discussed in relation to the academic social work world. There remains the organisational framework in the public service sector, within which social work is usually practised, and its relation to theoretical approaches.

The psychology of universal rules which focus on fixed personal traits and the ensuing division between the 'person' and 'society', as well as the linear conception of intervention, lend themselves very well to the requirements of the bureaucracy of public services administration. Explanations based on fixed personal properties enable the categorisation of needs, the territorial division simplifies the planning of services and interventions defined in terms of set goals is readily scrutinised.

The fit between the bureaucratic approach to the administration of public services and the definition of knowledge in terms of universal rules might explain the continuing dominance of this approach, in spite of its inherent incongruity with the subject matter of social work practice. For example, the tendency to demarcate territory by geographic-administrative criteria, and not by the nature or function of the relationships developed between a worker and a client, often intrudes grossly on the services required. One need only think of the all-too-common practice of the division of care into separate services that are provided to a child placed in a foster family and to his parents. As acknowledged by the Children Act 1989, this practice hardly enhances the goal of helping the child and the biological family maintain some contact or even of promoting the possibility that the child will return to his family.

Moreover, the fit between the expectation that practitioners adhere to universal rules and the expectations that they will adhere to the bureaucratic structure limits the practitioners' autonomy and is expressed by the definition of social work as a 'semi-profession' (Toren 1972). Indeed, social workers' professionalism is often measured in terms of their accountability to the administrative structure and not in terms of their responsibility regarding the choices made by them vis-à-vis their clients (Mass 1977).

Much in the same way, however, that the adherence to universal rules and striving for objectivity fail to capture the nature of the human event, the limited autonomy granted to practitioners in the public sector fails to reflect the nature of the critical decisions practitioners are called upon to make concerning their clients in their everyday practice. This gap between the limited autonomy implied by the supremacy of bureaucratic processes which expect social workers to follow guidelines over the practitioners' discretion and the gravity of the decisions practitioners are required daily to make adds to the feelings of stress and futility experienced so often by social workers (Pottage and Evans 1992; Jones 1993). Much in the same way that the adherence to the psychology of universal rules robs clients of their individuality, the adherence to bureaucratic procedures robs social workers from their professional autonomy and their unique contribution to social work knowledge.

To replace accountability with responsibility as a measure of professionalism and to view the construction of knowledge and of the assessment of practitioners' competence in terms of sharing and not in terms of control might be seen, therefore, as disruptive of the hierarchical structure of public service administration. Nevertheless, it is precisely this which is proposed as a means of lifting the barrier between these two contrasting orientations, the bureaucratic and the professional, and of serving as a bridge between them.

The previously privately-held personal knowledge, now based on systematic inference from daily practice, must be placed on the same footing as that of universal rules – in the public domain. Social workers will then be expected to assume responsibility for choosing one construction over another and will be able to examine the course of action indicated by this construction. A dialogue between the constructions made by practitioners and the view based on organisational procedures can then follow. Practitioners would become participants in a dialogue, not recipients of guidelines. A sense of confidence might replace the ever-present sense of stress.

Summary

The process presented here is akin both to the process required by social workers in their everyday practice and to the empiricism required by the academic-scientific community, as well as by the public sector. At the same time, it differs from each of these processes. It builds on inductive reasoning reached by practitioners in their daily encounters with their clients, not on deduction from theoretical and administrative rules. As such, it is likely to enhance the worker's confidence, building on professional skills and understanding. On the other hand, it requires the worker systematically to examine this reasoning and expose it to public scrutiny, not leave it within the privacy of the relationships with clients. The deliberate choice made by the worker in building and examining his/her construct holds the worker responsible, not only accountable, vis-à-vis the clients and public service. This, in turn, represents a position which is more consistent with the nature of the critical decisions practitioners are called upon to make.

This process of knowledge construction conceives of social behaviour as contextually constructed and, as such, may better serve the dialogue between the profession and society. Social work practice may then become better understood by societal institutions and, as a consequence, be less prone to public attack. This would make a meaningful contribution to the practitioner's sense of professional confidence.

CHAPTER 9

Social Worker or Policeman?
Stresses of the Moral Guardians

Roger Woods

The care/control dilemma for social work has been a long-standing point of debate and, perhaps, of stress. It would seem that currently the view is that social workers are increasingly expected to be engaged in social control to the detriment of the caring role. This extension of its policing role is frequently related to the declining share of resources available to social services departments and the subsequent concentration on statutory work to the detriment of preventative work. Whether or not the present interest in family welfare in the area of child protection should be seen as a move back from this tendency is uncertain, but squeezed resources impose their own logic.

This chapter will explore some of the contradictions that arise from the dual responsibility of social work to provide care to the vulnerable in society as well as control of those who in some way cross the bounds of the socially acceptable. Initially, the way in which social workers construct their role in relation to the care/control dichotomy will be examined, in particular by using a recent case example. This suggests that social workers operate with, at least, two repertoires of actions of containment dependent on whether a situation is deemed to require a response of care or control. However, the work of Michel Foucault will be used to question the difference by focusing on the common function as modes of social regulation. This will be illustrated through historical material, examining how policing had, prior to the nineteenth century, a markedly different meaning. The development of social work in Britain through the establishment of the Charities Organisation Society in 1869 demonstrates that at its origins, social work was as much a controlling force as one concerned with care as it attempts to distinguish between the deserving and the undeserving poor. The system of moral judgements employed to make this distinction can also be seen to underlie aspects of recent approaches to normalisation. In this context, the care/control dichotomy is reframed into the regulation of individual behaviour and relates to another long-standing dilemma for social work: should the focus be on changing the individual or on changing society. Finally, the problems of the care and control of the client is shifted to how social workers are managed and controlled. It is, perhaps, here that the question of stress is best addressed.

Social workers' construction of role

In some cases, such as mental health, these two functions may be closely linked: the control imposed to prevent a person suffering a mental illness from harming themselves can also be seen as providing the only care that at that moment can be usefully given. In other cases, such as in child protection, controlling an abusive parent may be regarded as the necessary first step to care for the abused child. These cases, however, are relatively simple. Frequently, particularly since the introduction of the purchaser/provider split, these functions are divided within the organisation between different postholders. Balancing the tasks of care and control becomes more difficult where the social worker has to change tack from one to the other. In particular, this is most likely to be stressful where a relationship of providing a caring service has to switch, often suddenly and perhaps in the course of a meeting with a client or family, to one in which the social worker must become a 'social policeperson'.

The question of the compatibility of the functions of care and control was explicitly posed in *A Child in Trust*, Louis Blom-Cooper's report on the death of Jasmine Beckford in 1985: 'Can the social worker fulfil a policing role, firmly and efficiently, if he has also to gain the family's confidence, and to convey the personal warmth and genuineness necessary for him to provide the support which will enable them to become better parents?' (p.15).

The immediate answer to this is that 'the duality of approach is by no means impossible to achieve, providing that the worker is crystal clear about the nature of the job' (ibid). This requires that allegiance is owed both 'to the agency (and society) which requires him to be a child protector' as well as to the parent. The condemnation of the social worker and her team leader in this case were, of course, that the allegiance to the parents in working with them to improve their parenting skills in caring for Jasmine and her sisters over-rode the necessity to be vigilant as a child protector.

Dealing with situations where the care relationship has to quickly switch to a controlling one thus requires a very careful approach. The following example also illustrates the stressful nature of negotiating with the care/control dichotomy and raises some interesting issues. This is an account of a weekly visit during a lengthy piece of therapeutic work with a family. Whilst the social worker is seeing one child, the mother suddenly locks another child in her bedroom. The social worker explained:

There's a care and control dilemma. The child was shouting 'Let me out, let me out, let me out' and I knew the minute I got into a control number, I'd had it… I knew that she'd feel really criticised, so I did a dead pan, stopped the session with the older girl and said 'What's going on?' knowing perfectly well what was going on. And she said she's done this and this and this again, and I've told her again and again and again, she's going to have to stay there, and she's only going to let her out after I've gone. Which was her way of saying she was going to let her out. And I said, now I'd like to say goodbye to her, you know I always do (which I do, we always have a bit at the end with the whole family), so it's important that she's there as well. She gave me this nonsense about the door handle falling off, she's (the child) taken it off deliberately which is why she can't get out. I didn't challenge it, I didn't get into any debate about how it was that this little girl couldn't get out of her room. In the end she (mother) looked furious, but finally dragged her in from the other room, and I did say goodbye to her.

Not surprisingly, the social worker found this very stressful. She felt that it had worked because she had underplayed it. If she taken a heavier line, she thought that would have undermined the mother and made her feel even worse because she felt out of control.

In discussion, it was suggested that the mother's loss of control might have forced the social worker to have to step into the situation and take control. However, what the mother was doing was to try to reassert her control over her daughter who was not doing what she was told. For the social worker to have asserted control would have been counter-productive, instead, in the 'most one-down position that I could think of', she had to give control back to the mother and let her agree to the social worker saying goodbye to the little girl before she left.

However, acting in this way had to be based on knowing the family and on the level of abusiveness that it represented. It was suggested by a colleague that if there had been more prior concern about the mother, the response would have been different. She felt that the preconception of the situation gave rise to different sets of thoughts: 'if it's likely the child might be seriously at risk of abuse, its one set of thoughts, if they are not, it's a whole different set of thoughts. So, in a way, the whole care and control thing goes on in your mind.'

That is, social workers need to have a repertoire of actions and responses based on an assessment of a situation as being abusive or, more generally, one in which control has to be asserted and another repertoire where the situation is considered not to require a controlling but more of a containing reaction. The repertoire that is brought into play depends on the construction of the situation, a construction based on previous knowledge of the family as well as more general previous experience. However, it was agreed that it is much easier to make these decisions with a family seen for the first time. Where there is a working relationship with the family, it is 'much more complicated, much, much harder to switch roles'.

Is the distinction between control and containment valid? Both would seem to require the exercise of power. Putting oneself in a 'one-down' position is an issue of presentation, it does not give power to the other, only the image of it. The containment of a disturbed other through interpretation or a demonstration of empathic understanding is founded on the person's recognition that the social worker is in a position of power with regard to the disturbance. They are powerful enough to hold it.

One might, at this point, identify a distinction between morally correct or morally incorrect applications of power determined in terms of whose good and in whose interests power is being exercised. However, Michel Foucault's concept of power provides a route to a richer understanding.

The power of the social worker: a Foucauldian perspective

For Foucault, power is productive: 'it induces pleasure, forms knowledge, produces discourse. It needs to be considered as a productive network which runs through the whole social body, much more than as a negative instance whose function is repression.' (1980, p.119). It is productive because it produces reality, what is 'really true'. A discourse – a way of using language to think about and talk about a particular area of knowledge – authorises certain statements as true and proper knowledge because it is articulated from a position of power. For example, the 'scientific' discourse of Western allopathic medicine provided a position for medical practitioners to sound authoritative and to act in accord with those truths, that is to prescribe a course of treatment based on a diagnosis.

This example is relevant to the problem of care (containment) or control in two ways. First, one of the enduring difficulties for social work, and why its professional status is always insecure, is that it lacks the certainty of a common knowledge base or a discourse from which statements can be uttered with conviction. Its certainties come from its use of other discourses, whether borrowed (a therapeutic discourse) or imposed (the law). Thus, in contrast to the doctor's ability to diagnose and prescribe treatment using a well-established vocabulary of terms, the social worker must largely use borrowed terms that carry no guarantee of certain translation to other members of the profession. The tools for analysing a situation such as that presented above, whether at the time or in retrospect, are imprecise. Any authoritative definition of 'care' and 'control' is impossible to make.

Second, power is productive, in part, because it fixes identities. The knowledge I have of myself – my self image – is the product of the discourses that circulate in society at this moment in time. The politics of identities, that has been such a powerful force in the last twenty years, precisely rests on this. An identity as Black or as Gay is the product of discourses of resistance against dominant discourses that marginalise minorities. This fixing of identities, however temporarily, also occurs at a micro-level. In the example above, the woman loses her identity as a 'good mother', that is as one who can control her children. Through the nature of the intervention of the social worker, she is enabled to regain it. A more anxious response by the social worker, attempting more directly to control the woman and the situation, would have reinforced her identity as a 'bad mother' unable to control her children. It is not difficult to recognise how such identities of inadequate parents and of good enough parents can be constructed over time by the language and actions of social workers.

From the viewpoint of an approach following Foucault, care and control are very much sides of the same coin. They are both modes of social regulation, both techniques for the ordering and disciplining of individuals. Foucault was concerned to map the development of disciplinary power as a primary characteristic of modern societies, which are also characterised by increasing democracy and the 'dangers' inherent in citizens 'misusing' their new-found political power. New citizens had to be made 'good citizens' (Garland 1985). From the end of the eighteenth century onwards, this involved a vast process of categorising modes of behaviour – for example types of madness, forms of sexuality, degrees of criminality – and classifying individuals, those that transgress the norm, through these categories. This process of normalisation, as noted by Hewitt (1992), 'became the principal means of discipline in democratic-welfare-capitalism, more appropriate to freely constituted subjects than repressive forms of coercion.' (p.158). 'Normalisation' has, of course, within social work, an apparently more positive reading. This will be returned to after an examination of the historical roots of social work.

Policing: the forerunner of social work

Is the problem for social workers of having to combine a caring and a controlling role a recent one? From my experience of teaching social work students, some tend to believe that it is. My view is that it may be best understood as an enduring myth of social work, which secretly constructs as a past, a never achieved ideal of caring. Was there – could there have been – a moment when social work was exclusively about caring, where the social worker was on the side of the client against those aspects of the state concerned with social control? Was social work forced into playing its part as social regulator – as moral police – only in order to maintain its 'proper' function of social carer?

Policing, which now is primarily focused on the maintenance of property rights, including those of the body, was a development of the nineteenth century. In the two hundred years before that the modern state was in its period of formation from the medieval era. During this period, 'police' was a term much used in writings on good government to refer to the general regulation of good order to ensure the welfare of members of society.

Pasquale Pasquino (1978), a follower of Foucault, cites Georg Obrecht, a high-ranking academic and municipal official of Strasbourg, who, in 1608, identifies as the three key tasks of police: 'First, information, conceived as a sort of statistical table bearing on all the capacities and resources of the population and territory; second, a set of measures serving to augment the wealth of the population and enrich the coffers of the state; third, public happiness' (p.113).

Nikolas Rose (1989) comments: 'Policing entailed the elaboration of a complex of regulations concerning all the details of life that might be conducive to the promotion of happiness, tranquillity, virtue and the public good' (p.221). But policing becomes, during the course of modernity, changed to its contemporary and more limited meaning of the maintenance of public order. But further, this must be internalised. The citizen is expected to take into themselves and to be responsible for their own policing – in both the earlier and later forms of the term. Thus 'new modes of self-evaluation were to be inculcated in schools, supervised through the activities of health visitors, doctors, and social workers, and spread through the writings of experts. Each individual was to become an active agent in the maintenance of a healthy and efficient polity, exercising a reflexive scrutiny over personal, domestic and familial conduct' (Rose 1989, p.224). In other words, they were to contain their own self-control as responsible autonomous citizens.

A key role of social work was to facilitate this self-regulation. But is this process of facilitation better achieved through the provision of care or through the imposition, or the threat of imposition, of social control? The observations of Jacques Donzelot (1980), whilst writing specifically of the French experience, are relevant to consideration of social work more generally. He notes that from the start of the twentieth century, a range of new professions, that can all be termed 'social work', have appeared and argues that '[these] occupations are currently in process of full expansion. Rather marginal at the beginning of the century, the social worker is gradually taking over from the teacher in the mission of civilising the social body.' (p.96). Donzelot sees the primary task of this new profession to be the intervention into 'the less-favoured classes' to deal with 'children in danger – those whose upbringing and education leaves something to be desired, and dangerous children, or delinquent minors' (p.96). This is 'a consistent revision of the old attitudes of repression and charity, the promotion of a boundless educative solicitude, more concerned with under-standing than with the application of judicial punishment, replacing charity's good conscience with the search for effective techniques' (p.97).

The Charities Organisation Society: the judgmental birth of British social work

The Charities Organisation Society (C.O.S.), seen by various commentators as a key element in the origin of social work in Britain (e.g. Abbott and Wallace 1990), provides a good example of the formation of this process in Britain. The C.O.S. was established in London in 1869 to combat the mushrooming of charities, often in competition with each other and with poorly developed systems of discriminating between who should receive relief and in what form that relief should take. Young and Ashton (1956) note contemporary references to 'good hearted, somewhat sentimental workers [who] all to often were taken in by apparent distress that they tended to give relief as a matter of course' (p.93). The task was seen, in the Annual Report of the C.O.S. in 1875, as providing existing charities and individual philanthropists 'with a machinery which will enable them to dispense relief more wisely and more effectively' (cited in Young and Ashton 1956, p.98). This machinery, developed to distinguish between those among the poor seeking assistance who were deserving from those who were not, took the form of case work (called as such from about 1885). Only those who were in need of help through no fault of their own, and were able to show that they were or could be thrifty and self-disciplined, should receive assistance. The undeserving 'clever pauper' seeking aid rather than work, or who spent what they had on drink or gambling, should only find relief through entering the workhouse.

Clarke (1993) notes the mixture of compassion and fear that lies behind much nineteenth century social work – the compassion that motivated the provision of assistance to the poor and the fear that limited it because '[unconditional] charity was seen as a recipe for social chaos so it was necessary to evaluate the cases and select only the deserving' (p.19). Clarke sees this complex relationship of compassion/fear translating into care/control: 'the provision of a personalised assistance uneasily combined with powers to evaluate, direct and make decisions affecting the client's life' (ibid).

An example of these developments is found in the work of Octavia Hill, the 'grandmother of modern social work' (Young and Ashton 1956, p.115), who, in 1870, took charge of the C.O.S.'s Walmer Street, Marylebone district in London. She instigated detailed case work and, rather than continue with the provision of coal vouchers, free meals and cash hand outs, found and arranged employment for local residents. In a not dissimilar way to how contemporary workfare schemes are regarded by some, this was bitterly resented. Whilst this strategy can be understood as giving control back to the unemployed, to empower them by finding them work, the recipients of this care regard it as control. Is it control to contain, empowering disadvantaged people to 'better themselves', or is it to force a socially marginal group of 'spongers' into a socially acceptable participation in the labour market? No one 'objective' answer is possible because the answer is ideological. This empowering, albeit an empowering through the withdrawal of benefits, is difficult to resist. Such attempts to make people become wage-earning members of society is, perhaps, also akin to contemporary uses of normalisation programmes.

Normalisation: the individual and society

Normalisation as a means for working with people with learning difficulties was developed in Denmark in 1959 and was introduced in the UK from the late 1960s, although the model used in this country has tended to be strongly influenced by the work of Wolfensberger in the United States (Emerson 1992). Wolfensberger argues that certain groups in society are devalued because they are labelled as deviant. This leads to their segregation from mainstream society or, in extreme cases, to their destruction. Normalisation is, therefore, intended to reverse the process of social devaluation by providing 'valued social roles for people who are at risk of social devaluation' (Wolfensberger 1983 cited in Dalley 1992).

The three major criticisms identified by Dalley with this conception of normalisation are closely related to the issues raised above in relation to care and control. First, Wolfensberger's approach to normalisation can be criticised for its conservatism. Although the norms to be promoted for devalued people are seen as culturally-specific, there is no recognition of a plurality of cultures within a society. The dominant culture is taken as the norm, for example the person with a learning disability may be encouraged to express their sexuality as long as it is heterosexual.

Second, it is morally authoritarian. In aiming to train people to behave in ways that are not 'deviant', there is an implication of acceptance of the initial assessment of the person as deviant. The teaching of new modes of behaviour is primarily designed to lessen social stigma, rather than to otherwise increase the person's quality of life.

Third, Wolfensberger's notion of normalisation stresses conformity to social norms, for example he states in an early paper: 'wearing a hearing aid may be a greater obstacle to finding and keeping a job than being hard of hearing' (1972, p.28 cited in Dalley 1992).

Dalley places these techniques of normalisation in the context of the on-going ideological conflict between possessive individualism and collectivism. She concludes that, as conceived by Wolfensberger, whilst it has an affinity with the latter in its struggle to give full rights to devalued people to participate in society as citizens, 'the emphasis on changing people, through modification of behaviour, appearance and attitudes rather than focusing on the paramount need to change society's attitudes towards disability, runs counter to the egalitarian principle of valuing individuals for themselves whatever the nature of their (dis)ability.' (1992, p.110).

This is a clear statement of the dilemma of whether social work should focus on changing the behaviour of the 'deviant' individual or family to fit with social norms or whether it should work to effect social changes to accommodate the 'misfits'. This debate was most dominant during the 1970s within the radical social work movement and its call to community social work. Since the rise of cash-limited departments and the individual pathologising of poverty under Thatcherism, the option of working for social change has appeared less and less viable other than through the key strategy of anti-discriminatory practice (ADP). A formative principle of ADP is that no one set of social norms should be dominant, that a person should not be judged against a set of criteria that does not reflect their own cultural practices. Of course, there are limits to and contradictions within this. The statutory framework and the interests of others (and of self) determine that certain practices are outlawed.

What does this mean for the care/control dilemma? If the exercise of power is, in part, about the fixing of identities, the techniques of control can be seen to have become more specific and subtle. The norms against which behaviour is assessed, and towards which the individual or family should be directed, are no longer – at least, according to ADP principles – those of the dominant culture. However, whether the strategy of intervention is through care containment or through a more overtly controlling approach, the social worker, or, perhaps, more correctly, the institution of social work, necessarily maintains the power to categorise and classify. Necessarily because, as Foucault argues, power produces realities, that is produces a framework for us to share, at least relatively, an understanding of the social and moral world.

The care and control of social workers

In this role as 'technicians' of the moral maintenance of social reality, social workers must be managed. In a comparable way to the analysis of care/control as two sides of one coin, Friedman (1977) examines the apparently polar opposite management strategies of 'direct control' and 'responsible autonomy'. 'Direct control' is the strategy whereby managers control work by close specification and supervision of tasks and, in general, aim to reduce the skill levels of their workers. 'Responsible autonomy', on the other hand, works by ensuring that workers internalise the values and cultures of the organisation, identifying with it, as a 'caring employer', so that they will act responsibly with minimal supervision. However, both are intended to maintain managerial authority – the first by ruthlessly asserting it, the second by giving some of it to employees to control themselves. This dichotomy of means to maintain authority is identical in effect to that of social work: the direct regulation of a client's behaviour through 'control' and the encouragement towards self-regulation through strategies of 'care-containment'.

Although Friedman was primarily concerned with the management of manual labour, his model also has resonance in the context of the management of more professionalised work such as social work. The control of the social worker as a trained *professional*, reliant on their internalisation of values and competencies, is unmistakably responsible autonomy, whereas the wish by a social services department, or by the Department of Health, for social workers to follow checklists and strict procedures is a clear move towards the strategy of direct control.

Howe (1992) observes that this process of bureaucratisation is most acute within the area of child protection. In the attempt to identify 'dangerous parents', the Department of Health guidelines and local procedures have redefined the social work role:

> Her role has become that of investigator, reporter and 'gatherer of evidence'. The analysis of the information is no longer left to the discretion of the practitioner. Other actors, including managers, case conference members, and the formulae that indicate levels of dangerousness, help assess the information and reach decisions. (p.502)

Arguably, this loss of professional freedom returns social work to a position not dissimilar to that of the C.O.S case worker. However, the contemporary social worker as moral technician has less authority than her predecessor to determine final outcomes, whether these be to pursue a strategy of care or control.

Parton (1994) has also noted that social workers are no longer 'constituted as case workers drawing on their therapeutic skills in human relationships' (p.100). Instead, they have become care managers within a wider inter-agency network of care/control that has become established because of '[the] apparent failure of professional expertise and knowledge(s) to ameliorate problems and meet needs' (p.101).

Perhaps, then, it is in the strategies of control of social work that the care/control dichotomy causes greatest stress for social workers. Put simply, is it more stressful to feel that you are relying on your training and experience to reach decisions about a client or family or to be concerned that you have properly followed procedures? It is well established that stress is most damaging to health when a person has limited control over their decision making. In England and Wales, within the critical area of child protection, this is compounded both by the stress on procedures and checklists and by the 'process of institutionalised polarisation' that Cooper (1992) identifies in his comparison of French and English systems of child protection. Such differences stem from the different criminal justice systems of these two countries. Based on an adversarial system in England, the 'care and control' dilemma is subject to such a polarisation between the 'values and practices of law and of social work' (p.120). On the other hand, in France, which practices an inquisitorial approach to criminal justice and where there is greater structural integration of the law with social work, care and control is united in the figure of the Children's Judge. He argues that the English system gives rise to much higher levels of anxiety:

> Where power and responsibility for the primary task are structurally disconnected from each other, and where there is difficulty about access from social work to the legal part of the system, then the scope for anxiety increases in particular ways. This manifests itself as both a *blockage* to the possibility of conflict resolution, and as a *lack of containment* for felt destructive potential on the part of workers. (p.123 original emphasis)

Conclusion

Social work has always been constructed through a series of apparent dilemmas: how to distinguish the deserving from the undeserving; should the focus be on changing the individual or on working to change society; and how does one balance the provision of care with the need to exercise control. The split between the pre-modern form of 'policing' as a means of social regulation into social work and the modern police, in general, has satisfactorily coped with the care and control problem. The police and the legal system developed as the primary means of maintaining social control and enforcing behaviour to comply to established norms. Social work, on the other hand, emerged, initially outside of state mechanisms, as a 'softer' form of judging and rectifying behaviour towards established or perceived norms. The student or the new social worker might find the tasks of control required of the profession onerous but the vast majority soon learn the appropriate 'repertoires' of action necessary to deal with different situations. That is, as shown by the case study example at the start of this chapter, they become increasingly able to rapidly assess a situation in terms of the choice of responses and actions appropriate to it. It is not necessary in most meetings with clients to consider the use of a control repertoire, although, in some cases and, sometimes, within a volatile encounter, these must be brought into play. But the experienced social worker will rarely be confused about which type of repertoire – of control or of care – is required.

However, as we move away from modern times into post-modernity, some of the long-established strategies for maintaining social control are becoming less effective (see Howe 1994 and Parton 1994 for discussion on post-modernity and its impact on social work). For example, social pluralism, and a population that perceives itself in terms of an increasingly non-hierarchical range of identities, poses a wholly new set of problems for agencies of social control. There are no longer a coherent set of social norms that can realistically be used to judge behaviour. The adoption of anti-discriminatory practice, although seen by Howe (1994) as a modernistic attempt by CCETSW to impose a single 'truth', is a response to this aspect of post-modern society.

It is a matter for debate whether the recent developments in the management of social work in the UK are to be understood as part of these social changes or, rather, are out-moded strategies that are no longer compatible with contemporary life and moralities. The role of the social worker as 'investigator, reporter and gatherer of evidence', returning it back to its origins for judging the deserving from the undeserving poor, does not seem the answer in these times of pluralism and consumer rights. Indeed, the reliance on checklists and formal procedures is wholly out of step with the approach to management that involves, at least for the core workers, an emphasis on the organisation's culture and the internalising of its values. This tendency to manage by giving workers 'responsible autonomy' has become predominant within most large companies since the early 1980s.

The bureaucratisation of social work is not, of course, absolute. Social workers, as was illustrated in the example at the start of this chapter, can work in a more therapeutic way, exercising discretion and judgement based on internalised knowledge and experience. This may well be stressful and the wrong decisions can have devastating effects for the client, the social worker and for the organisation for which they work (as was the case in the Jasmine Beckford and similar tragedies). But such cases are fortunately rare and, despite the profession, and the state, sometimes pretending to have an omnipotent ability to stop them, they are inevitable. As moral guardians, competent social workers can negotiate the moves between the care and control of clients but, perhaps, are most at risk from attempts by the state to control them.

CHAPTER 10

Stress at the Top

David Townsend

Most Directors of social services were once social workers. As a result, they have experiences, maybe no more than distant memories, of the sort of pressures and stress that are faced in the direct delivery of services. Those experiences are, of course, useless when it comes to affording insights to survival at the top of the organisation. So too are the rare management qualifications that some directors possess. In the milieu of town hall politics you might as well to be equipped with a diploma in mud wrestling as an MBA or some such.

Broadly speaking, the problems that most directors and their senior colleagues find to be stressful come from five or six different directions. Sometimes, like London buses, they arrive in threes – which is the time for directorial prayer for a few and a possible visit to the GP for the rest. Top of the list is the unprotected isolation of the job, highlighted by the very public nature of it. The evidence of this is most frequently revealed by grim-looking photos of a director in the local or national press under the headline: 'Director denies "poor services" allegation.'

The isolation is given strength by the fact that a director's employers, the councillors, are neither colleagues nor distanced, as government ministers usually are from civil servants. Councillors appoint chief officers and, after that, order them as they wish. Ministers do not appoint the civil servants, who, as a separate service for the government, can give independent advice without fear or favour.

Looking for trouble?

Correct rules of engagement between councillors and officers are barely understood by the employers in the worst run sort of local authorities. It is the received wisdom that these problems are most intense in London. Indeed, the opposition group of councillors in an authority may choose to attack a director personally, and in public, as the most visible (and perceived) representative of the majority controlling group. They may be assisted by trade unions, who sometimes make common cause, even if their real interests are not the same. The controlling group cannot always be relied upon to defend a director. He or she may feel a certain despair at apparently being co-opted into one group or another. Occasionally, an unwise director may feel obliged to make quasi-political statements. It is a mistake that will come back to haunt him or her.

The publicity about a case of child abuse, for example, is difficult enough for a member of staff dealing with that child and the family. For the director, it can become a nightmare of radio, TV and newspaper items that bring in their wake literally hundreds of letters from opinion formers, opinionated people and the plain deranged. All are addressed personally to 'The Director'. Apart from the obscenities, there are those containing various forms of curses, threats of violence and messages from retired vicars hoping that the director will honourably and immediately resign. There are also those who want to know the names and addresses of the staff responsible. Time for a director's holiday.

The staff themselves, up to 10, 000 in some social services departments, are as reasonable as directors but, under threat of some kind, tend to band together to blame someone else. 'Lack of resources' is a favourite and 'Whose fault is that?' Grievances that personally name the director or assistant directors are regularly launched. Staff themselves have the protection, rightly, of their trade unions. Directors do not easily fit into a union that may represent many of those whom they manage. The director's professional trade union, good as it is, tends to be called in only to diagnose a condition known as 'about to take early retirement', and then, helpfully, to undertake the funeral negotiations.

Perhaps the biggest difficulty for a director is similar to that of a meteor-ologist predicting the weather. He must divine accurately what kind of pressure is moving in on the council's majority group, is it a high or low? It is very important to know. Last year, for example, one director was 'escorted off the premises' of the local authority without warning. She had done nothing wrong or incompetent. She was merely the victim of internal turbulence in the majority group. In recent years, two other directors found themselves 'removed' over a weekend, again without any pre-warning, and their offices locked against them. Once again, the reason was internal political bickering and had nothing to do with the quality of work of the director.

There is little acknowledgment and rarely sympathy for the pressures and stress at the top of the department. Staff and councillors both tend to agree that, since directors are, in their view, paid an enormous salary, they should suffer no stress. Money is thought to ward off the problem, probably as garlic is alleged to defeat vampires. Any sensible director knows how to smile politely at the wit and joviality of councillors who comment on the style of the director's clothes, car or holidays. These drolleries are especially enjoyed at the evening committee seances with councillors, of which there may be three or four a week.

A director also knows how to put up with the views of shop stewards remarking upon vast pay differentials. Interestingly, the pay differentials of white collar staff to directors have tended to narrow in the years since the establishment of social services departments.

Some 'official' stress is also provided, for example through the Health and Safety Executive and the Ombudsman. Of course, accidents and injuries to users of services and staff need to be investigated but, ultimately, in the most serious cases, it will not necesssarily be the member of staff who caused an accident but the director who is up before the Beak. The Ombudsman frequently receives complaints from people who make a hobby of complaining, but whether the complaint has a sound basis or not, it will often be supported by a councillor who is sometimes a member of the Social Services Committee. It is, again, a question of directors being found between a rock and a hard place. However, the worst and most prolonged pressure is caused by the great and expensive public enquiries into something awful in the department's work. Usually, these enquiries result in 'blame' for everyone and no one. More procedures are usually demanded.

When pressures like this apply, the support of a peer group ought to be available. Every local authority has some sort of chief officer's group who face, in varying degrees, similar problems. But co-operation or sympathetic understanding is not necessarily available. Some chief officers' groups meet very irregularly. And the chief executive may believe it is in his or her best interest not to promote too much of a 'corporate culture'. Some councillors do not welcome that either, believing not only that chief officers are overpaid but also that they are overmighty. Reported conversations between chief officers can all too easily been translated into 'conspiracies' by excitable councillors. So, in the worst of all worlds and local authorities, a director may find no personal support in a crisis.

The future looks pear-shaped

And yet no other job in social services expects 'leadership', 'dynamism', 'commitment to equality/ quality/innovation', 'managerial excellence', 'intellectual rigour', 'a record of achievement', 'sound track record at senior management level', 'good communication skills' and 'evidence of good budgetary management'. And those are just some of the public requirements of directors of social services taken from recent advertisements.

Similar sorts of personal qualities are demanded of assistant directors. The holders of these jobs are presumed to be near super-human. Unhappily they are not and, for most, their salad days are relatively brief. Early retirement, 'in the interests of the efficiency of the service', 'on health grounds' or as a result of 'reorganisation and redundancy', is the most common flight path of a career as a director. Cynically, it could be said they go as they come, fired with enthusiasm. Since most directors know this before they begin their ascent of social services, they can try to prepare themselves for what will be a wholly different experience from working at the base camp. Even so, the experiences and the isolation of the job will create stresses that they will, at times, find intolerable and, sometimes, overwhelming.

In the 1970s, when directors jobs were invented, a working life as a director could reasonably expect to reach 65 years of age. Certainly 60 years was quite common. Now not many go beyond 55 years of age and even fewer last 10 years in the job. 'Are we breeding wimps for this bit of public service?' a recently defeated MP put to me over the canapés at a reception for directors. The answer is 'no'. Directors are much the same as they always were: idealistic, optimistic and with a desire to fulfill the description which the late Lord Joseph, the midwife of modern social services, used of them. 'Directors', he said, 'are powerful new advocates for the poor'. What has changed utterly is the public attitude to welfare in general and to social services in particular.

From the early 1980s, public opinion, as expressed by the media and, especially, the press, has more often been hostile than sympathetic to the work of social services departments. Whilst some of that criticism is fully justified, the constant attention of newshounds to particular cases (mostly, though not always, relating to child abuse) and the personalising of the enquiries to individual workers or their managers has made the job extremely stressful. Alas, the aggressive way in which the press conduct themselves, at times, as self-appointed champions of the public is increasingly mirrored by councillors. This is one area of work that was always hard to manage but has become more difficult with an apparent need to fix 'blame' somewhere. Some authorities have recognised their own deficiencies in the way they have managed things in the past. Their adverts ask for the same high personal qualities of director applicants but at least acknowledge past failures in their conduct of public affairs and delivery of public services.

Quarts into pint pots

The personal pressures at the top of the social services organisation stem not only from a changed public perception but also from the shift in relative importance within the local authority of the department. It is now the last big department still directly managed by the local authority. Council control of education and housing was seriously eroded during the 1980s and 1990s. For example, education departments lost control of polytechnic education and now have reduced powers over schools through the introduction of local management. In housing there was an end to significant building programmes and the increasing use of Housing Associations to manage council-owned properties.

This left the local authority, and its respective directors of those services, with a 'commissionaire' role; they can tell users who may have entry to the service but not be responsible for what goes on in it. Witness the thousands of children, nationally, who are now excluded from school education, often referred to social services accompanied by the wringing of hands of education directors, or the immediate referral of anti-social tenants to the social services department by housing departments.

Social services, on the other hand, have had powers and responsibilities handed to them, albeit with ropes attached. This has principally meant community care money transferred from central government, with accompanying legislation, defining how and where it may be spent. It was a reluctant transfer, only brought about because the then Prime Minister was persuaded there was no alternative. However, those extended responsibilities have brought with them strains of a different order on two fronts: first, through the regulation of a private residential care sector that had not been properly supervised before – either in the imposition of cash limits or in the assessment of actual need – and second, and much nearer home, some members of councils (sometimes aided and abetted by directors of finance) believed that the transferred cash was 'new' and the authority could consequently look to reduce its own contributions to social services. Up to a quarter of most social services departments' budgets is now made up of transferred money.

The other problem about community care is that some councils do not, for political reasons, like the private sector. Nor do they welcome the inevitable cost comparisons it brings. Yet the regulations governing the use of the cash require a director of social services at least to shake hands with the independent part of the welfare business, if not embrace it. As, a result, conflicts can arise, and they do. How they are resolved is a matter of diplomacy, or bad luck, for a director.

The fact that new legislation and its operation can provide grounds for difficulties between a director, who must interpret and fulfill the council's legal obligations, and his or her employers who may not quite see it that way is only one of the stresses at the top of the hierarchy. Asking for more resources at a time when the fashionable parrot cry is 'Education, education, education' or pressing the case for bathing facilities for elderly disabled people or respite care for the parents of children with multiple disabilities, for example, risks a collision. It raises frustration and angst amongst councillors who simply do not have the budgets available to them to make easy decisions for everyone.

In these circumstances a Social Services director might expect to find amongst the chief officer peer group a personally supportive network and a mutual interest in presenting councillors with proposals that are consensual. In the best run authorities they do. In the worst they can find all-out competition and concealed games being played with leading councillors. Most councils are somewhere in between, governance by curate's egg. The role of the chief executive may or may not be pivotal in this. He or she may be the 'ceremonial' type – organiser of visits by minor royalty or wearer of the official wig at council meetings – or the chief executive may be an arch schemer intriguing with an eye on his own prospects. The best chief executives are open and communicative and have an interest in the welfare of their director colleagues. I believe a few exist.

Dirty work at the crossroads

Generalisation is all very well but some detailed examples of the nature of life at the top will help illustrate the problems faced by directors. Directors are responsible for maintaining equal opportunities policies and ensuring probity in the use of public money, not only in their own departments but in a voluntary service world that is heavily dependent on grant aid from the local authority. Imagine, then, a well-established women's centre in London that received around £50,000 a year from the local authority.

A review of the work of this organisation was put in train apparently with the co-operation of the centre's management committee. There had been some delay in producing audited accounts and a business plan was proving elusive. Because domestic violence had become a potential election issue in the forthcoming local election, the (male) director agreed with the chairperson of the social services committee that he would take a personal interest in the work with the centre, in conjunction with his voluntary sector grants officer.

As the weeks went by, a number of concerns arose. First, a Black woman member of the women's centre staff was suspended without, it appeared, good grounds or equal opportunities procedures having been followed. Second, the business plan did not appear and offers of help from the social services department received no response. Third, accounts were not submitted and there was prevarication over them.

After weeks of fruitless correspondence and cancelled meetings with the centre's management group the director held discussions with the authority's finance, legal and personnel departments and informed both the outgoing chairperson of the committee and the new chairperson that he believed it would be right to recommend suspension of the grant to the centre. In the circumstances, a reasonable professional decision and one within his authority.

Not surprisingly, he received little response from the chairperson of the defeated administration and no comment at all from the incoming chairperson – who had expressed great concern about domestic violence before the election and was in fact a trustee of the women's centre.

A letter was issued by the director to the women's centre management committee telling them that a recommendation to suspend funding would be made to councillors unless and until satisfactory discussions about the perceived problems could be held. The letter provoked a furore.

The new leader of the council was a close friend of at least one member of the women's centre management committee. She did not care to hear what the evidence might be for the director's decisions. She took charge. The new chairperson of social services was told to keep clear. The chief executive was told to inform the director that he should play no further part in the matter of the women's centre. The chief executive told him 'that the leader's confidence in him had been damaged'.

But the real issue for the leader was a web of lies spun by those who wanted no investigation of the centre's affairs. It was alleged that the director was having an affair with the suspended Black member of staff at the centre. The allegations and rumours were wholly untrue but were peddled by the leader.

The chief executive even sent one of his junior members of staff around the social services offices to see if the rumours could be substantiated. He did this without informing the director and the social services staff were interviewed and asked to say nothing to the director. In fact, one did and so the process came to a halt. When confronted by the director, the chief executive explained that the enquiry was to 'clear the director's name'. No report or further comment was forthcoming from the chief executive.

Despite this pressure, the director believed that it was his duty to ensure fair play, to maintain public probity and to investigate the racism in the case. He advised the leader, the chairperson and the chief executive that, in his considered opinion, the case would result in an industrial tribunal claim for unfair dismissal and racism by the suspended member of staff. The director also advised that allegations of harassment against the staff member by the management committee were a fiction and that he believed council money was being, or had been, stolen.

A final memorandum from the chief executive warned him that his position as director was at risk if he continued to investigate or take any further action in respect to the women's centre. The leader refused to meet him. The chief executive would not facilitate such a meeting. The director of personnel and the council's solicitor, answerable to the chief executive, did nothing to support the director. All this lasted for several months. The stress created was enormous. The personal rumours were damaging to the director's reputation – staff knew of them and individuals in the wider community knew of them. There was no way of putting an effective end to them because, of course, they had, in part, been spread by the director's employers. Why else would the director be 'taken off the case' unless they were true?

Surviving that was, for the director, a matter of self-belief. Even the fact that, on all the particulars, racism, industrial tribunal and theft of £10,000 by the treasurer of the centre committee, the director was proved to have been right did nothing but increase the hostility towards him. Sound professional advice, which, after all, was what a director is paid to offer, was regarded as 'he told us so'. The only outside personal support he received was from individual Black members of staff and Black community activists who believed a serious injustice was being perpetrated by councillors and the women's centre management committee. He remains very grateful for that.

That is an example of personal stress for a director; it is not rare. This year a well-respected female director was made 'redundant' for similar sorts of reasons by a London council that similarly lacked integrity. The more usual scenario for disagreement is over budget setting. Social services always face increased user demands, not least because of demographic change. In that, social services resembles the health service, although it does not receive financial growth on the scale of the health service. Social services is always in the business of cutting and saving, reinvesting and redrawing priorities. That disappoints local politicians who try to please as many people as possible. Here is one example of intense stress created by attempts to recommend new priorities.

A sheltered workshop, part of social services in a London borough, was making losses of between £500,000 and £750,000 a year. It employed about one hundred adults with disabilities. In a time of reductions in expenditure it was on an equal footing with services for severely disabled adults and children who, in some cases, could not move, let alone go to work. In terms of need, the workshop workers were a lower priority than those who could not fend for themselves.

A series of options supported by the chairperson and some, though not all, of the social services majority group councillors, was pursued for the workshop. The options were: a reduction in the number of jobs in the workshop that would save money or, more drastically, the workshop would close and some of the savings would be invested in alternative work opportunities away from an institutionalised setting. A last option was that the management and cost of the workshop should be transferred to the public works department, on the grounds that this was work for people with disabilities rather than disabled people needing welfare-based work.

The chairperson continued to support the ideas and, after research, concluded that closure and reinvestment in different forms of work was the best option. At that point, many other majority group councillors, not known for their interest in social services, intervened. The opposition opposed, naturally, but the real turmoil came in the argument within the majority group. At a meeting chaired by the leader, the assistant director and director were abused by councillors as being 'unhuman'(sic), 'unfeeling', 'incompetent' and incapable of 'running a whelk stall.' Staff were encouraged by councillors to oppose the proposals, as too were parents and the workers themselves. The stress caused to the assistant director was obvious to see. The director wrote to the leader and the individual councillors concerned to express his strong dislike of personal and unreasonable attacks on staff who were unable to defend themselves. He offered to discuss these matters with them.

The leader replied privately to say that she had been unable to control the meeting and regretted what had happened. One councillor believed the director's letter had exceeded his authority. Councillors could 'say what they like when they like about senior managers'. He wanted the director to be disciplined for his insolence.

The results were far reaching. The chairperson of the committee was deposed and the director was invited to meet with a tribunal of councillors to hear what they thought of him. The trade union saw the change of policy as a victory. The chief executive sat on his hands. A shiver ran round the chief officers' group but found no spine to run up. In the event, the director simply ignored the kangaroo court invitation. It was a dangerous move, but all that was left to him. The new vice-chairperson of the committee, three months later, was one of the kangaroos, who had on his private agenda the removal of the director. The election of councillors to committees with the sole purpose of 'getting someone' is not unknown.

This example draws attention to the danger of close working relationships with the chairperson of a committee (it may also say something about the political nous required of a chairperson). Yet the essence of a director-chairperson relationship is analogous to that of chairman and managing director of a company. The difference, however, is that there are not twenty-odd, under-employed board members waiting in the wings, anxious not to be spear carriers but to have speaking parts, as there are in a political group.

A much more stressful area of work for senior managers is the maintenance of departmental standards and, from time to time, the need to take disciplinary action. There are a number of opposing forces in 'disciplinaries' (if the matter is racism, the force is usually with those who deny it). Complaints about staff, misdemeanours by staff or wrong decisions in cases may all end up in disciplinary proceedings.

Local government has a complex system of disciplinary hearings and rights to appeal can vary from one authority to another. The onus to prove wrongdoing is not as heavy as in a court of law and sometimes impels some councillors on appeals panels to try to prove that they would have made successful criminal lawyers. The trade union role in disciplinaries is not at all predictable. It is not always outright opposition to management but, when it is, reason is not always evident. Two examples follow that show the amateurish nature of the proceedings and limited awareness of the issues at stake.

The first example occurred a few years ago in a London authority. A six foot two, male shop steward employed as a care assistant in an old people's home was alleged to have shouted at, and then thrown, a 100-year-old lady, who had no arms, onto a bed. The departmental enquiry found the facts were as stated. The man was dismissed. There was an appeal to councillors. The trade union vigorously supported one of its own stewards. At the hearing the union secretary demanded the presence of the 100-year-old lady to answer a few questions. In fact, she was, despite her age and infirmity, willing to appear but the councillors on the appeal panel intervened. They asked a question of the deputy director who was presenting the case, a question that had never crossed his mind: 'Was this care assistant told not to do what he did during his training?' The appeal against dismissal was upheld on this point and the deputy director was, in effect, reprimanded about the quality of the department's training programme. The care assistant was reinstated. Subsequently, he was dismissed for a further assault on a resident and for being drunk on duty.

The second case, some years later in a different authority, shows how 'maverick' decisions, damaging to the reputation of a department's standards, the protection of vulnerable members of the public and to the professional integrity of senior managers, are still being made by councillors on appeals panels.

In this instance a driver in the social services department, was alleged to have buggered two women with learning disabilities. The police took statements from the two women and believed their story but did not press charges on the grounds that their evidence would be destroyed in court by the defence lawyers. The department then launched a disciplinary enquiry led by an assistant director, who was also an experienced magistrate. The man was dismissed. The evidence was well ordered and well presented to the appeals panel. The driver denied the charges. He produced his ex-wife as a witness, who subsequently admitted to lying. On this occasion the trade union was not supportive of the appeal because of a personal antagonism between the branch secretary and the driver. That did not matter in the event. Two of the three councillors insisted that there should be a strict time limit to the hearing. They both had other things to do; one had to walk her dog. She was also, coincidentally, sponsored by the trade union of which the driver was a member. The third councillor left the proceedings declaring that the other two had made a farce of them. The result became a foregone conclusion. The two remaining councillors declared that there was insufficient evidence to justify dismissal. They said the man should be found alternative work. He remained on full pay. A year later, no work had been found and he received a redundancy payment.

Both these cases were demoralising, and not only for senior managers. In disciplinaries, other members of staff – colleagues of those alleged to have done wrong – give evidence. It is highly stressful for them and to see reinstatement opens up the prospect of years of friction and, possibly, worse ahead. The message goes out to staff: 'Do not get involved in giving evidence!' Maintaining standards does not receive the sort of support it should from employers. Senior managers are less able to reassure public, users and other members of staff that quality is important and will be upheld.

What can be done?

The picture above is a gloomy one; it emphasises the worst sorts of problems. But there are many more well-run authorities than bad and thousands of committed, highly competent councillors. However, the way local government is organised allows a well-run authority, for example on a change of political control or on the election of one particular councillor to a significant position in the authority, to set that authority on a downward spiral. There are, probably, too many councillors with nothing worthwhile to do. There are as a result too many meetings and making decisions becomes diffuse, long-winded and stale, with the prospect that the lowest common denominator will be the choice of all those who take part in any decision.

For chief officers, and ultimately for all staff, it is not difficult for a political culture to inhibit or damage equality in the delivery of services, fail to be supportive of quality and to be one that is based on whimsical interference by councillors to gain an ascendancy. Chief officers are accountable to their local authorities but they should not be fearful in their advice to councillors that an unpopular measure may lead to something unpleasant for them. Adopting a 'safety first' approach to policy making, especially in social services, may be a short-term way of keeping councillors off the department's 'back' but, in the long term, it will restrict the service's ambitions and prevent the public receiving the services they need.

A new Labour government might usefully look at the possibility of some reforms in local government as part of its constitutional programme. Possible reforms might be to reduce the number of councillors in local authorities and to examine seriously the idea of elected mayors who would be supported by a small executive in local authorities. As I have also indicated, a properly regulated relationship between chief officers and councillors would be an important step forward. With some necessary structural changes such as I have suggested, whilst there will always be stress at the top, it could become enjoyable and creative.

CHAPTER 11

Roots in the Air
Stress and Survival in Psychiatric Social Work

Tony Manning

Introduction

Psychiatric social work (PSW): what does the name of my profession signify? Acquaintances might reasonably enquire whether we are 'some kind of psychiatrist' or 'some kind of social worker'? Or are we, perhaps, more one than the other? My own response is that the profession stands somewhere in between practices and beliefs that locate 'Mind' within the person and their individual mental and biological processes, and those that suggest that the person and, indeed, their own experience, can only be understood in the context of family and social systems. Relative clarity about our professional identity, and about the value of our perspective, enhances both our practice and our self-esteem. The same 'information' is capable of more negative constructions: that we lack a strong and exclusive body of knowledge, or even that we are professional 'jacks of all trades'. I think we can afford to be assertive, secure in the knowledge that intervention in the social and community domain is generally a crucial component of the recovery of health. At the same time, we do not need to be overly competitive, acknowledging that life is lived both intra- and inter-personally, and avoiding the conundrum: 'Which came first, the physiological event, or its social construction?'

PSWs form part of services that are increasingly recognised as essential to the health of the nation – in addressing problems now and in preventing future problems – yet there is profound insecurity in terms of funding. This creates a further area of tension for workers when they receive discrepant messages, that their work is both vital and dispensable. For psychiatric social workers in particular, no longer sure of their place in any department, survival as a distinct profession becomes a serious concern.

Survival – the orchid metaphor

Nature is replete with examples of unlikely life-forms that have somehow adapted to their particular ecological conditions. The most precious orchids, for example, rely on the supportive structure of their host plant, while not being parasitic. Unable to draw water for sustenance from the ground, one might imagine that the specie's survival would be precarious, if not impossible. However, their adaptation to feed from the air allows them to thrive, providing that their host remains healthy. Students of child and family consultation teams might equally suggest that their structure is such that their survival is unlikely. They lack the means of independent existence and are attached to structures that may fail to feed them, since the provider departments' perceived priorities are elsewhere. Health is, perhaps, preoccupied with acute medicine, education with the national curriculum and social services with the 'sharp end' services, for example child protection. Small wonder, then, that from the Brunel Report (1976) onwards, observers have been perplexed as to how a clearly needed set of services can prosper without radical change. Such teams can indeed seem likely to self-consume amid the woes of structural confusion, marginalisation and a lack of clear and agreed leadership. The need to respond to such threats has at last been recognised, following the publication of the Health Advisory Service report on Child and Adolescent Mental Health Services, allowing a strategic approach to planning and funding such services.

Our orchid-like service might be considered to be involved in a symbiotic relationship, providing benefits in exchange for the supports it receives. These benefits consist of the clinical work we do (indeed our presence attracts types of work that the team would otherwise be ill-equipped to undertake), the special perspectives we provide and the access to other networks and their resources which we bring to the team. Beyond the realm of the clinical team are the key relationships in the wider network that need to be nurtured. These relationships not only enhance the effectiveness of our work but also help to build effective systems capable of supporting innovation.

Unhealthy organisations are preoccupied with their own survival, while progressive ones realise that the resolution of professional and organisation stresses is ultimately useful only in so far as it enables the delivery of increasingly effective services to those who need them. There are stresses at the delivery level too, in the struggle to create a therapeutic process, to define and redefine the nature of the problem and so on.

This chapter will, therefore, address, within a relational framework, the following areas of stress in the profession:

1. Professional identity and purpose

2. Clinical work

3. Multi-disciplinary team relationships

4. Wider system relationships, including the challenge of change.

First, however, it is important to think about what we mean by 'stress' and why its understanding is an important consideration in our work. I will also say something about resilience, that is those qualities that make for hardiness, endurance and, ultimately, survival.

Pressure and stress – how to make a difference

Wilkie (1995) points out how mystifying it is to find the word 'stress' used 'to refer to both a cause of nervous system overload and the result of nervous system overload.' (p.8). Modern approaches distinguish between environmental events, that the subject appraises as a threat or stressor, and the outcome of such a process, that may involve a stress state, with negative consequences for physical and psychological health.

'Stress-related episodes of impairment [may occur] when stress exceeds an individual's vulnerability threshold', that is affected by ambient or day-to-day stresses of family, household, social activity and work-related spheres; life-events, such as the loss of a job, or the death of a close friend or family member; the coping behaviour of the subject. (Falloon *et al.* 1993, p.??).

To this 'menu' I would add the impact of unpredictable, and usually sudden, external trauma or disaster. Additionally, the support system available to the individual, in terms of timely practical help and emotional support, is vitally important. This, as well as innate/inherited characteristics, contributes to the person's 'hardiness' and ability to survive, actually and spiritually, in the sense of retaining integrity and positive beliefs about the meaning of his life.

There will be instances, of course, when the immediate stressor does not fully account for the response, which appears to be disproportionate to the event. In such cases it may be that the 'last straw' incident has re-awakened an earlier, largely unprocessed but heavily defended, loss or trauma. These are important concepts to keep in mind since overburdened staff may be carrying vulnerabilities from their personal life histories that are not appreciated by their colleagues but which may contribute to an eventual 'burnout'.

Boss (1987) refers to learning from Carl Whitaker about 'boundary ambi-guity as a major variable to explain family stress. Symbolically, there can be loss and absence even in an intact family. This is the "crazy maker", the stress producer. Fathers were there but not there. They were physically present but psychologically absent. Coping was blocked because clarity was lacking on whether or not he was in or out of the system' (p.155).

On the other hand, intermittent pressure to carry out meaningful tasks within one's capability can be both stimulating and creative. Stress states tend to involve a series of mismatches, where the demands are or are taken to be, relentless and inescapable, so that all other life needs are squeezed out, resulting in a lack of balance. The fulfilment of the tasks seems pointless or morally odious; one is asked, or demands of oneself, performance beyond one's gifts, energies and training; one can no longer 'see the wood for the trees', either in terms of immediate task effectiveness or in achieving a 'fit' between one area of one's life and the very many others.

It can be argued that our most intractable cases, that have defeated and frustrated numerous professionals, are often those where at least one member of the family is carrying a high level of stress or where the stress is visceral, unconscious, carried as a secret at the core of the person and, often, the family. It is, therefore, not readily amenable to language as a processing medium. The stress that cannot be put into words, perhaps because it was never adequately processed by such means at the time of the critical event, will resist such a cognitive and, essentially, language-based approach. Individuals presenting with borderline states, repetitive and apparently compulsive self-injury, witnesses to unspeakable tragedy or violence or who have endured serious emotional and sexual abuse challenge our ability to reach these deeper structures.

Coping and resilience

It is heartening that there is an increasing interest in discovering what it is that makes some individuals able to withstand – and even grow through – crises and stresses that will disable others. While the tradition has been to analyse the negative impacts of stress, there is now the possibility of further work to enhance coping abilities through education and novel therapeutic approaches. Walsh's (1996) concept of family resilience 'concerns both vulnerability and regenerative power' and is 'forged *through* adversity not *despite* it'. This is a concept that matters to psychiatric social workers because:

- how we have incorporated our own difficult, or even critical, events, experiences and transitions is important material for our growth, our empathy and our work generally;

- awareness of the concept reminds us to look for it in the story of the family over time and to work to enable a 'schema' of competence and mastery to come to prominence over a destructive dominant story (Hawley and De Haan 1997)

- the concept is connected to an important strength, sometimes called 'tough-mindedness'. Psychiatric social workers need to be able to listen, certainly, but also to hold their ground and to stay with issues our clients may be uncomfortable with

- ° the way that our team models (or fails to model) mutual support in times of stress and disorder affects our esteem and effectiveness.

Clinical work can be tough and clinicians, like athletes, need to be hardy, positive and near the top of their form much of the time. Williams (1994) suggests that those who are watching for clues of optimum performance should look out for 'energy and enthusiasm; alertness; high morale; good humour/cheerfulness; a positive "can do" approach; calmness; quick decision-making' (p.118). Earlier, he explains the importance of the context in which one views one's job. He tells a story of three different stonemasons who were asked in turn what they were doing. One replies that he is cutting stone, the second that he is making stone blocks, while the third says that he is helping to build a cathedral.

Stress in the system 1: professional identity and purpose

Psychiatric social workers are concerned with the psychological life of the individual, with an active orientation to the family and community settings in which distress is experienced.

It is, therefore, important for them to explore how they experience and manage stress in themselves, in their face-to-face work and in their work settings. It is not necessary, nor indeed is it possible, for psychiatric social workers to be stress free, but it is reasonable for a person in difficulty or distress to expect the professional, to whom they turn for help, to have mental space available for them as well as the capacity to be reflective, resourceful and positive. The professional is required to be able to tell the difference between the stresses they themselves carry into the situation from other sources and those that form part of the therapeutic relationship. The latter may be regarded as sources of energy that can be understood and turned to good purpose.

The history of the profession demonstrates a rehabilitative purpose and a strong interest in resolving the tensions between the 'outside' and the 'inside', the family and the patient and the hospital and the outside world. As such, psychiatric social workers have long been interpreters and go-betweens. This includes our availability to help professional colleagues to understand the social, relationship, environmental and contextual pressures that have been the catalyst for the individual's distress or dysfunction.

How stressful an occupation is psychiatric social work?

While there are many 'soft' factors, such as individual perception and temperament, that play a part in determining whether or not a given job or set of conditions is experienced as stressful, there may be intrinsic aspects of particular jobs that create a loading towards stress. Cooper and Payne (1988) have devised occupational stress ratings that locate social work as a 'very stressful' occupation, although within its sub-group it rates lower than the jobs of teacher, nurse and doctor. Indeed, shorn of the child protection and other statutory roles of mainstream social work, one might argue that the stresses of psychiatric social work should be considerably reduced. Or is this a case of 'comparison being odious'? After all, psychiatric social workers are exposed to the direct, and at times draining, work with a wide range of children and families in distress. It is rarely sufficient to assess and refer on, or to provide simple information, and the resources at one's disposal are largely one's skills and personal qualities.

The emphasis is on the worker's personal availability, rather than on any bag of professional tricks that might create distance from the person seeking assistance. The work thus has a high potential for stress and the clinician has to safeguard his psychic health through development of professional and personal support systems – I refer here to supervision, personal psychotherapy and well-maintained personal and family relationships as well as health and cultural interests.

Stress in the system 2: clinical work

The person of the therapist

At different times we might think of our work as to do with information or with transformation. One level exposes our knowledge, the other, our self. Even where we construe our task in a providing-recipient framework, we discover that our knowledge and insight is often 'strictly non-transferable' other than through the medium of a relationship. The healthier and more integrated the recipient, the more straightforward this process is. In our particular specialism, however, many clients have difficulties that have resisted simple advice-based solutions and they transact at two levels simultaneously: the surface or concrete and the relational or symbolic. The problem may start as the 'figure' but move to be the ground against which relative realities are reprocessed and reorganised. 'Keeney suggests that symptoms must be seen as metaphoric communications about the ecology of the patient's relationship systems – an ecosystem of which the therapist becomes a part' (Hoffman 1981, p.343).

Permitting oneself to become sufficiently immersed in the family's process and pain, if only to be able to describe it back with more accuracy and empathy, involves a number of risks. Their situation may hold reminders of our own past conflicts and, where we feel we have resolved them, we may be impatient with family members' efforts. Where these remain unresolved, our own feelings are likely to colour our perceptions and interventions. We may move from taking part to taking sides. Minuchin's (1974) view was that there was nothing wrong with this, just as long as everyone got their turn! Whitaker and Keith (1981) recommend that the more psychotic a family's transactions are, the greater is the need for a co-pilot – to be available to take the controls at the inevitable points where the 'explorer' might become irretrievably lost.

Reaching new and deeper understandings through language is important too. Whitaker is celebrated for his ability to say the 'big things that can't be said that need saying'. This seems to be based on a deep awareness of personal foibles and a humble acceptance of how difficult life can be. It implies more than a spectator's interest in the life of those seeking – and, apparently, resisting – help. It requires a process of getting inside, being 'captured' by the family, feeling their experience and seeing things their way.

Different workers will put more or less emphasis on the impact of their person on the healing or helping process, yet however rigorously we may pursue a methodology, we will come unstuck unless we can access and utilise our experience beyond our cognition. 'Hypotheses as well as poems are the product of imaginative thinking. Scientific discoveries happen to people not by magic or luck, but by people being open to discovery, by their listening to emotions and responding to intuition.' (Boss 1987, p.147). Similarly, Pascoe (1980) suggests that the creative and mature therapist can stay with even negative feelings such as hopelessness during a period of impasse, connecting with family emotions and trusting their own efforts and abilities.

Finally, what the professional learns from their own experience of stresses – minor or major – and what of this they are prepared to make available to the therapy process is of considerable importance.

Models and muddles

Tensions exist in how we conceptualise our approach to therapeutic work. What sorts of questions are likely to be effective? (Tomm 1987; Palazzoli *et al.* 1980). How much interest will we show in relation to the past, or the past in the present, in terms, for example, of attachment to history colouring current relationships (Byng-Hall 1995)? How will we position ourselves in relation to the family and to the responsibility for change? Will we try to stick with one model (each of which may have several off-shoots, factions and gurus) or attempt to move between them, more as a set of techniques than 'church membership'? How do we think about the nature of 'problems' and what is involved in producing change? What kind or level of change do we have in mind?

Will our emphasis be on the *technical* or the *personal* (the 'centred', non-ego-tistical accepting presence) or the *structural/political* (the conditions of society in terms of encounters with difference, such as gender, race and social class)? Perelberg and Miller (1990), for example, point out some of the limitations of the family therapy model: 'Systems theorists can become entrenched in the study of systems as if they have no political, social or economic context. Systems practitioners can become so focused on the inner consistency of a given formulation that they lose sight of the larger realities that structure and shape it.' (p.26).

The past forty years have seen a profusion of ideas and models in the area of family therapy. If you have been around for even half of that time then you have been a 'leader' (Haley 1976) and a neutral 'conductor', you will have sung in choruses both 'Greek' (Papp 1980) and Norwegian (Andersen 1987), 'hypothesised' (Selvini Palazzoli *et al.* 1980) and 'restructured' (Minuchin 1974), trawled for 'three-generational myths' (Byng-Hall 1979) and 'co-constructed new futures' (Penn 1985), attempted to 'master resistance' (Anderson and Stewart 1983) – unaware that it had been 'dead for some time' (deShazer 1984) – and struggled with 'circularity' (Selvini-Palazzoli *et al.* 1978), 'triangulation' (Bowen 1978), 'double-bind' (Bateson 1972), 'hermeneutics' (Paré 1995, quoting Sellick), 'paradox' (Fisch, Weakland and Segal 1982; Palazzoli-Selvini 1978) and 'autopoesis' (self-creation) (Maturana and Varela 1980) until you were as dizzy and suggestible as you may have wished your most difficult families to be.

Many of these models have been intellectually quite challenging, highly systematised and prescriptive. They have tended to emphasise head over heart, and a culture of questioning that can become tyrannical, while believing itself to be open and reflective (Launer 1997). Since such practice tends to suggest excessive devotion to 'gurus' and theories, Pocock (1997) talks of 'using theory lightly' (p.294). In addition, there has been no shortage of posturing, with a tendency at times to debunk the 'old' theory rather than to attempt any synthesis. Happily, there are signs of the tolerance that comes with maturity, with attempts to achieve greater synthesis (for example, Breunlin, Schwartz and Kune-Karrer 1992).

Recruitment and engagement

At the point of referral there will be, typically, a range of opinions within the family about the need for sessions to explore difficulties. Such 'difficulties' are more likely to be symptom- and individual-focused and considered in terms of relationships only in so far as the symptoms annoy or distress family members or interfere with normal life.

The very earliest points of contact are crucial in setting the scene for subsequent work, in thinking through who is needed at sessions to maximise the potential for understanding the issues and achieving change and in actively working to get them to attend. A common element of 'stuck' cases is lack of commitment to the process, with crucial family members having dropped out or never having been tempted in (for fuller discussion of recruitment and engagement issues see Treacher and Carpenter 1982; Carpenter and Treacher 1983; Stanton and Todd 1982).

Having gained initial co-operation, we then need to keep people involved in the process for long enough to make a difference. This entails understanding the fears that clients may bring to the situation as well as acknowledging that 'motivation' is mutually negotiated (Kingston 1984).

We face the frustrations of patients who quit during the 'getting worse phase', for example adults abused as children who 'splurge a great deal of abuse-related material in first sessions... They may have a history of "dumping" such material on unsuspecting counsellors in first sessions, never to be seen again; leaving the counsellor feeling somewhat abused. This may reflect an unconscious leaking of aggression and persecution from otherwise passive "victim" personalities' (Dale 1996, p.332). Additionally. there are the dynamics of the abusing family of origin, steeped in secrecy for years, and 'in action...a far greater potent force upon the client than the therapist...at the point in therapy when the client is poised to talk about the abuse, sudden and significant changes in mood may occur, suicidal thoughts may occur or return, and the client may suddenly behave in a withdrawn or angry way with the counsellor. These can be very challenging and stressful times for the counsellor, who needs to pay a good deal of attention to counter-transference reactions, including the not-uncommon one of feeling like an abuser' (Dale 1996, pp.334–336).

One important question that may arise, during assessment or later in treatment, is whether confidentiality can be preserved when immediate child protection concerns are evident. This situation has the potential for a stressful dilemma for the psychiatric social worker in particular. He is faced with the wish to pursue therapeutic issues on the one hand and the need to fulfil statutory obligations on the other.

The therapeutic encounter

In relation to practice and service delivery, between 40 and 70 per cent of our working day is likely to be spent on clinical work, so the impact of stresses arising from this area also bears examination. It is important to understand what makes a particular case stressful. Are there characteristics of 'case' or 'family' types that account for this? Is it the role we play in relation to the case? Does our theory or model that underlies our approach make a difference? Since it is an individual who delivers the service, it is important to look at the use of self, gut feelings, instinct, and how our own relationships, past and present, can influence our work for good or ill.

Some element of stress is to be expected at points during therapy, and this is true of all therapists and methods. Indeed, for the helping relationship to be comfortable might suggest 'a conspiracy to do nothing' (Egan 1994, p.17) or to avoid the responsibilities and action that follow from the abandonment of a victim position. A common element in the endeavour is the renegotiation of the nature of the problem. Typically, the transition from a limited perspective that tends to locate the problem in one person and that utilises blame and projection to protect the system to one that permits wider and deeper analysis is likely to produce stress. This stress might be considered to derive from boundary ambiguity as the therapy system, that includes the therapist, struggles with change. This state will, hopefully, be temporary and transitional. While immersed in such a process, stress might present as boredom, a sense of being lost or ineffective or of being rejected as one's credentials are challenged by failed appointments, escalation to ensure the old perspective predominates or a demand, subtle or otherwise, to be referred to someone else. It is important to take time to get to know and like the family, to understand 'where they are coming from' and, indeed, where they were trying to get to before they lost the map, 'immersed in the time-capsule of a problem-determined world' (Anderson and Goolishian 1986). As this exploration takes place, a process that implies a conditional permission to enquire beyond the realm of the confined problem, themes of the human condition, come to the surface through stories of loss, rejection and abuse, accounts of trying to cope with real or perceived differences, of struggling with the problems of social and economic disadvantage, of 'turning points' in experience. Inevitably, some of the themes that emerge will have an emotional connection with the therapist's personal experience and may be 'skirted over' as a means of avoidance of pain or obsessively pursued because of their valency for the therapist rather than for the needs of the family or individual in treatment.

Supervision is important in promoting reflectiveness so that there can be recognition of such processes, enabling their incorporation in the therapy, rather than have them block it. Some therapists might opt to own the counter-transference overtly, allowing the theme to be discussed afresh.

It may be that stress will be provoked in the therapist by families operating at the extremes of interactional styles. At one extreme are the rigid and enmeshed families with marked communicational deviance, where opportunities for change and growth appear to be snuffed out as the spark appears. At the other extreme are the disengaged families who refuse responsibility for their problems, fail appointments wherever they are set up and seem to live in a chaotic permanent present. Each family style embodies fundamental discrepancies. The family in rigid transaction states that 'We are a close family' but also operates rules that no one may state, or experience, differently. The disorganised family tends to make a lot of noise about its rules and sanctions, often involving violent threats, yet fails to notice that their threats are as rarely delivered as their promises or that the parents are models for the aggressive behaviour they complain about in their offspring. While it is hard to progress with such families, and tempting to give up, one needs to recognise the significant problems posed by untreated problems of this kind, both for the individual himself and for those who may be affected by unbounded and self-serving behaviour. These risks include dropping out of school, alcohol/drug abuse, anti-social personality, marital disruption, interpersonal problems and poor physical health (Herbert 1993). The highly enmeshed families tend to generate confusion coupled with high emotion and somatised stress – in the therapy room as well as at home. Again, the consequences of failed treatment are potentially severe for the young people concerned, for example persistent mood disorders and long-term psychosomatic dysfunction.

Success and failure

The ideal time to be thinking about success and failure is at the beginning of contact. Where families drop out of treatment, or the problems persist or even worsen, it is important to consider how this failure is processed by the therapist. There are personal elements to this, such as family of origin roles and how these feed into the need for conspicuous success or difficulty in accommodating to failure. Dealing with failure, or apparent failure, is worth studying but is often neglected. Indeed, not to do so is to act like the gambler who only remembers the winners. Treacher (1989) had the courage – and the curiosity – to conduct unannounced 'failure follow-ups' and learned much that was instructive, and, at times, surprising, from doing so.

Thinking through what we mean by 'success' and framing this as a responsibility shared with service users is both responsible and protective for workers since we are not limited to 'production-line' thinking about quality. It may be reasonable in some cases to consider that there was a favourable outcome even where problems persist if, for example, there is evidence that some learning or attitudinal changes towards the child or helping systems has taken place.

Stress in the system 3: multi-disciplinary team relationships

Boundaries – what's mine?

Throughout Nature there is a strong tendency for species to seek security by marking and protecting territory that has been selected for its utility in preserving the species. Symbolic behaviours, involving loud cries and warning displays, are used to deter incursions, but where these do not suffice, actual violence may ensue and this is more likely when current environmental conditions enforce severe competition. In multi-disciplinary teams it can be difficult to establish which areas, based on profession or skill, 'belong' to a particular group. Sometimes it hardly seems to matter, whereas at others it seems to be a matter of survival. For psychiatric social workers, the 'territory' might be thought of as family and community but this is not exclusive. Twenty years ago, roles may have been clearer, if not rigidly defined, with parallel assessment of psychiatric, educational, internal and family/social functioning as the norm. Since then, boundaries have become more blurred, although there are current pressures on staff to clarify their roles and, perhaps, particularly for psychiatrists to do so. Furthermore, high referral rates make it difficult to preserve much joint or parallel work, other than via workshops or second opinions. Clinical teams will have to work on a number of fronts to capitalise on the diversity of skills and knowledge in the wider team, to continue to challenge and learn from each other and to provide a flexible and comprehensive service to users. When we work alone, do we consider that we represent the team, incorporating skills and viewpoints from the other disciplines and constantly aware of the possibility of their intervention, directly or indirectly? If we have difficulty in accessing sufficient collaboration, even though we seek it, the concern may revolve around boundaries and resources and the solution will involve negoti- ating realistic contracts that support quality, teamwork and a reflective, pro- gressive organisation. To do this will involve setting boundaries that may restrict access to the service, and this sits uncomfortably with the desire to have a highly available service capable of early intervention.

Internal tensions

Team members face competing pressures both to function as team players and to wave the flag of their own particular discipline. When pressures are manageable and morale strong, there seems no need for conflict about this, or at least it is avoided. However, as the pressures mount, fewer people arrive for clinical meetings and many who do have no space to take on new work. There start to be murmurings that one of the reasons for this is that certain team members have over-committed themselves in another setting, indeed that the multi-disciplinary team has become a secondary setting for their work. Whether this was true in the beginning, there is every risk of it becoming true since 'detached' work is much more direct, simpler to manage and may tend to support and confirm a particular role.

Over time, therefore, each discipline may develop important, but separate, networks and supporters which then provide the opportunities for new projects. The risk, as in families, is that from being too close and protective an organisation, the structure may be too loose, all satellite and no core identity.

Stress in the system 4: wider system relationships

An organisation is a structure to which people belong, that is 'united and constructed for a particular end' (Collins Concise English Dictionary). The sense of belonging derives from awareness that the organisation has a job to do, is clear about the reasons why it is a job worth doing well and thus looks after those who see that its tasks are carried out. Ideally, it operates a culture that is open to learning, responding to changing conditions and feedback, and is proactive in reviewing its performance to construct a viable future. It should seek to find a level of growth that is realistic, and tolerable to its staff and users, while aware that changing too much and too often is disorientating and destabilising and may tend to produce the inertia and conservatism it was designed to sweep away. Too little change, on the other hand, while providing some security and comfort, offers no real challenge or excitement and the longer staff stay, the less equipped they will be to leave. Warren and Toll (1993) comment that conditions of understress and overstress can co-exist in an organisation through 'stress blockage' with managers critically overstretched and the talents of their staff underused.

Perhaps the first question to ask about psychiatric social workers in relation to their wider system is 'Who do they seem to belong to?' Allegiance may be to the profession, to the speciality within that profession, to the employing organisation or to the team in the work setting. One cannot guarantee a good fit amongst these possibilities.

Change is inevitable, whether the small and constant rebalancing moves to keep the apples on the cart, and to keep things recognisably 'the same', or the more radical shifts that upset the apple-cart and question its usefulness in the new environment. For PSWs, and the teams which they are part of, there is an increasing need to understand their market, remembering that a quality product is not necessarily a successful one – like some British cars in the USA, where potential customers might have said: 'Great cars! No spares!'. Similarly, therapists in the public service can no longer focus exclusively on the sanctum of the therapy room, ignoring the business elements necessary to their own and their organisation's prosperity. We are in an era where we must communicate what it is that we do distinctively and well. We need to innovate, market and evaluate and, crucially, to become familiar with the world of numbers – including those on balance-sheets.

Whether elements of the team seek to develop different markets or pursue cohesive development will vary according to a complex set of factors to do with history, locality, strategy and personality mix as well as conscious and unconscious conflict. Some teams will become expert bridge builders, capitalising on the common ground of shared interests and marketing flexible, yet diverse, services successfully. Less happily elsewhere, stress fractures may start to show between professionals and professional groups or between the clinical team and particular parts of the network.

While it is clearly the responsibility of others, from Government down, to ensure that market-forces operations do not get out of hand, the demand for a business orientation to running our services is unlikely to go away. This leaves us with a dilemma: what must we stop doing, or do differently, if we are to take on all of these new demands and tackle them successfully? As the song says: 'something has to give!'. Facing the dilemma involves difficult decisions, unfamiliar work and new challenges. Ducking it, as we have seen throughout this chapter, brings stress to individual and organisation alike.

Summary

This chapter has explored four main areas that require attention to minimise stress as a limiting and destructive force and to optimise the positive and creative practice of psychiatric social work. An assumption throughout has been that in an exposed profession such as mine, not only is stress unavoidable but it offers opportunities for inter-personal understanding and growth, both with one's clients and one's colleagues, in the pursuit of satisfying, productive and co-operative experiences.

CHAPTER 12

The Inner Impact of Work with Disturbance

Robert Fleming

Introduction

Much of social work is about being in close contact with people in crises. What happens psychologically to the social worker in such relationships? The sight of human beings struggling, for example, to be parents to their offspring and being overwhelmed or destructive in the process can be saddening and chastening. I often recall feeling that I was unequipped to deal with the emotional issues being raised and certainly unsure of how to understand what was happening to my inner world. What did I do with my experiences of families in an unrelenting series of losses and broken attachments, of disadvantage and sheer misery? Perhaps I would not be alone in admitting that one way of dealing with this kind of onslaught is to try to deny and resist the impact of such experiences. The tendency seemed to be to rush into action, to focus on external matters, to the detriment of what was happening internally, both to me and the client. There seemed to be a wish to switch off the part of myself that could be in touch with another's human condition. The stress involved in being emotionally true to both oneself and one's client in such an environment is considerable.

Recently, I read, with fascinated horror, a diary-type account in a national social work journal of the removal of a child from its parents by a social worker accompanied by a police escort. The candour and accuracy of the description had a chilling effect. This is not a task that all social workers do every day but it is a glimpse of the sort of work the social work profession can face and a hint at what happens to that experience:

> When I go into the office tomorrow they will ask me, 'How did it go?' And I shall reply 'Oh, it was OK. We managed'.
>
> But oh, that isn't true. It was dreadful, utterly dreadful...

The child protection team had been unanimous: pre-birth registration in the category of likely neglect. An Emergency Protection Order (EPO) was to be sought and police protection organised. We had a plan. It was all straightforward, all under control. And in a sense it was, except that you cannot plan pain and raw emotion and fear...

As soon as we knew it was born I filled in the blanks on the paperwork... However tiny, this is for real. 'Can you manage?' they asked 'Of course,' I replied...

The special care baby unit is waiting, the parents are waiting. We zoom off feeling like the Flying Squad, except for my stomach which is giving subtler messages.

My client and her boyfriend are waiting for us in the hospital cafe... The pain of it hits me again. What am I doing? It's inhuman.

We are all very reasonable. I serve the order. One more hurdle over...

The couple are stroking the baby, attaching a balloon to his cot, crying and mouthing soft words. What am I doing? They take him out of the cot for a cuddle and the nurse raises her eyebrows at me. 'It's OK', I try to signal back with my eyebrows. 'Let it be OK,' I silently pray.

After a while I risk it. 'We'll have to go soon – just a few more minutes'. To my relief they put the baby back in the cot and say goodbye, tears splashing over him. I walk with them to the door. Don't show your fear, I tell myself. This is the difficult bit. They leave the unit. The door locks behind them. Another hurdle over...

I have time to look at the bundle properly. A screwed up little face and tiny hand. God, is he still breathing. Is he warm enough? The enormity of it all hits me again. Such a tiny little life, such an eventful beginning, and what a long way to go.

We head back down the motorway hardly talking. My stomach begins to unknot. I am incredibly tired. Tomorrow, when I go into the office, shall I say 'No sweat. It was OK'? Or shall I find a listening ear for an hour and tell them the truth?' (Anon 1994, p.7)

At other points in this article this social worker wrote with some humour but it was clear that the emotional impact of the awful task she had to complete was enormous at the time and, perhaps, more importantly, would be subsequently.

 It is crucial, in my view, for the mental health of the workers involved, that the mechanisms underlying these situations can be thought about and understood. In this chapter I would like to explore some features of the casework relationship and ask what happens when a social worker truly allows herself to face her own internal world and that of her clients, to ponder the consequences of really being stirred up by the state of mind of another human being in crisis.

Towards a model of understanding stress

A good starting point for this exploration would be to use ideas about the psychological development of human life and, thus, the basis of all relationships. To do this I will utilise some background concepts from the field of psychoanalysis and, in particular, Melanie Klein, who was a major contributor in this area. Her experience of work with children led her to describe the psychic development in original ways. In an attempt to suggest fluidity, Klein describes 'positions' with the clear implication of movement. The earliest position describes the inner world of the first months of the infant as it struggles with the limited resources available to him. The infant, despite having some innate abilities to respond in a relationship to the 'other', does not have the full facility of perceiving the mother or consistent caregiver as a whole person. The mother is regarded as a series of pieces or 'part objects'. These might include the breast, nipple, eyes, etc. The part objects are not related or connected to each other in the infant's mind. As a result, the terrifying, but sometimes gratifying, world is divided into distinct and separate camps. The 'good' parts of the mother that feed and console the infant become idealised and separated from the painful, absent and frightening 'bad' parts of mother that do not meet the infant's needs instantly.

These 'part objects' are not the anatomical parts of the mother but represent the functions the mother provides for the infant. In this way, the feeding breast or the holding arms, for example, are known for their feeding and holding respectively, rather than as physical parts of the mother's body.

Juliet Mitchell (1986) tells us that to understand and benefit fully from this part of the work of Klein, we need to understand her use of the defence mechanisms of splitting, projection and introjection in particular:

> The ego makes use of these defences to cope with the inner world and the constant interaction between inner and outer. Its own destructive feelings – emanations of the death drive – make the baby very anxious. It fears that the object on which it vents its rage (e.g. the breast that goes away and frustrates it) will retaliate. In self-protection it splits itself and the object into a good part and projects all its badness into the outside world so that the hated breast becomes the hateful and hating breast. Klein describes this as the paranoid-schizoid position. (p.20)

This is the first position that is described above.

Roughly around the second quarter of the infant's first year, some important physical and psychic changes can be seen. Klein attempted to describe these universally observed changes in her unique way. In the next, more integrated, position, the infant has a slowly growing awareness of the mother as a whole person. The mother, who, in some part of the infant's mind, is the withholding and terrifying mother, is seen to be the very same mother who reappears and gives comfort, etc. The infant has to accommodate the fact that the destructive rage that the infant felt towards 'bad' mother would also have been on the 'good' mother. The fear that the good mother may be permanently injured or destroyed by this rage is a great source of anxiety to the infant. The resultant concern for the mother is crucial for the subject's development. It leads to feelings of responsibility in later life and is the basis of future creativity. This movement leads to the second position, which Klein (1935) called the 'depressive position'. This concept in Klein's model does not connote illness but, rather, the bearing of painful reality. Winnicott (1963) referred to the more or less same phenomenon as the 'stage of concern'.

Returning to the concept of the earliest and primitive paranoid schizoid position, we can see that the split-off, idealised and denied world of part objects in the first few months of the infant's life is a rapidly changing and multi-dimensional stage. One of the many clinical discoveries Klein made was that from birth the infant attempts to export both good and bad aspects of its experience. Symbolically, the infant tries to mentally enter the other with part of its self and this can lead to a changed perception of itself and the relationship it has to the other. This is the process by which the infant imagines himself to be inside another person. This can give the infant a sense of control and allow it, for example, to withstand its own fear of annihilation and lack of power. Klein (1946) named this mechanism 'projective identification'.

More recently, this concept of projective identification has been used more broadly in terms of a primitive communication through which the subject makes the object feel what it is like to exist as that person. It can also be seen as a way of defending the subject from a very painful internal world. Thus the 'bad' split-off parts are pushed into the object. Projective identification is also used in relation to control. The infant, patient or client in the grip of some primitive emotion may attempt to use projective identification to control the object's mind or body. This fusion with the other prevents the possibility of separation. In a sense, the perception of the isolating space between the subject and the other (technically called the 'object') has been changed to reduce the pain of being dependent.

The valuable concept of projective identification was developed by many subsequent thinkers and clinicians through their work with very disturbed people (Sandler 1988; Rosenfeld 1987). It helped to explain and understand some of the clinical phenomena faced in working with mental disorder. Bion

(1957), in particular, adapted it and provided us with yet another important tool for understanding experience. He took the idea of projective identification and elevated it to a different level of theory that could attempt to explain human interaction at a broad level. In doing so, the term is applied to 'normal' as well as pathological development. Bion built on the original idea of projective identification as a description of one person somehow being in some way *in* the other. He expanded the concept beyond the interrelationship between the infant and its mother, which had important implications for the very nature of the therapeutic relationship.

Bion (1962) wrote of the relationship between the infant and the mother in terms of the capacity the latter had to be a 'container' for the terrors of the infant. He used the term 'Maternal Reverie' to describe the process in which the mother has a state of mind in which the infant's projection (fears, terrors, unwanted bad parts, etc) can be placed within the mother. The mother in maternal reverie is open to this onslaught and able not only to survive the experience but respond in a positive and constructive manner. The mother processes these projections and then allows the infant to introject the experience through her understanding and tolerance of the pain. This detoxification makes the unthinkable thinkable, the unbearable bearable.

Hanna Segal (1981) described the process concisely when she wrote:

> When an infant has an intolerable anxiety, he deals with it by projection into the mother. The mother's response is to acknowledge the anxiety and do whatever is necessary to relieve the infant's distress. The infant's perception is that he has projected something intolerable into his object, but the object was capable of containing it and dealing with it. He can then reintroject not only his original anxiety but an anxiety modified by having been contained. He also introjects an object capable of containing and dealing with anxiety. The containment of anxiety by an external object capable of understanding is a beginning of mental stability. (p.134)

This process of 'containing' the powerful projections is not, therefore, a luxury. It is crucial to healthy development in that it allows the infant (or person projecting) to have a sense of being held and understood and thereby allows the next more integrated phase of accepting good and bad in the same object. This, in turn, leads to the reparation and responsible attitudes by the process mentioned earlier.

If, for any reason, the maternal object fails to offer this process of under-standing and containing the projections of the infant, Bion (1962) feels that it runs the risk of facing a terror of enormous proportions. He refers to this as 'Nameless Dread' and describes it as the sense of meaning ebbing away from the world and a frightening feeling of unknown taking over in the mind of the infant.

The cause of this failure in maternal reverie can be thought about in many ways. For example, the mother may have no space in her mind to accommodate the projections of the infant. She may, in this way, be psychically absent and preoccupied by her own issues (Murray (1991) has, for example, confirmed the impact of post-natal depression in the infants of depressed mothers and stressed the terrible effect on their emotional and cognitive development). The infant might be in the grasp of such envy of the maternal object that the vital factor of reintrojection is not possible. The containing function of the mother may be destroyed in the mind of the infant and this will similarly destroy the crucial link of reintrojection. Alternatively, in reality, the containing function of the maternal object might not be capable of standing up to the infant's onslaught. The psychic demands of an infant might overpower the psychic resources of the mother or, in extreme circumstances, the external world may be so dangerous that it prevents the facilitation of the relationship.

The impact on the social worker

What can this model of relationships have to offer the social worker trying to grapple with the inner impact of work with disturbance? It is true to say that the task of social work has changed dramatically in the past decades. The cash nexus has crept into nearly every aspect of life and the social work profession has not escaped. From the tragic death of Maria Colwell to the Cleveland and Orkney debates, from the chronic under-funding of local government to the savage and, at times, ill-informed attacks by the press, social work has been the focus of scrutiny. The legislative framework has been altered dramatically by the Children Act 1989 without a corresponding change in resources. In short, the social work of today seems very different to that of its predecessors. Policing high-risk families and an ethos of 'covering your back' would not be an inaccurate description of the attitude and state of mind of many inner-city social workers.

However, despite this possible move away from the primacy of the casework relationship, it would be dangerous for both clients and social workers to believe that the emotionality of the relationship can be relegated or ignored. Only by having space to think about the complexities of the human condition will the social worker be able to feel human and to respond humanely. One might even argue, in the terms of the current atmosphere of budget-led structures, that it is only by paying close attention to the psychological aspects that social workers can act efficiently in the long term. To properly finance a department of professionals to work with the crises of human life, one needs to strategically budget for space to allow the professional to think clearly about the complex situations facing them and impacting them. To avoid this is not to understand the true costs involved.

In an ideal world, social work could make an enormous contribution to the understanding of our social systems. What other profession works at the interface of the individual and society and is, therefore, uniquely placed to understand the tensions of modern life for the individual and the family in all its forms? If social workers are effectively siphoned off into another form of police force, as some current political circles suggest, the efficiency that could be claimed in terms of a full understanding of the real dynamics of society is reduced. This is the efficiency that could have come from the harnessing of the creative power of human relationships.

Returning to the psycho-dynamic model for thinking about the emotionality of relationships and human exchanges, what are the symptoms of this kind of stress likely to be in the social work task? It would be trite to attempt a simple list of ways in which the containing function of the social worker might falter and how this would manifest itself – there will always be unique aspects to every situation. However, sickness rates and 'burn-out' in heavily bombarded teams of social workers may have some relationship to this aspect of stress and failing containment.

When *Community Care* carried out a survey of 524 social workers across the profession, around 96 per cent regarded their jobs as stressful. King (1991) reported on the survey findings. Seventy-seven per cent of the sample said that they had noticed, or were aware of, physical symptoms of stress in colleagues, such as headaches, high blood pressure, insomnia and ulcers, while 58 per cent admitted these symptoms themselves.

The commonly held view of some sleepless nights being the result of psychological issues is only a very simple aspect of the mind-body link. The body is clearly capable of expressing many complex and powerful emotions. Indeed, some of the most exciting research in progress at the moment is in exploring the psychological components of disease and, especially, the interrelationship with what was once thought purely organic conditions – for example hypertension, stomach ulcers, bowel complaints, bronchial asthma and eczema (Taylor 1987).

The widely reported High Court decision in November 1994 in favour of Mr John Walker illustrates the seriousness of the stress in social work. This area manager in a busy social services department warned his employers on a number of occasions, over a number of years that the workload of child protection cases he was expected to manage was having a serious impact on his mental health. The temporary support provided by his employers following his first crises was removed and this manager had a 'nervous breakdown' serious enough to prevent him ever returning to his twenty year career in social work. The judgement on the case clearly stated that the employers were responsible for the situation that led to this man being 'severely mentally wounded'. Mr Justice Colman (1995), in his judgement on this case, is reported to have said:

I am satisfied that although sheer volume of work often imposes stress which can cause psychiatric damage to a normally robust personality, the character of the work itself imposes stresses capable of causing psychiatric change, regardless of volume of work. A given normal personality may develop mental illness when the work which has to be undertaken is intrinsically stressful, while less stressful work of equal volume might have no detrimental effect.

The intrinsically stressful character of child abuse cases would clearly be expected to bear heavily on field social worker. I am, however, quite satisfied that not only would such cases give rise to stress in field workers, but also in those who, like Mr Walker, had the responsibility of participating in the decision-taking which such cases demanded... (p.8)

One can easily imagine a social worker having a physical and/or psychological reaction to an unprocessed or unacknowledged psychological experience in her case work. In the terms of the model being discussed here, it would not be hard to view the social worker as being the target of projections. Inevitably, containing and processing them will be a drain on the worker's inner resources. To withstand, for example, the sometimes powerful, sometimes perverse, sometimes murderous aspects of a damaged psyche is extremely hard work. To add to the task by attempting to be thoughtful and containing and resisting the urge to, perhaps, reject, distance, judge or ignore is even harder. I think this will be especially true if the unconscious dynamic is never addressed, with the task seen in terms of the external constraints only. If, for example, the supervision focus is more clearly on the 'throughput' and management of cases rather than the underlying emotional dynamics of the people involved, the containing quality and ability of the social worker is seriously diminished. A manager may feel that the unallocated cases are being dealt with sooner but at what cost to the containing space required to fully understand the dynamics of the crises and the people involved?

To truly survey one's own inner responses to another person's crises takes a level of honesty and insight that, perhaps, few can claim to have without considerable struggle. Our natural and, arguably, necessary defences against the anxieties involved in emotional pain are complex. Without time and space and a skilled other (team, supervisor, consultant, therapist) to probe and grapple with the content of our responses, we run risks of acting out many of the powerful projections that are inevitable in work with disturbance. When the projections become intense and there is, perhaps, no venue for these to be expressed, the tendency would be to enact them in some form. Perhaps the simplest description of this would be the troubled day at work that becomes the inexplicable row at home. The unprocessed experience is being acted out in another venue. Given the nature of the projections in many disturbed clients of social services, this could be very dangerous.

I recall joining a social work team where the morale and the staffing levels had been at rock bottom for some time. The supervision had been *ad hoc* and rushed. One veteran social worker with many years of experience was amazed to discover how the impact of the work had gradually eaten into his life in so many respects. One case stands out in particular. An adolescent, with a turbulent relationship with his inconsistent and, at times, rejecting parents, had managed to convince the social worker that his input was 'rubbish'. Nothing was good enough and everything was given to him for an ulterior motive. Slowly, the experience of this brought the social worker to the point that he began to believe wholeheartedly that everything he was giving the boy was indeed 'rubbish' and the task was hopeless. My experienced colleague's self-esteem was at rock bottom. His skills and his career held no value for him any longer. It was only when the team created a containing space to really think about what the boy needed to communicate (put into) to my colleague that the reality of the situation was perceived. The boy had to 'place' all the unbearable aspects of himself into the social worker; the projection could be said to stand as a communication of what it was like to exist as that boy. My colleague was 'acting out' the message that was coming so strongly from his client. He had received the communication about the client's fears of himself (that he had nothing of value) and was unable to properly place it.

Using the concept of splitting, we might also explore some of the serious reactions to the primitive anxieties underlying much of the social work task. The tendency, when faced with such a powerful set of situations that arrive when human beings are in distress, might easily lead to the kind of 'exporting' of the experience which is described above in terms of splitting and projection. For example, a social worker might feel the impotence and anger from a case and respond by attempting to psychologically split off the experience. She might feel a wish to, for example, place the blame in another colleague, another department, another section of society, anything to avoid the full impact of being in touch with the raw emotionality oneself or to be put in touch with that part of ourselves.

We all, at times, find ourselves using this defence, but perhaps an example from someone at the start of their career might illuminate the issue clearly. A social work student, from a rather over-protected and, possibly, naïve background, was, in her first case, faced with many issues that rocked the very basis of her life. That the client, a young woman the same age as the student, could have such a radically different position in society stunned her emotionally. The client was the product of a family where parental containment was in short supply. As she grew up she sought to find some source of love and loving for herself by having a child. When the infant inevitably failed to give the love that she was so hungry for, this young mother retreated from life.

On return to the office, the situation, which was already known to the duty social worker, was presented in material terms only. The Department of Social Security became a target for the student's anger. The student, faced with the emotionality of the experience of meeting another human being in distress, was thrown by the facts of a life that had not included love and parental concern. The impact was too much and the experience had to be defended against. In this case, it was only after very careful and rare supervision that the student could begin to see the underlying dynamic that she was having difficulty facing and to begin to be more in touch with the client's emotional state. The full impact of a loveless neglected early life on an under-resourced adult was devastating for the student. It could not be tolerated and so was converted in her mind into a simple material deficit for which a bureaucratic agency could be blamed.

Winnicott (1982) once described a bravely honest concept of 'hate in the counter transference'. In these days of empowerment and individual rights via charters, this thought may initially strike the reader as shocking. However, it may cast light on an area that would be dangerous if not acknowledged. Winnicott was telling us that the impact of human disturbance needs to be felt. To resist really feeling it, or to deny the emotions involved in being the recipient of primitive feelings from other times, is to run the risk of the reaction appearing in another form. Thus, if we are not aware, sometimes, of our angry feelings at being filled up by the apparently inappropriate projections of clients we are striving to help, we run the risk of acting out this feeling in other areas.

Although not all social work is with children and not all social work with children is about abuse, it is the public perception that this is what social workers do. The hatred and violence that has followed some social workers caught up in the public furore of social work inquiries suggest to me that the concepts of splitting, projection and containment can offer an understanding of this dynamic between the profession and the public. The primitive nature of the impact of repeatedly hearing that some children are being hurt or abused brings out echoes of our own early experiences and deepest fears of our own annihilation. Klein's intensive work with children led her to argue that the fear of being completely wiped out is an important part of the development of infants. As we mature and grow older it is easy to understand that this frightening and primitive state will have strong reverberations in our adult life. One can imagine that in order to keep the memory of this state away from our adult awareness, the notion of an innocent and trouble-free infancy was created. With this delusion we could convince ourselves that the infant is not having to grapple with anxiety that had developed out of fear of its own destruction.

When the facts of child abuse appear, the bubble is burst and society has to face the reality of violence and aggression aimed at children.

The need to control (and deny) the aspects of ourselves that might lead to aggression and destruction is strong. The hate etched on the faces of the crowds outside courts where child abuse cases are being held seems to suggest that the rage is intolerable and has to be projected outwards. With this model of projection we can easily see that it might be placed in others in a controlling manner. When society impossibly demands that social workers prevent all child deaths, it can be seen as a manifestation of this. When, from time to time, there is an inevitable failure of the system, society can rail against the profession, thereby allowing it to avoid the pain (it has been almost entirely placed in the social workers) and idealise the 'good' within, whilst attacking the 'bad' without. Society can feel itself to be the 'good parent' that never feels destructive, whilst attacking the 'bad parent' that has failed to protect.

The failure to appreciate the stress involved in being the recipient of projections from disturbed clients and society is dangerous. The impact on the social workers can be devastating. However, the most important issue is the eventual impact on the client. We know from the theories of psychoanalysis and the close observation of infants that when the projected terrors are not contained and are not, therefore, available for safe reintrojection, the basis for mental instability is formed. When we fail to understand and contain our client's projections because of our own stress, we re-emphasise their primitive fear of being unloved and omnipotently destructive.

CHAPTER 13

Emotional Repair for Organisations
Intervening in the Aftermath of Trauma

Liz Webb and Tony McCaffrey

Introduction

In the recent past there have been a number of definitive events of a shocking public nature:

- In Dunblane a gunman invaded a primary school and, in a hail of bullets, murdered eighteen children and one teacher.

- In Sheffield, at the Hillsborough Stadium, a crowd surge led to a horrific pile-up of bodies, resulting in the deaths of dozens of football fans.

- In North Wales organised rings of sexual abuse were uncovered, the tentacles of which were found to spread deeply into the local authority Childrens' Homes.

- In Cambridge a child was murdered, strangled, disturbingly, in his own anorak.

These tragic events have a deeply upsetting effect on the victims, survivors and on the public at large. However, they can also be seen as forming the tip of another particular iceberg. In each case, professional workers have had to deal with the immediate impact and then the aftermath. In this intensively stressful work there is a danger that the needs of workers themselves do not get met and untold damage can be done in the longer term to the individual workers and to their teams and networks.

    This chapter describes a consultancy intervention into a particular system – a children's home – in which it emerged that the staff team had been seriously traumatised to the extent that they lost their capacity to look after the children effectively. The intervention extended over a relatively lengthy period, with two referrals for consultancy being made over the course of a year. In the following we will first detail the key staff involved and then describe the development of this consultancy intervention. Finally, we will conclude by identifying the key issues which emerged from this piece of work.

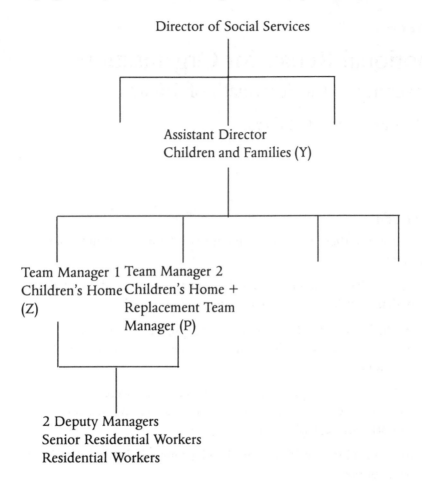

Figure 13.1 Organisation chart

The first referral

One of the authors was first approached by the team manager (Z) on behalf of the staff group as a whole. Z described problematic relationships within the staff group. There was a pattern of scapegoating within the team, with talking going on behind people's backs such that the team was not able to function effectively. The team manager himself accounted for these difficulties by blaming his appointment of deputies, who were unable to fulfil their management responsibilities.

A two-day workshop ensued. The picture that emerged from this work was that the staff's task was felt to be overwhelming. In the culture of complaint, the children had learned to use their new found 'citizen's charter'-backed power. Staff felt their hands were tied behind their backs and control of the children was being lost in a welter of vindictive and/or mischievous complaining by the young people.

Management became the target for blame. External senior managers took the brunt of the projections, being treated with contempt and held responsible for the staff's helplessness in the face of the challenge presented by the children. Internal management was unconsciously let off the hook. Staff seemed to obliterate the formal hierarchy in their minds. The two male deputy managers were purposefully ignored by the staff and thus rendered ineffective. They worked on the rota as if they were ordinary members of staff and were thus effectively hidden. The power vacuum was filled in the following way: in place of the formal hierarchy, a 'family' model was superimposed and Z joined with a particular female member of staff (E) to act as if they were 'mother' and 'father' to a squabbling family of naughty children. When these dynamics were interpreted, it helped the staff to begin to disentangle their difficulties. A few months later, the team manager reported, in a Christmas card, that the consultation had been helpful and that he was helping the deputies to develop their roles appropriately.

The second referral

However, six months later a more macabre slant appeared. The consultant was approached by the external manager responsible for the home (Y) with an urgent plea for help. It emerged that the children's home manager (Z) was part of a paedophile ring. He had been arrested and charged (and was subsequently imprisoned) for circulating obscene material. Suspicions lingered that some of the children, over the years, had been abused by him (though this was never proven). The senior manager wanted the consultant to work with the home's staff, who were, he reported, devastated by the disclosure. He also described the impact on the rest of the organisation. The wider department was shocked and intensely fearful of public exposure. There was talk of closing the home, suspending the staff and dispersing all the children. It seemed to us that the home was being experienced within the department as a kind of social 'Chernobyl', provoking a widespread fear of contamination.

At this stage it was felt that the dynamics were so difficult that two consultants would be needed and the second author became involved. We wondered if a useful way of thinking about the experience of the staff would be to see them as having been traumatised. We therefore developed a model of intervention based on the work of Caroline Garland and the Tavistock Clinic Trauma Unit.

Thinking about trauma

In her remarkable paper, Garland (1991) draws on the work of Freud, Bion, Klein and Segal to devise an approach to intervening in the aftermath of disasters. First, following Freud, she identifies traumatic events as having a fundamentally disruptive impact on mental organisation. She quotes from Freud as follows: 'We describe as "traumatic" any excitations from outside which are powerful enough to break through the protective shield...the concept of trauma necessarily implies a connection...with a breach in an otherwise efficacious barrier against stimuli.' She adds here: 'The breach in the stimulus barrier has profound economic consequences: it presents the mind "with an increase in stimulus too powerful to be dealt with or worked off in the normal way, and thus must result in permanent disturbances of the manner in which energy operates."' (p.509). Crucially, the traumatic event is seen as overwhelming the ego and thus creating a sense of helplessness and intense confusion. Symbolic and linguistic abilities are also overwhelmed such as to undermine the capacity for thought. Garland adds here:

> Through the very inarticulacy created by the scale of the breach in the protective shield, one experiences a projected fraction of the helplessness that overwhelmed the survivor: the blasting away of his normal psychic systems of mastery, control and defence, to leave him unprotected, disintegrated and suffering acute mental pain in the struggle to restore some kind of equilibrium. (p.510)

Traumatic events, then, involve a collapse into more primitive modes of functioning. As the capacity for linguistic and symbolic communication is lost or seriously damaged, the individual is forced to draw on more primitive communicative devices – in particular, using projective processes in an attempt to expel unwanted and painful thoughts and feelings. Garland states here:

> Projective identification is the name first given by Melanie Klein to an intra-psychic process whereby unwanted feelings, perceptions, attitudes, thoughts and fantasies are projected out of the self and perceived to be situated in the object. The object then becomes, in the mind of the projector, identified with those same feelings, attitudes, thoughts or fantasies. Although it was described as an omnipotent fantasy in that it paid very little attention to the actual properties of the object, by some process still not yet fully understood...the external object can be induced to feel or think or behave as though he or she did indeed possess these attributed properties – in other words, the object can get caught up in the reciprocal and complementary state of introjective identification. (p.518)

Such processes, however, also serve a communicative function. Thus Garland emphasises:

> Projective identification is not only the infant's primary way of dealing with unmanageable levels of distress, through getting rid of them wholesale, but it is also his earliest means of communication. It is how he lets his mother know what he feels like at a stage before other means of communication are available. (p.518)

The mother's capacity to contain and manage these feelings for the infant are then critical to subsequent development. Thus:

> The parent's capacity to contain the infant's anxieties without being overwhelmed by them – to know what sort of state of affairs exists in the infant without becoming too identified with it through introjection – enables the infant to begin to order and make sense of his own experience. (p.518)

Garland argues that these primitive modes of functioning co-exist in each and every individual alongside more 'mature' mechanisms. However, whilst every-day experience is premised on the continual shift between differing states of mind, traumatic events inevitably involve a collapse into these more primitive modes of functioning. She states:

> Since an external disaster plunges the individual back into a position of extremity, into the prolonged helplessness that characterises the earliest stages of infancy, inevitably projective identification becomes the primary means of managing it. The survivor is making a desperate and unconscious attempt to rid himself of intolerable state of terror and helplessness, and at the same time to let the object know about the condition of his internal world so that something can be done about it. (p.518)

The model she then develops for intervening in the aftermath of traumatic events is based on these theoretical assumptions. She argues that immediately after a disaster, 'the survivor's overwhelming need and wish will be to find something or someone he can perceive, even temporarily, as offering primary maternal care.' (p.525) and adds: 'At this early stage, what is needed are blankets, holding, warmth, the presence of another human being within physical reach and, above all, one who is in a state to sit and simply be with the survivor, rather than bustling about in a busy way.' (p.525). She identifies the second stage of recovery as extending up to three months after the event. During this period the focus is on the use of groups as a means of enabling individuals to talk about and share their reactions to the traumatic event – the aim being to repair the capacity to function effectively. The third stage then applies to the small group of individuals who remain severely disabled as a result of the convergence of the trauma with earlier infantile experiences. These individuals are seen as requiring longer term psychotherapy.

The consultation

We developed a model of intervention based on the second stage of recovery. As detailed in the proposal, the intervention was directed to a number of levels within the system. The children's home staff group were offered six group meetings (lasting one and a half hours), initially fortnightly and then on a monthly basis. The new team manager was offered role consultations (on an approximately fortnightly basis). Finally, milestone meetings were held with the senior manager and new team manager (again, approximately once a fortnight) to review the work and discuss other developments within the department. However, whilst the senior manager was keen to seek our involvement, there was some initial resistance from the staff group and from the interim manager. This was handled by working with the team manager to secure his support and writing a letter to the staff group (Figure 13.2 and 13.3). The consultation process started shortly afterwards and extended over a four-month period. In the following we will be drawing on the key themes which emerged during this period and relating these to the theoretical constructs discussed above.

Dear Y,

Proposal for Consultancy Work with Homes Staff Team
THE SITUATION AT HOME

The Home has lost its team manager and a second RSW in circumstances which are deeply traumatic to the staff team and will be traumatic, when the situation becomes apparent to them, for the children and young people.

You have asked P (the manager of another children's home) to step into the breech and run the home for an interim period.

The staff team may be doubly dysfunctional, due to the peculiar team dynamics exposed at a previous consultation – a culture of dependency on the team manager, an unofficial female leader and the abdication of the role authority of the male deputies.

The children and young people will require skilled help and support from the staff team to cope with these losses.

AIMS OF THE CONSULTANCY

- To help the *team* work through the trauma they have experienced, so that they are able to retain their competence in doing their jobs. If their capacity to cope with this distressing situation is supported, then hopefully they will then be able to offer the effective help and care that the children and young people will need throughout this difficult period.
- To support *P* with his onerous management task and to give him space for reflective thought in what is a very difficult leadership situation.

PROGRAMME OF WORK

- A sequence of *six meetings with the whole team*, of one and a half hours, facilitated by male and female consultants. These meetings would flow as follows:
    - A set of four meetings on four consecutive weeks, at a regular time and, if possible, outside the Home.
    - Two further meetings, at four weeks and then eight weeks after the first set.
    - *Role consultation* for P on a one to one basis, at a frequency to be agreed, say up to six meetings, before, during and after the group work with staff.
    - A number of one hour *progress or 'milestone' meetings*, say three, with consultants, yourself and P to review the programme. I suggest one before the start of the group work, one after the group work and one two to three months down the line.

Figure 13.2 Letter to Y (Senior Manager responsible for home)

Dear

X (the Director of Social Services) and his management team recognise that you have been through a most upsetting and distressing experience. They are determined that you should be offered appropriate help to deal with this. They have invited me and my colleague to work with you all as a group.

It is suggested that there will be six meetings. The aims of these meetings would be as follows:

1. To talk with each other about what happened to each person when the shock news about Z (the team manager) was uncovered, and how people are managing in the aftermath.

2. To reflect on the changes in each person's life, and how colleagues, families and friends are adapting to them.

It is important to understand that the meetings are *not* a continuation of the team building exercise that we recently shared (the first referral).

We suggest a series of six one and a half hour meetings in the following pattern:

- Four weekly meetings of one and a half hours on consecutive Fridays.
- Two further meetings spaced at one monthly intervals.

Unfortunately we cannot do the day of your regular staff meetings. We acknowledge that as RSWs the rota is of key importance in organising your life, and that this may make it more difficult for some of you. However, given the critical nature of your current situation, we hope that you will be able, with your managers, to make the arrangements to enable you all to attend.

We look forward to meeting you and enclose brief biographical details for your information.

Yours sincerely

Figure 13.3 Letter to the children's home staff

The first milestone meeting

This initial meeting introduced some key themes. There was an urgency about change. P (the new manager) felt that he needed to change everything in the home. He also felt like a 'mother', experiencing the staff group as needy and dependent. In addition, further anxieties about perverse behaviour had emerged within the home. D, a female staff member (a senior residential worker), had made a number of serious allegations against M (a male residential worker). D alleged that M (who had himself been in care) had, at some time in the past, procured fellow foster children to make an obscene video of homosexual rape. She also alleged that, more recently, he had engaged girls from the home in prostitution activities. In addition, D stated that her husband had sexually abused her with an iron pipe and that she had subsequently collapsed and 'died' and been resuscitated in the police station. Whilst D had since had a breakdown and been admitted to hospital, the nature of the allegations were such as to necessitate M's suspension pending a police investigation.

The first role consultation

In this meeting P elaborated on these themes. He was filled with woe and frustration and used the physical environment of the home as a powerful metaphor to express his feelings about the staff group: 'in the kitchen they polish the visible surfaces, but they don't see the grease on the floor, they don't see the filth under the cooker'; 'in the hallway they don't see the institutional paint, the broken hoover halfway up the stairs or the painting riveted to the wall'; 'and the garden, in comes a gardener, but no one asks what he does, they're unquestioning and he appears to do nothing, one tree has a broken branch which is left hanging'. Finally, these themes converged on the image of the water butt, which was filled up with broken bits of furniture, fag ends smoked by the kids: 'all the gunge is left there and it never gets sorted out'. The consultant linked this material with the unquestioning attitude of the staff group towards Z (the team manager) and the subsequent scapegoating of M. He suggested that the staff felt guilty about not getting behind the surface gloss such as to identify what Z was doing. They then mobilised D to attack M, with M being like the water butt, a scapegoat to be filled up with all the organisational 'gunge'. In confirmation, P responded: 'yes, yes, the kids actually piss in the water butt, it all fits'.

The first group meeting

This meeting confirmed the extent to which the allegations and subsequent suspension of the team manager had created confusion in the minds of the staff and disabled their capacity for thought. They were helped to articulate some of this confusion by our asking how they had heard about Z's suspension: 'a 'phone call from Y'; 'a stranger on the 'phone at work'; 'being overwhelmed by the police' and by 'police kindness'. Two of the staff reported having seen Z outside the home shortly afterwards: 'he looked smaller'. B felt angry with Z and disbelieving. E felt angry at being under scrutiny. Others were concerned for the informal 'deputy' (E), wondering 'how she would take it'. The sense of being 'tainted' by their association with Z was also clearly evidenced and vividly expressed by one staff member who referred to hiding the letter she had received and reading it furtively in the home's kitchen and, later, in the garage at her own home. Another added that she had not felt able to read the letter. Acknowledging these feelings of contamination permitted further shocking disclosures: some years previously, E had discovered obscene photos when an envelope addressed to Z, and coming through the mail, had burst open. At the time she had chosen to see these as part of some research project in which Z was involved. She never tackled Z but she did confide in two other staff members, who had colluded with her desire not to know what these might mean. She felt relieved when it all came out, but also relieved that she had not been the 'whistleblower'. F referred to a trip to Romania organised by Z under the umbrella of a Christian organisation and his suspicions that the apparently worthy explicit aims of this project concealed murkier intentions. Coming closer to home, anxieties were expressed about Z's relationship with a particular child who had been in the home some years previously. M's comment that 'everything's ruined' seemed to summarise the mood of the group, as anxieties extended across the possible closure of the home to the implications for future career prospects. As consultants we felt that we had entered a wasteland. Yet this despair appeared to conceal a deep ambivalence about their feelings for Z: was he the good children's home manager who had been well respected within the borough and developed innovative projects or was he the pervert who had used his position to abuse vulnerable children in his care? In the minds of the staff there was a deep split, the allegations having transformed the Z whom they had known and respected for many years into a pervert from whom they wished to dissociate themselves. When the consultants pointed out this ambiguity, the staff were able to acknowledge this and it freed them to begin to think about their use of projection and, in particular, the way in which Y and P (as the bearer of the news) had initially become the hated objects. M referred to having been under suspicion, comparing the experience to having 'demons floating past his head'. Finally, the group discussed how they might negotiate their new 'tainted' identities with others and, whilst there was no clear solution here, they explored what they might tell colleagues and partners and what they would do if they saw Z.

This session confirmed the traumatising impact of this event and the associated confusion and loss of competence within the staff group. As consultants, we were struck by the way in which the staff seemed to feel themselves as having been corrupted by their association with Z and their desire to avoid being stigmatised. They struggled internally with the need to re-negotiate a relationship with the now damaged picture of their erstwhile respected team manager. The urge towards concealment was also evident – at some level they knew or had known but hadn't wanted to know – such that their guilty feelings were then to be split off and transformed into attacks on the external managers.

The second group meeting

At the second group, the urge to draw on denial as a defensive strategy became more explicit. Initially it seemed that the intense feelings of guilt provoked by this situation were to invoke a desire to deny the seriousness of the allegations against Z: 'It all seemed a long time ago'; 'perhaps it wasn't so bad, Z had only circulated obscene material, it would have been different if he'd interfered with children'; 'after all they didn't really know, it hadn't come to court yet, maybe it wasn't so bad, what if he wasn't found guilty'. P emphasised that Z had admitted to some of the offences and, whatever happened, he wouldn't be returning to the home. However, the desire to minimise the nature of the offences seemed the dominant theme at this stage in the meeting. Suddenly, however, the mood shifted. N (one of the formal deputies) stated angrily that a number of children had broken into the flat in which Z had lived (which was on the premises). He argued that there seemed a desire to think that this meant nothing, adding that no one really knew what the children thought about it all. Others argued that it meant nothing, it's just something these children might do. N seemed on his own, asserting an alternative view in the face of the concerted minimisation of the other staff. Eventually he argued that he thought the children knew something. Also, if Z is an abuser, what does that make them in the eyes of the children? Maybe they don't feel they can trust anyone. Perhaps the break-in had been an act of revenge against Z – not so much that Z had abused them but that they had themselves been abused in the past. Some of the staff talked about having asked the children if Z had abused them and E referred to having been asked by the police to identify photos of children who had been in the home at some time in the past. The group explored what the children might or might not know about the allegations against Z. The absence of any formal knowledge (at that stage the children had only been told that he'd been suspended) had provided a fertile ground for rumour. The children did know something, they'd been told by friends, they'd been referring to Z as a 'dirty bugger', they'd also been saying that he'd been abusing little girls. The group became preoccupied with discussing what the children should be told. How could they deal with the children's questions when they felt so uncertain and confused themselves? They turned to one of the consultants for expert advice: she had been involved in similar situations in the past, what did she think they should do. The other consultant related the way the loss of external authority (in Z) appeared to have created a sense of loss of internal authority and expertise. Finally, a lengthy debate ensued on what the children could/ should be told, with different staff relating different view points. Ultimately, a group decision was made to formally tell the children about the reasons for Z's departure.

As consultants, we felt that the preoccupation with the 'break-in' told us something about how much the staff had felt intruded upon since Z's suspension. This meeting also confirmed the extent to which denial had been used throughout the system in an attempt to ward off the difficult and anxiety-provoking feelings aroused by this event – the decision not to tell the children what had happened clearly both reflecting and reinforcing the collective urge to draw on denial.

The third group meeting

This session opened with what might be thought of as a re-enactment. P informed us that M had been re-suspended. As consultants, we were shocked, traumatised and silenced by this news. Why we had not been fore-warned? After all, one of the consultants had met with P for a role consultation on the day that the suspension had occurred. Our feelings were mirrored in the group's responses: 'It's like a body blow, how much more can the staff take'. More paranoid feelings emerged: 'The finger is being pointed, it's put us back two weeks'; 'it's like East Germany, people are afraid to say anything; it's like the secret police; a waste of time'. The consultants interpreted the convergence of secrecy and denial: 'Everyone knew about Z, everyone knew he was bent but it wasn't challenged; perhaps everyone knew about M as well, but again was he ever challenged?' This permitted some acceptance of responsibility. Reference was made to the earlier consultation: 'Perhaps we are guilty, we learned about scapegoating in the team building, but it's one thing if we do it internally, it's another if it's taken up externally'. They thought about M and realised that they identified him, in his normal working practice, as a rule breaker, a boundary-breaker, in a sense he volunteered himself as a scapegoat. Yet no one ever confronted him, they just told the line manager and then nothing happened. D (who had made the allegations against M) was also seen as problematic. They related a history of disturbing incidents in which she had been involved. However, despite the fact that she was clearly disturbed, she had been promoted by Z to being a senior residential worker. Whilst they had worried about her practice, nothing had ever been done. There was some recognition that M and D served a function for the rest of the staff group: 'D fires the bullets on behalf of us all, and she fired them at M this time'. Reference to the difficulty in challenging decisions fuelled an attack on P for not having carried out the decision, which had been taken by the group the previous week, to inform the children. P responded by emphasising that a decision had been taken by the senior management group to tell the children next week, at the same time as the parents. One of the deputy managers then identified authority as a central problem: 'We want our bread buttered on both sides'. Others agreed: 'Everyone's a leader, it's like having six bosses'. As the failure of formal authority became a subject for discussion, P returned the group to a task issue. He identified the way in which authority was subject to re-negotiation at the beginning and end of each shift and the impact on handovers between the shifts.

The consultants felt that the shock disclosure had an unconscious communicative function: we were to be made to feel as the staff had done when the earlier news about Z and then M had been thrust upon them. Like them, we were to feel helpless and stunned. We were also to be undermined by the lack of fore-knowledge. However, what also became evident within this group was the extent to which any authority was to be perverted. As described by Chasseguet-Smirguel (1985), perversion involves a denial of both generational and gender differences. In this case, it then appeared that the perverse internal world of the team manager had been translated into a management structure in which hierarchical difference was denied and leadership flaunted. As the extent of conflict within the group became evident, splits between the consultants also appeared – one feeling drawn into taking authority whilst the other identified with the helplessness of the staff group.

The second milestone meeting

These projective splits were to prove critical to our attempts to understand, and work with, the dynamics of the staff team. Due to the exigencies of timing, immediately after this group we met with Y and P for a second milestone meeting (with hindsight we recognised that this had not left us with enough time to recover from the dynamics of the staff group and we were then sucked into the anxieties of the senior manager). Y was under intense pressure from the senior management group within the department. He conveyed a sense of extreme anxiety and an urgency to take some kind of action. He described a climate dominated by persecutory anxieties. These were particularly focused on the fear of public exposure (following the court hearing on Z). Y informed the consultant that some senior managers were demanding that the home be closed and the children dispersed widely. The staff group's sense of being 'tainted' seemed confirmed by these responses. Whilst Y had succeeded in stemming any immediate action here, he was also under some internal pressure to secure a scapegoat. He pursued us with questions about the quality of the staff in the home, interpreting our comments about the perverse management structure as a direct critique of the deputy managers (a view which was endorsed by P). Whilst we attempted to maintain our position as consultants, the drive to locate blame/ responsibility within this system was to prove overwhelming. The consultant who had identified with P found himself taking an increasingly managerial role, whilst the other consultant continued to feel somewhat helpless. We left feeling somehow tainted by this experience, the sense being that our neutrality as consultants had been undermined by the insistent drive within the organisation to secure a scapegoat.

Supervision meeting

These dynamics were, however, to become more clearly understood as they were re-played in the interaction between the consultants. A subsequent supervision meeting ended in disarray, with one of the consultants feeling criticised, even 'blasted', by the other consultant and the supervisor for failing to inform the group about the ongoing milestone meetings. This consultant was left with an overwhelming sense of shame and uselessness and could find no internal refuge from these persecutory feelings. This material, however, proved invaluable in facilitating our understanding of the dynamics within the staff group. Drawing on the work of Mollon (1996), we began to understand the way in which the perverse sexual behaviour of Z had instilled a deep sense of shame in everyone connected with this situation. As Mollon states:

> Many of the effects of sexual abuse on the sense of self are closely allied to shame… Shame is inherent in sexual abuse. Indeed sexual abuse is the ultimate shame, and probably that is its purpose – to transfer projectively shame from the abuser to the victim… Shame is for the self and for the connection to the abuser. (pp.54–5)

Referring to the treatment situation he later adds:

> Shame is contagious. If we connect empathically with another's shame we feel shame. Not surprisingly, both patients and therapists have tried to avoid contact with shame, preferring instead to focus on feelings of guilt, aggression and sadism – all of which can actually be fuelled by shame. (p.55)

This urge to divest the self of the sense of shame was then to create a volatile and precarious dynamic within the staff group – the shaming/ blaming process informing a focus on scapegoating which was re-enacted through all layers within the system and constructed a triangle of abuse which ensured the inevitable and relentless transformation of 'rescuers' into 'victims' and/or 'persecutors' (Pengelly and Hughes 1997).

Meeting with the senior manager

This experiential learning, whilst intensely uncomfortable, was critical to our subsequent work with the staff group and senior manager involved in this situation. We decided that we needed to share our understanding of these dynamics with Y and one of the consultants arranged an additional meeting with this senior manager. The consultant used the imagery of the 'waterbutt' to illustrate the powerful impact of the scapegoating processes and the way in which these had reverberated through the entire system. The manager was shown how, within the staff group, D had been mobilised to attack M and the staff had criticised and undermined P, while P and the staff group together had been driven to re-enact these themes in their relationship with the consultants. In the wider system, the threat of public exposure (and shaming) had created a climate of persecutory panic, such that Y was to feel pressurised to identify culprits who could be blamed and then expelled. Finally, the consultant described how we ourselves had been drawn into these dynamics in the group meeting, the milestone meeting and subsequent supervision session. We explained how we had thus colluded in a process of blaming the deputies and then re-directing the attacks internally. The consultant also described the intense sense of shame that he had experienced following the supervision meeting. Y responded well to this intervention. He was able to share his own sense of shame, commenting that he felt 'dumped' with something and also felt that he too was tainted by his association with Z. He worried about the implications for his career. Whilst the rest of the department were using a current departmental review to 'feather their own nests', he and one of the other senior managers were left 'minding the shop'.

The fourth group meeting

The group initially felt stuck, reiterating that they were 'no further forward'. There were still 'unresolved issues to do with D and M' and they felt 'treated like naughty kids, not being told what was going on' and 'not being trusted'. They challenged P to give more information (which he did). The consultants then used the triangle of abuse to talk about the way in which blaming processes seemed to be re-enacted through the system. This permitted some greater acceptance of their own powers and responsibilities: 'we have to accept our own responsibility', 'whether or not M is guilty we do this as a team, this is us'. Reference to 'secrets and things they couldn't confront' facilitated further exploration of their failure to confront incidents of poor practice and the associated undermining of any formal authority within the home. S talked about the way in which no one had challenged him when he had driven the van with more children than permitted for insurance purposes. The lack of authority given to, or taken up by, the deputy managers was also discussed. However, what also emerged was the extent to which the group was disabled by a long-standing fear of confrontation. One member referred to an 'unconscious rota' whereby the staff group never met in its entirety – the concern being to avoid any conflict or confrontation since this was imagined to be 'explosive' and, therefore, catastrophic. S stated: 'We need to get through the door, not stop in the corridor'. As the possibility of difference and then challenge began to emerge, the group then returned to the story of the van driving and began to think about what actually had taken place.

The final group and milestone meetings

The final meetings identified the way in which an understanding of the shaming/blaming dynamic had permitted a return to task-focused issues. In the final milestone meeting, Y demonstrated the extent to which he had been enabled to withstand the pressures in the department towards scapegoating and closure of the home. He had also encouraged further training days for the staff group to address the structural difficulties which had emerged during this consultation. This sense of clarity had clearly impacted on the staff group. Thus, in the final group meeting, we were struck by the way in which the concern to challenge the perverse management structure seemed concretely represented by the seating arrangements. The new manager and one of the deputies chose to sit together and between the two consultants. They also increasingly took over the leadership of the group, continuing the previous discussion about work-related concerns. The possibility of some closure in respect of Z seemed reflected in the opening discussion about the outcome of his court hearing. Some concern was expressed for Z: how would he manage in prison, given the way in which paedophiles were treated by other inmates? However, the primary focus here was on the sense of relief at the lack of media interest – such protection from public exposure also allowing some valuing of senior managers. Thus, whilst someone commented that 'it had all been a damp squib', others acknowledged that this, in part, reflected the work of the external senior managers, adding that 'perhaps, after all, they had done a good job'. The discussion then shifted towards the possibility of change. Reference to the subsequent training days provoked an ambivalent response. Whilst most of the staff welcomed the possibility of change, anxieties were expressed about the extent to which any proposals here were driven by the sense of contamination. Did everything have to be changed in order to divest the home of any association with Z? Or was it possible to reclaim prior areas of expertise and competency? The group became preoccupied with questions of authority, with various staff arguing the need to assert their own authority within the workplace. Finally, the team members started talking about the children currently placed in the home, with recognition of their difficulties provoking a plea for specialist help. As the discussion gradually extended to a consideration of the specialist needs and difficulties of various individual children, the ability to re-focus on task issues seemed increasingly evidenced.

Conclusion

In concluding, we would like to reflect on what we, as consultants, learned from this experience. First, we wondered why it was that no one had identified the team manager as a paedophile, despite his lengthy employment within the borough and the evidence, which emerged during the consultation, of some carelessness on his part in respect of such activities. We were also aware that this failure to identify paedophile tendencies and behaviour was not atypical, given the recent history of disclosure of sexual abuse within residential settings. In thinking about this issue, we drew on the experiences of one of the consultants who had previously been employed in just such a role. He argued, first, that children's homes tend to operate as closed systems within the broader department; the closeness of working creating a sense of intimacy and inter-relatedness which would be less dominant in fieldwork settings. He also identified the way in which knowledge, power and authority tends to be projected onto the team manager from both supervisors and subordinates, thus encouraging a sense of omnipotence on the part of the manager. These organisational projections would then seem to permit a situation in which the children's home becomes a microcosm in which a perverse team manager can operate with little fear of identification.

These processes also provide some explanation for the organisational distortions identified within this children's home. Thus, given the projection of power and authority into the team manager, as combined with the difficulty in providing any effective external oversight of a residential environment, the manager is likely to have a powerful influence on the way in which the home is run. Effectively, the organisation of the home is then likely to reflect the internal world of the manager. Under such conditions, if the team manager is perverse, as was the case with Z, one might, perhaps, expect to find the distortions of authority and hierarchy which were prevalent in this home.

However, this consultation also brought home to us the inevitability of the traumatic experience being primarily conveyed through projective processes. The early sessions demonstrated the confusion and inarticulacy of the staff group following the disclosure of the team manager's involvement in perverse activities. Yet, whilst these early sessions both with the new team manager and the staff team clearly identified the way in which the feelings of contamination were to be defended against by the use of splitting and denial, it was only when we ourselves were drawn into these dynamics that we were really able to understand what was happening both within the staff group and within the wider organisation. The re-enactment of the sudden expulsion following allegations of perverse behaviour proved critical here, provoking a sequence of interactions through which we too were to experience the power of the shaming/blaming dynamic. Ultimately, our understanding of the impact of this dynamic, both intra- and inter-psychically, was then to prove critical to our ability to help the staff group and the senior managers in their attempt to restore the capacity to work.

Finally, we would then want to underline the extent to which this consultation confirmed the impact of such events on individuals, staff groups and the wider organisation and the value of such interventions in enabling a return to work following traumatic experiences within the workplace. Thus, as emphasised by Caroline Garland (1991):

> Disasters of this kind have a tremendous and lasting impact on those caught up in them – survivors, the bereaved, the emergency services, relief workers, social services, local psychiatric and psychological services, the community at large, in ever widening if diminishing waves of disturbance. This is implicitly acknowledged in the way disasters are named after their location. It implies an effect upon an entire social network, not just a large number of individuals. (p.507)

Contributors

Sonia Appleby is a qualified social worker with over twenty years' experience. She works as a practitioner, consultant and trainer for local authorities and other agencies, specialising in child care/protection issues, and organisational difficulties mirrored by the client/worker/manager interaction. She is also a qualified psychoanalytic psychotherapist in private practice.

Richard Davies is a principal adult psychotherapist at the Portman Clinic. He teaches social workers and probation officers on the psychodynamic approach to casework and also supervises and consults to professionals in the health, social and probation services. He has a private practice and consults to the Samaritans and to organisations in the private sector. An associate member of the British Association of Psychotherapists, the British Confederation of Psychotherapists and a founder member of the International Association of Forensic Psychotherapy, he has a background in probation, psychiatric social work and teaching. He has contributed chapters to *Forensic Psychotherapy* (Jessica Kingsley Publishers 1996) and *Violence in Children and Adolescents* (Jessica Kingsley Publishers 1997).

Robert Fleming is Head of Child and Adolescent Psychotherapy in child and family psychiatry in Lambeth, working with very disturbed children and adolescents. He also teaches and consults to many professional disciplines including social work. He has a private practice. Formerly a senior social worker in Lewisham Social Services, he later worked in Child Guidance in America and the NSPCC in London, before undertaking psychotherapy training.

Alison Jones is a senior probation officer currently managing a Family Court Welfare team. She has worked for many years as both a main grade probation officer and as a manager of a criminal court-based team. She has retained an involvement in social work education as an external assessor for the Diploma in Social Work. She is joint author of *The Probation Handbook* (Longman 1992) and *Probation Practice* (Pitman 1995).

Linda King is an experienced senior probation officer and manager in Oxfordshire and Buckinghamshire. Formerly she worked as a main grade probation officer in south east London. In her roles both as practitioner and manager she has become acutely aware of the circumstances in which stress can arise among colleagues and staff and has utilised her experience in her work for the benefit of others.

Brynna Kroll is Senior Lecturer in Probation Studies at Brunel University College and an external assessor for the Diploma in Social Work. She has previously worked as a probation officer, guardian ad litem and court welfare officer. She is the author of *Chasing Rainbows: Children, Divorce and Loss* (Russell House Publishing 1994) and joint author of *The Probation Handbook* (Longman 1992) and *Probation Practice* (Pitman 1995).

Ann Kutek is a psychotherapist and Clinical Director of Counselling in Companies (part of WPF). She was formerly Head of Strategies Planning for Hammersmith and Fulham Social Services, and a Child Protection Coordinator for a London Borough..

Tony Manning is a psychiatric social worker in Redbridge. He has extensive practice experience with children and families, having previously worked in Dorset and Buckinghamshire prior to Seebohm reorganisation. He has incorporated his wealth of experience of major organisational upheaval, and the faded idealism and excitement of generic social work, in his work and in his contribution to this book.

Mili Mass is Senior Teacher at the Paul Baerwald School of Social Work at the Hebrew University Jerusalem. She is the author of a number of publications, relating in particular to the subject of parenting, and also to different approaches to social work practice.

Tony McCaffrey is a psychoananlytic psychotherapist whose practice includes group psychotherapy with adolescents and adults, and the provision of clinical supervision to professional groups in the health service. In a related consultancy role, he consults to a number of social services departments and NHS trusts, and is a member of Opus Consultancy Service. He also acts as an independent social worker, and is a principal lecturer at the Centre for Community Care and Primary Health at the University of Westminster.

Isabel Menzies Lyth is a psychoanalyst in private practice, and a consultant to organisations. She was formerly a consultant at the Tavistock Institute of Human Relations.

Martin Ruddock is a manager in a Family Service Unit in south east London. He formerly worked for a number of years in Local Authority Social Work both as a practitioner and as Team Manager.

David Townsend was until recently Director of Social Services in Croydon and was formerly Director in Haringey and Deputy Director in Camden. He has served as Special Adviser to the Secretary of State for Social Services, as a councillor in Lewisham, and as a member of a London Health Authority. He has held chair positions in the Association of Directors of Social Services and has been a member or representative on a number of groups and working parties including the Race Equality Board of the National Institute of Social Work, and has also written chapters in *Future of the Welfare State* (Heinemann 1983) and *Public Issues Private Pain* (Insight and Nottingham University 1988).

Paul Van Heeswyk is Consultant Psychotherapist to the Cotswold Community, a therapeutic community for deprived and abused young people, and is also Head of Child and Adolescent Psychotherapy in the Lewisham and Guy's Mental Health NHS Trust. Prior to this, he worked as a lecturer in a college of further education, and as a residential social worker in a special school and two children's homes.

Liz Webb is a psychoanalytic psychotherapist, organisational consultant and social worker. She has worked in clinical practice and management positions in local authority social work. She has based her chapter on consultancy work in a local authority residential setting.

Chris Wilmot is a (recently retired) service unit manager of a children and families team in Lewisham. He has worked in local authority social work for 27 years, mainly in the field of statutory child care. In his role as manager he has always been a strong supporter of the 'front line social worker' and an advocate of individual casework.

Roger Woods is a senior lecturer in Social Policy and Organisational Sociology at the University of Luton and also runs a module on Organising Care for the Diploma in Social Work. He previously had many years experience in an inner London social services department in a variety of development roles.

Bibliography

Abbott, P. and Wallace, C. (1990) 'Social work and nursing: a history.' In P. Abbott and C. Wallace (eds) *The Sociology of the Caring Professions.* Basingstoke: Falmer Press.

Ackroyd, S., Hughes, J. and Soothill, K. (1984) 'Public sector social services and their management. '*Journal of Management Studies 24, 6,* 603–619.

Allsopp, M. (1995) *Social Workers' Perceptions of Risk in Child Protection.* Nottingham: University of Nottingham, School of Social Studies.

Andersen, T. (1987) 'Reflecting teams: dialogues and metadialogues in clinical work.' *Family Process 26:4,* pp.415–428.

Anderson, C. and Stewart, S. (1983) *Mastering Resistance.* New York: Guilford.

Anderson, H. and Goolishian, H. (1988) 'Problem determined systems: toward transformation in family therapy.' *Journal of Strategic and Systemic Therapies 5, 4.*

Anon. 'But what was it really like?' *Professional Social Work,* April 1994, p.7.

Arrud, J., Cooper, C. and Robertson, I. (1995) *Work Psychology: Understanding People in the Workplace.* London: Pitman.

Balint, M. (1954) 'Method and technique in the teaching of medical psychology, II: Training general practitioners in psychotherapy.' *British Journal of Medical Psychology 27,* 37–41.

Balloch, S., Andrew, T., Ginn, J., McLean, J., Pahl, J., and Williams, J. (1995) *Working in the Social Services.* London: National Institute of Social Work.

Barber, J. G. (1991) *Beyond Casework.* London: Macmillan.

Barkai, M., & Mass, M. (in press) *The meanings of 'parental capability' and the 'best interests of the child' as reflected in supreme court decisions regarding the adoptions of minors.* (Hebrew) Jerusalem: The Harry Saker Institute for Legal Studies, The Faculty of Law, The Hebrew University of Jerusalem.

Bateson, G. (1972) Steps to an Ecology of Mind. London: Paladin.

Beckford Report (1985) *A Child in Trust: the Report of the Panel of Inquiry into the Circumstances Surrounding the Death of Jasmine Beckford.* London: Borough of Brent.

Beels, C. and Ferber, A. (1969) 'Family therapy: a view.' *Family Process, 8, 2.*

Bell, L. (1990) 'Social services departments: preparing for the 1990s.' *Public Money and Management* Spring 1990.

Benjamin, A. (1994) *Object. Painting.* London: Academy Editions.

Bhaskar, R. (1978) *A Realist Theory of Science.* Sussex: The Harvester Press.

Bion, W.R. (1962) 'A theory of thinking.' *International Journal of Psychoanalysis, 43,* pp.306–310.

Bion, W.R., (1957) 'Differentiation of the psychotic from the non psychotic personalities.' *International Journal of Psychoanalysis, 38,* pts 3–4.

Bion, WR. (1961) *Experiences in Groups.* London: Tavistock Publications.

Borkowski, M., Murch, M. and Walker, J. (1985) *Marital Violence: The Community Response.* London. Tavistock.

Boss, P. (1987) 'The role of intuition in family research: three issues of ethics.' In R. Garfield, A. Greenberg and S. Sugarman (eds), *Symbolic Experiential Journeys, A Special Issue of Contemporary Family Therapy, 9, 1 and 2.*

Bowen, M. (1978) *Family Therapy in Clinical Practice.* New York: Jason Aronson.

Brearley, J. (1985) 'Anxiety in the organisational context: experiences of consultancy.' *Journal of Social Work Practice 4.*

Brearley, J. (1991) 'A psychodynamic approach to social work.' In J. Lishman (ed) *A Handbook of Theory for Practice Teachers in Social Work.* London: Jessica Kingsley Publishers.

Breunlin, D., Schwartz, R. and Kune-Karrer, B. (1992) *Metaframeworks.* San Francisco: Jossey Bass.

Brunel Institute of Organisation and Social Studies. (1976) *Future Organisation in Child Guidance and Allied Work.* Working Paper H/21. Uxbridge: Brunel.

Byng-Hall, J. (1979) 'Re-editing family mythology during family therapy.' *Journal of Family Therapy 2.*

Byng-Hall, J. (1995) 'Creating a secure family base: some implications of attachment theory for family therapy.' *Family Process 34, 1.*

Carpenter J. and Treacher, A. 'On the neglected but related arts of convening and engaging families and their wider systems.' *Journal of Family Therapy 5, 4.*

Chasseguet-Smirguel J. (1985) *The Ego Ideal: A Psychoanalytic Essay on the Malady of the Ideal.* London: Free Association Books.

Chen, C.C., David, A.S., Nunnerley, H., Mitchell, M.J., Dawson, J.L., Berry, H.., Dobbs, J. and Fahy, T. (1995) 'Adverse life events and breast cancer: case-control study.' *British Medical Journal 311.*

Clarke, J. (1993) 'The comfort of strangers: social work in context.' In J. Clarke (ed), *A Crisis in Care?: Challenges to Social Work.* London: Sage.

Clulow, C. and Vincent, C. (1987) *In the Child's Best Interests? Divorce Court Welfare The Search for a Settlement.* London: Sweet and Maxwell

Colman, J. 'Case Book.' *Professional Social Work,* January 1995, p.8.

Coleman, J.C. (1974) *Relationships in Adolescence.* London: Routledge and Kegan Paul.

Cooper, A. (1992) 'Anxiety and child protection work in two national systems.' *Journal of Social Work Practice 6 (2),* pp.117–128.

Cooper, C. and Cartwright, S. (1996) *Mental Health and Stress in the Workplace: A Guide for Employers.* London: HMSO.

Cooper, C. and Payne, R. (eds) (1988) *Stress at Work.* Chichester: John Wiley.

Cournoyer, B. (1988) 'Personal and professional distress among social caseworkers.' *Social Casework., The Journal of Contemporary Social Work,* pp 259–264.

Crompton, S. (1996) PSW Survey Results. *Professional Social Work,* May 1995. Birmingham: BASW

Dale, P. (1996) 'Counselling adults abused as children.' In S. Palmer, S. Dainow and P. Milner (eds), *Counselling.* London: Sage, pp.325–338.

Dalley, G. (1992) 'Social welfare ideologies and normalisation: links and conflicts.' In H. Brown and H. Smith (eds), *Normalisation: A Reader for the Nineties.* London: Routledge.

DeShazer, S. (1984) 'The death of resistance.' *Family Process 23, 1.*

Dockar-Drysdale, B. (1990) *The Provision of Primary Experience.* London: Free Association Books.

Dockar-Drysdale, B. (1993) *Therapy and Consultation in Child Care.* London: Free Association Books.

Dominelli, L. (1988) *Anti-Racist Social Work.* London: Macmillan.

Donzelot, J. (1980) *The Policing of Families: Welfare versus the State.* London: Hutchinson.

Eeklaar, J. (1991) *Regulating Divorce.* Oxford: Clarendon Press.

Egan, G. (1994) *The Skilled Helper.* Pacific Grove, California: Brooks/Cole.

Emerson, E. (1992) 'What is normalisation?' In H. Brown and H.Smith (eds), *Normalisation: A Reader for the Nineties.* London: Routledge.

Emery, F.E. and Trist, E.L.(1972) *Towards a Social Ecology Contextual Appreciation of the Future in the Present.* London, Plenum Publishing Co.

England, M. and Cole, R., (1995) 'Children and mental health: how can the system be improved?' *Health Affairs 14* (3), 131–138.)

Erikson, E.H. (1965) *Childhood and Society.* London: Penguin

Escalona, S., and Heider, A. M. (1959) *Prediction and Outcome.* New York: Basic Books.

Even-Shoshan, A. (1988) *The New Dictionary.* (Hebrew) Jerusalem: Kiryat Sepher.

Falloon, I., Laporta, M., Fadden, G. and Graham-Hole, V. (1993) *Managing Stress in Families.* London: Routledge.

Firth, H. and Britton, P. (1989) 'Burnout, absence and turnover among British nursing staff.' *Journal of Occupational Psychology 62,* 55–59.

Fisch, R., Weakland, J. and Segal, L. (1982) *The Tactics of Change.* San Francisco: Jossey-Bass.

Foden, A. and Wells, T. (1990) 'Unresolved attachment: role and organisational ambiguities for the divorce court welfare officer.' *Family Law,* May 1990: 189-91

Foucault, M. (1980) *Power/Knowledge.* Brighton: Harvester.

Friedman, A. (1977) *Industry and Labour: Class Struggle at Work and Monopoly Capitalism.* London: Macmillan.

Fryer, P. (1984) *Staying Power. The History of Black People in Britain.* London: Pluto Press.

Garland C. (1991) 'External disasters and the internal world: an approach to psychotherapeutic understanding of survivors.' In J. Holmes (ed), *Textbook of Psychotherapy in Psychiatric Practice.* Edinburgh: Churchill Livingstone: Longman UK Ltd.

Garland, D. (1985) *Punishment and Welfare: a History of Penal Strategies.* Edinburgh: Gower.

Gergen, M. G., and Gergen, K. J. (1984) 'The social construction of narrative accounts.' In K.J. Gergen, and M. G. Gergen (eds), *Historical Social Psychology,* (pp. 173–189) Hove: Lawrence Erlbaum Associates Ltd.

Glisson, C. and Durick, M. (1988) 'Predictors of job satisfaction and organisational commitment in human service organisations.' *Administrative Science Quarterly 33,* 61–81.

Goldberg, D. (1972) *The Detection of Psychiatric Illness Questionnaire,* Oxford: Oxford University Press.

Greenfield, T. and Attkinson, C. (1989) Steps toward A Multifactorial Satisfaction Scale For Primary Care and Mental Health Services. *Evaluation and Program Planning 12,* pp.271-278.

Gyford J, Leach S, Game C. (1980) *The Changing Politics of Local Government.* London: Unwin Hyman.

Haley, J. (1976) *Problem Solving Therapy.* San Francisco: Jossey Bass.

Hamilton, G. (1959) *Theory and Practice of Social Work.* New York: Columbia University Press.

Handy C. (1985) *Understanding Organisations.* London: Penguin.

Harré, R. (1981) 'The positivist-empiricist approach and its alternative.' In: P. Reason and G. Rowan (eds), *Human Inquiry.* (pp. 3–17) California: John Wiley.

Hawley, D. and DeHaan, L. (1997) 'Toward a definition of family resilience: integrating life-span and family perspectives.' *Family Process 35,* 3.

Herbert, M. (1993) *Working With Children and the Children Act.* Leicester: British Psychological Society.

Hester, M. and Radford, L. (1996) *Domestic Violence and Child Contact Arrangements in England and Denmark.* Bristol: Policy Press.

Hewitt, M. (1992) *Welfare, Ideology and Need: Developing Perspectives on the Welfare State.* Hemel Hempstead: Harvester Wheatsheaf.

HMSO. (1989) *The Children Act 1989.* London: HMSO.

Hoffman, L. (1981) *Foundations of Family Therapy.* New York: Basic Books.

Home Office. (1992) *National Standards for the Supervision of Offenders in the Community.* London: HMSO.

Home Office. (1995a) *National Standards for the Supervision of Offenders in the Community.* London: Home Office Public Relations Branch.

Home Office. (1995b) *Dealing with Dangerous People: The Probation Service and Public Protection Report of a Thematic Inspection.* London: HM Inspectorate of Probation.

Home Office. (1995c) National Standards for Probation Service Family Court Welfare Work. London: HMSO.

Home Office.(1996) *Three Year Plan for the Probation Service 1996–1999.* London: Home Office Communication Directorate.

Hornby, S. (1993) *Collaborative Care.* Oxford: Blackwell.

Howe, D. (1992) 'Child abuse and the bureaucratisation of social work.' *The Sociological Review 40* (3), pp. 491–508.

Howe, D. (1994) 'Modernity, postmodernity and social work.' *British Journal of Social Work 24* pp. 513–532.

Hoxter, S. (1983) 'Some feelings aroused in working with severely deprived children.' In Boston, M. and Szur, R. (eds), *Psychotherapy with Severely Deprived Children.* London: Routledge and Kegan Paul.

Jackson, C. (1992) 'Reporting on children: the Guardian ad Litem, the court welfare officer and the Children Act 1989.' *Family Law,* June 1992: 252–256.

Jackson, J. (ed) (1970) *Professions and Professionalisation.* Cambridge: University Press.

James, A. and Hay, W. (1992) *Court Welfare Work: Research, Practice and Development.* Hull: University of Hull.

James, H. (1897) *What Maisie Knew.* London: Penguin.

Jones, M. L. (1993) 'Role conflict: cause of burnout or energizer?' *Social Work 38,* 136–141.

Journal of Family Therapy 11, 2.

Kakabadse, A., Ludlow, R. and Vinniecombe, S. (1988) *Working in Organisations.* London: Penguin.

Kaplan, A. (1964) *The Conduct of Inquiry.* San Francisco: Chandler.

Kaufman, J., and Zigler, E. (1987) 'Do abused children become abusive parents?' *American Journal of Orthopsychiatry 57,* 186–192.

Keith, D. (1987) 'Intuition in family therapy: a short manual on post-modern witchcraft.'
In R. Garfield, A. Greenberg and S. Sugarman (eds), *Symbolic Experiential Journeys, A Special Issue of Contemporary Family Therapy, 9, 1 and 2.*

Kessen, W. (1979) 'The American child and other cultural inventions.' *American Psychologist 34*, 815–820.

Khan, R.L., Wolfe, D.M., Quinn, R.P., Snoek, J.D. and Rosenthal, R.A. (1964) *Organisational Stress: Studies in Role Conflict and Ambiguity.* Chichester: John Wiley.

King, J.(1991) 'Taking the Strain.' *Community Care*, 24/10/91, p.16.

Kingston, P. (1984) 'But they aren't motivated...' *Journal of Family Therapy 6, 4.*

Klein, J. (1987) *Our Need for Others and its Roots in Infancy.* London: Tavistock Publications Ltd.

Klein, M. (1935) 'A contribution to the psychogenisis of manic-depressive states.' In *The Writings of Melanie Klein*, Vol. 1, pp.262–289. London: Hogarth.

Klein, M. (1946) 'Notes on some schizoid mechanisms.' In *The Writings of Melanie Klein*, Vol. 3, pp.1–24. London: Hogarth.

Knapp, M. (1997) 'Economic evaluations and interventions for children and adolescents with mental health problems.' *Journal of Child Psychology and Psychiatry 38 , 1*, pp. 3–25.

Kniskern, D. (ed) *Handbook of Family Therapy.* New York: Brunner/Mazel.

Kouzes, T. and Mico, P. (1979) 'Domain theory: an introduction to organisational behaviour in human service organisations.' *Journal of Applied Social Studies 15, 4*, 449–469.

Kraemer, S. (1994) 'On working together in a changing world.' *Association of Child Psychology and Psychiatry (A.C.P.P.) Newsletter 16, 3.*

Kroll, B. (1994) *Chasing Rainbows: Children Divorce and Loss.* Lyme Regis: Russell House Publishing.

Laing, R. (1971) *The Politics of the Family.* London; Tavistock.

Launer, J. (1997) 'Systemic discourse: or, some thoughts about words.' *Association for Family Therapy Context*, Spring, 33–34.

Lester-Levy, I. (1992) *In Quest for a Line: Social Workers' Need to Find a Linear Relation between their Efforts and their Effects on their Work.* (An unpublished term paper in Hebrew) Paul Baerwald School of Social Work, The Hebrew University of Jerusalem.

Liddle, H. (1983) In B. Keeney (ed), *Diagnosis and Assessment in Family Therapy.* London: Aspen.

London Borough of Greenwich (1987). *A Child in Mind: Protection of Children in a Responsible Society.* The Report of the Commission of Inquiry into the circumstances surrounding the death of Kimberley Carlile.

Manicas, P. (1987) *A History and Philosophy of the Social Sciences.* Oxford: Basil Blackwell.

Marshall, J. and Cooper, C. (eds) (1985) *Coping with Stress at Work.* Aldershot, Hants: Gower.

Mass, M. (1977) 'Back to the individual in the teaching of casework.' In S. Spiro (ed), *Innovations in Teaching Social Work in Israel.* Jerusalem: The Council of Schools of Social Work in Israel, pp.65–78.

Mass, M. (1983) *Parenting: A Study from the Parent's Perspective.* Unpublished doctoral dissertation, University of California, Berkeley.

Mass, M. (1994) 'The need for a paradigm shift in social work.' *Social Work and Social Science Review, 5(2)*, pp.130–145.

Mass, M. (1997) 'The determinants of parenthood: power and responsibility.' *Human Relations, 50(3)*, pp.241–260.

Mass, M. and Alkrenawi, A. (1994) 'When a man encounters a woman Satan is also present: on professional encounters in the Bedouin society.' *American Journal of Orthopsychiatry 64*, pp.357–347.

Mattinson, J. (1975) *The Reflection Process in Casework Supervision.* London: Institute of Marital Studies.

Mattinson, J. and Sinclair, J. (1979) *Mate and Stalemate: Working with Marital Problems in Social Services Departments.* London: Institute of Marital Studies.

Maturana, H. and Varela, F. (1980) *Autopoesis and Cognition: The Realisation of Living.* Dordrecht, Holland: D.Reidl.

McCaughan, N and Palmer, B. (1994) *Systems Thinking for Harassed Managers.* London Karnac Books.

McGowan, P. (1996) 'Social worker wins £175,000 for breakdown over job stress.' London: *Evening Standard* 26 April.

McKenna, E.F. (1987) *Psychology in Business.* Hove: Lawrence Erlbaum Associates Ltd.

Meehl, P. (1973) 'Some methodological reflections on the difficulties of psychoanalytic research.' *Psychological Issues 8*, 104–117.

Menzies-Lyth, I. (1988) *Containing anxiety in institutions.* London, Free Association Books.

Menzies, I.E.P. (1959) 'The functioning of social systems as a defence against anxiety: a report on a study of the nursing service of a general hospital.' *Human Relations 13*, 95–121. Also in: Menzies, I.E.P. (1988) *Containing Anxiety in Institutions* , pp.43–85 London: Free Association Books.

Minuchin, S. (1974) *Families and Family Therapy.* Cambridge, Mass: Harvard University.

Mitchell, A. (1985) *Children in the Middle.* London: Tavistock.

Mitchell, J. (1986) (ed) *The Selected Melanie Klein,* p.20. London: Peregrine.

Mollon P. (1996) *Multiple Selves, Multiple Voices: Working with trauma, violation and dissociation.* Chichester: John Wiley.

Murch, M. (1980) *Justice, Welfare & Divorce.* London: Sweet and Maxwell.

Murray, I. (1991) 'The impact of maternal depression on infant development.' *Journal of Child Psychology and Psychiatry 33*, 3, 543–61.

Nathan, J. (1993) 'The battered social worker.' *Journal of Social Work Practice, 6, 2.*

Palazzoli-Selvini, M., Boscolo, L., Cecchin, G.F. and Prata, G. (1980) 'Hypothesizing – circularity – neutrality: three guidelines for the conductor of the session.' *Family Process 19:1*, pp.73–85.

Papp, P. (1980) 'The Greek chorus and other techniques of paradoxical therapy. *'Family Process 19, 1.*

Paré, D. (1995) Of families and other cultures: the shifting paradigm of family therapy. *Family Process 34 ,1.*

Parkinson, L. (1987) *Separation, Divorce & Families.* London: Macmillan.

Parton, N. (1994) 'The nature of social work under conditions of (post)modernity.' *Social Work and Social Sciences Review 5 (2)*, pp.93–112.

Pascoe, W. (1980) 'Overcoming blocks to creativity in family treatment.' *Journal of Family Therapy 2, 2.*

Pasquino, P. (1978) 'Theatrum politicum: the genealogy of capital police and the state of prosperity.' In Burchell, G. *et al.* (eds) *The Foucault Effect: Studies in Governmentality.* Hemel Hempstead: Harvester Wheatsheaf.

Pengelly, P. and Hughes, L. (1997) *Staff Supervision in a Turbulent Environment.* London: Jessica Kingsley Publishers Ltd.

Penn, P. (1985) 'Feed-forward: future questions, future maps.' *Family Process 24, 3.*

Perelberg, R. and Miller, A. (1990) *Gender and Power in Families.* London: Routledge.

Pink, G. (1995) *People and the New World of Work..* London WPF Counselling.

Pocock, D. (1997) 'Feeling understood in family therapy.' *Journal of Family Therapy 19:3*, pp.283–302.

Pottage D., and Evans, M. (1992) *Work Based Stress: Prescription is not the Cure.* London: National Institute for Social Work.

Pottinger, J. (1995) 'Preventing Stress at Work.' Address to the conference on Stress at Work in the Social Services. London AMA/NISW.

Radford, L. and Woodfield, K. (1994) 'Domestic violence & child contact arrangements in England and Denmark.' Draft discussion paper on interim findings and the implications for family court welfare work.

Rahe, R.H., McKean, J.D. and Arthur, R. J. (1967) 'A longitudinal study of life change & illness patterns.' *Journal of Psychosomatic Research 10:3*, pp.55–66.

Reason, P.L. and Rowan, J. (1981) 'Issues of validity in new paradigm research.' In P.L. Reason and J. Rowan (eds), *Human Inquiry* (pp.238–249). California: John Wiley.

Reeves, C. (?) 'Maladjustment: psycho-dynamic theory and the role of therapeutic education in a residential setting.' *Maladjustment and Therapeutic Education 1, 2.*

Reeves, C. (1983) 'The role of milieu therapy in the treatment of sexually abused children.' *Child and Youth Care Forum 22, 2.*

Richards, M.P.M. (1990) 'Parental divorce and children.' In B.T. Tonge, G. D. Burrows and J.S. Werry (eds) *Handbook of Studies in Child Psychiatry.* Oxford: Elsevier Science Publications.

Robinson, M. (1991) *Family Transformations Through Divorce and Remarriage.* London: Routledge.

Rogers, L. and Rayment, T. (1995) *Sunday Times* Focus feature 'Stress Explosion'. London: 31.12.95.

Rose, N. (1989) *Governing the Soul: The Shaping of the Private Self.* London: Routledge.

Rosenfeld, H. (1987) *Impasse and Interpretation.* London: Tavistock.

Ruddock, M. (1987) *Personal Submission to the Kimberley Carlile Inquiry.* Unpublished.

Rutter, M. (1987) 'Continuities and discontinuities in socio-emotional development: Empirical and conceptual perspectives. 'In R.N. Emde and R.J. Harmon (eds), *Continuities and Discontinuities in Development* (pp. 41–64). New York: Plenum Publications.

Salzberger-Wittenberg, I. (1970) *Psychoanalytic Insight and Relationships: A Kleinian Approach.* London: Routledge and Kegan Paul.

Sandler, J. (1988) (ed) *Projection, Identification, Projective Identification.* London: Karnac.

Scott, W.R. (1966) 'Professionalisation in bureaucracies: areas of conflict.' In H.M. Vollmer and D.M. Mills (eds), *Professionalisation.* Englewood Cliffs, New Jersey: Prentice Hall.

Secord. P.F. and Harré R. (1972) *The Explanation of Social Behaviour.* Oxford: Basil Blackwell.

Segal, H. (1981) 'A psychoanalytic approach to the treatment of psychosis.' In M.H. Lader (ed), *The Work of Hanna Segal.* London: Free Association Books and Maresfield Library, p.134.

Selvini Palazzoli, M., Boscolo, L. Cecchin, G. and Prata, G. (1978) *Paradox and Counterparadox.* New York: Jason Aronson.

Selvini Palazzoli, M., Boscolo, L., Cecchin, G. and Prata, G. (1980) 'Hypothesizing circularity – neutrality: three guidelines for the conductor of the sessions.' *Family Process 19, 1.*

Selye, H. (1975) *Stress without Distress.* London, Hodder and Stoughton.

SeQueira, R. (1995) *Working in the Social Services: Stress and Strains in the '90s.* Address to the conference on Stress at Work: in the Social Services London AMA/NISW.

Spence, D. P. (1986) 'When interpretation masquarades as explanation.' *American Psychoanalytic Association 34,* 3–23.

Stanton, M.D. and Todd, T. and Associates (1982) 'Principles and techniques for getting 'resistant' families into treatment.' Chapter 5 of *The Family Therapy of Drug Abuse and Addiction.* New York: Guilford.

Stevenson, O. and Parsloe, P. (1978) *Social Service Teams: The Practitioner's View.* London: HMSO.

Stone, N. (1991) *Family Court Welfare Law.* Norwich: University of East Anglia.

Sutherland, V. and Cooper, C . (1993) *Understanding Stress. A Psychological Perspective for Health Professionals.* London: Chapman and Hall.

Taylor, C. (1977) 'What is human agency?' In T. Mitchell (ed), *The Self: Psychological and Philosophical Issues* (pp.103–135). New Jersey: Littlefield.

Taylor, G. (1987) *Psychosomatic Medicine and Contemporary Psychoanalysis.* New York: IUP.

Temperley, J. and Himmel, S. (1979) 'Training for psychodynamic social work.' GAPS Discussion Paper 4, London: CAPS.

Tomm, K. (1987) 'Interventive interviewing: Part II. Reflexive questions as a means to enable self-healing.' *Family Process 26, 2.*

Toren, N. (1972) *Social Work: The case of a Semi-Profession..* Beverly Hills: Sage.

Treacher, A. (1989) *Termination in Family Therapy – Developing a Structural Approach.*

Treacher, A. and Carpenter, J. (1982) '"Oh no! Not the Smiths again!" An exploration of how to identify and overcome "stuckness" in family therapy.' *Journal of Family Therapy 4, 3,* pp.285–305.

Tugendhat, J. (1990) *What Teenagers Can Tell Us About Divorce and Stepfamilies* London: Bloomsbury.

Unison/BASW (1996) *Dealing with Violence and Stress in Social Services.* London: BASW.

Vecchio, R. P. (1995) *Organisational Behaviour.* Orlando, Florida: Harcourt Brauand Co.

Walczac, Y. and Burns, S. (1984) *Divorce: The Child's Point of View.* New York: Harper and Row.

Wallerstein, J.S. and Blakeslee, S. (1989) *Second Chances.* London: Corgi.

Wallerstein, J.S. and Kelly, J.B. (1980) *Surviving The Breakup: How Children and Parents Cope with Divorce.* London: Grant McIntyre.

Walsh, F. (1996) 'The concept of family resilience: crisis and challenge.' *Family Process 35, 3.*

Warren, E. and Toll. C. (1993) *The Stress Work Book.* London: Nicholas Brealey.

Whitaker, C. and Keith, D. (1981) 'Symbolic-experiential family therapy.' In A. Gurman and D. Kniskern (eds) *Handbook of Family Therapy.* New York: Brunner/Mazel.

Wilkie, W. (1995) *Understanding Stress Breakdown.* Alexandria, Australia: Millenium.

Will, D. and Baird, D. (1984) 'An integrated approach to dysfunction in inter-professional systems.' *Journal of Family Therapy 6, 3.*

ormance. London; Kogan Page.
sference.' In *Through Paediatrics to*

he capacity for concern.' In (1990) *The*
nment. London: Institute of Psychoanalysis

rmalization in Human Services. Toronto:
n.
isation: a proposed new term for the
dation 21 (6), pp.234–239.
nxiety and the Dynamics of Collaboration

milies during life transitions: matching
Process 26, 2, pp.295–308.
itish Social Work in the Nineteenth Century. London:

ories: The Perception of Choice and the Perception of the
brew.) Jerusalem: Paul Baerwald School of Social
Jerusalem.
Adaptation. (A Master Thesis in Hebrew.) Jerusalem:
Work, The Hebrew University of Jerusalem.

Subject Index

Author Index